ENDORSEMENTS

By the Voices of Success

This book presents an original penetrating look at the notion of success, full of unique insights and interesting conclusions. A must read for anyone who aspires to be a success.
—Frank Sciame
Entrepreneur of the Year in Construction

Vincent Roazzi shows us not only how to achieve emotional and financial success but also how to maintain it. Turning conventional wisdom on its head, he demostrates that authentic success comes only from authentic living—an invaluable lesson that goes well beyond the workplace to touch every corner of our lives with affluence, well being, and gratitude. —Patti Breitman
author of *How To Say No Without Feeling Guilty*

Roazzi's ideas on goal setting are insightful! If you define things too much, like with goals, there is no room to maneuver! —Aubrey Balkind
Entrepreneur of the Year in Advertising and Media

Vinny's ideas about goal setting are correct. Goals are for companies, not entrepreneurs!
—Wade Saadi
Entrepreneur of the Year in Technology

A fabulous book on the strategies of life, using guidance positively and effectively, and having the vision to create goodness from within. We can learn from *The Spirituality of Success*.
—Irvin Sternberg
Entrepreneur of the Year in Apparel and Textiles

Vince's principles on success are correct! With determination and dedication, one can achieve one's dreams in this blessed country like no other place in the world!
—William Ungar
Master Entrepreneur of the Year

SUCCESS TRAINING TESTIMONIALS

The best part of the training was seeing so many previously unsuccessful people become very successful and build wealth for their families.   —David Becker, NJ

Vinny is one of the best success trainers and motivators that I have had the privilege to be trained by. I have been to many seminars with such people as Zig Ziglar, Oliver North, Norman Schwartzkopf, and Dexter Yager, just to mention a few. Vinny is among the best. His success training has changed many lives, including mine.
—Gary Holder, MI

I had the pleasure of experiencing his training and motivation, which enabled me to rebound from a dire financial situation. —Forrest Harrell, NC

I can only say that the new perspectives based on Vinny's principles have, indeed, set me free from an old mind-set which held me back from being successful. —Janet Schultz, GA

The principles that Vinny teaches are life changing. —Mike Wehner, OH

I can recommend Mr. Roazzi's training system without reservation for those who want to succeed. I use his training system to this day, twelve years later. —Richard Weisglas, NJ

Anyone can be successful in their chosen field if they will apply the success formulas that Vincent Roazzi has laid out in his training. Mr. Roazzi has a gift for turning ancient truisms and complicated theories into street smarts. This stuff works! —Jo Taylor, CA

Even after all these years, I find myself following his ideology and using the techniques. —Bill DeRoss, NJ

I was a fledging sales rep that wasn't supposed to make it. I owe a great measure of gratitude to Vinny's training. It held before me a vision of success that exceeds the boundaries of simple material attainment. —Michael Ring, SC

The training has given me a system to follow each day that will not fail me. —Sal Spedale, NY

In 1993, I attended a seminar at which Mr. Vincent Roazzi was enlightening the audience on "Steps to Success." Little did I know what an impact this would make on my life! If I were asked to name several people that made an impact on my success in life, Vinny would definitely be one of them. —Joseph Sansonetti, FL

The training has the ability to make people look inside themselves and maybe for the first time in their lives be honest with themselves. Thank you Vinny for helping me put my life on the right path. —Michael Weiner, PA

I had to be in Pittsburgh for a training with Vinny. I tried everything I could think of to get out of it. I am still unsure how he did it, but the information and knowledge that I received over that weekend has propelled and enhanced my career so much that I could never thank him enough. —Troy Holder, IN

The training addresses the basic needs of success, which are not taught in class and can only be learned from someone who has been on the road, earned their way, and paid their dues. —Wayne Baldock, FL

For sure, without your success training, my effectiveness would be greatly diminished. —Carl Baratta, NJ

I personally witnessed the training make a remarkable impact on individuals, who in many cases, were embarking on their business careers and benefited enormously from Vinny's training program. —Joseph Romano, DE

Your training has done more for me in a couple of days than I can thank you for. —Helen Russell, MN

Vinny trained us to understand that our success had to be based on how we helped others to succeed. I have used the system with much success. I am helping people achieve their dreams. —Diane Elkins, IL

Vinny's training is a unique combination of "been there-done that" and "here's how you can do it too." —Dennis McCuistion, TX

There is no doubt that the trainee will have his horizons expanded by as much as one can absorb. It will take several readings for the material to sink in. I for one, ten years later, still go back and reread some of the material that was presented to me during Vinny's initial training. —James Berenson, NJ

Vinny's training has the ability to promote a structured plan for success, and at the same time, make you feel an obligation to be successful for yourself and your family.
—Gary Socha, SC

Learning from you has proved to be a most important part of my continuing development.
—Albert F. Courter III, NJ

He has an uncanny way, through his training, of allowing you to look at your world from a different perspective—always in a way that will help you, if you want to be helped.
—Lynn and Dave Bower, PA

Because of your training we've been able to hire better people and increase retention…the motivational techniques have increased sales. —Gary Alloy, GA

Vincent's theories, put into practice, assisted me to do what I had to do to advance. I attribute a portion of my personal success to his training.   —David Norkus, NJ

Mr. Roazzi's training deals with the real matters of success, the building up of people and relationships.
—Stephen J. Tarbe, CT

His training has been able to build entire sales teams from little or nothing to the number one team in the U.S. He is the E. F. Hutton of sales.   —Rick Pertile, FL

and many, many more—too numerous to print.

Your testimonial could be the next one!

THE SPIRITUALITY OF
SUCCESS

THE SPIRITUALITY OF
SUCCESS

GETTING
RICH
WITH INTEGRITY

Vincent M. Roazzi

BROWN BOOKS
DALLAS

For information, please contact Brown Books
16200 North Dallas Parkway, Suite 225, Dallas, Texas 75248
972-381-0009   BrownBooks.com

First Printing, 2002
ISBN 0-9706988-7-9
LCCN 2001117757

Acknowledgements

I would like to humbly acknowledge some of the teachers I have encountered in my lifetime. Naming all of them would be impossible because everyone we encounter teaches us something if we allow them. I would like to thank my grandfather, Fortunato Chirieleison, for teaching me to love life; my father, Mike, and my mother, Rose, for teaching me what to do and what not to do; and my children, Daria, Jessica, Vincent, Dana, and Victoria.

I would like to pay tribute to those who have given of themselves so that I may learn—Dave Keeler, Anne and Frank Sciame, John and Susan Roazzi, Helen Russell, Jeff Holloway, Dennis and Niki McCuistion, Ron Jensen, Sal and Marianne Spedale, Tony Teska, Juan Peña, Ricky and Barbara Sciame, Gary and Debbie Socha, Deepak Chopra, Stuart Wilde, Jerrilynne and Frank Vanella, Bob Thomas, Steve Salvatore, Fred Hill, Rick Pertile, Patti Breitman, Chuck Rock, Dave Milks, Victor Lugo, Jim Dawson, Irwin Sternberg, Wade Saadi, Aubrey Balkind, William Ungar, Kurt Adler, Napoleon Hill, Zig Ziglar, Joe Sansonetti, Dave and Lynn Bower, and the thousands I have trained who allowed me to share in realizing their dreams of success.

Most of all, I thank my wife, Marlene. Through the years she has been my best friend and confidante, and my greatest teacher. But what I remember most is that she stood by me through all the trials and tribulations that were necessary in order for me to become who I am today.

x

THE SPIRITUALITY OF SUCCESS

GETTING RICH WITH INTEGRITY

FOREWORD

This is one of those rare opportunities that I get to write about my dear friend and business partner, Mr. Vincent Roazzi, and he is not in a position to debate, negotiate or navigate my views and opinions of either him or our road of success together. Our story goes back much further and deeper than these few pages will allow me to tell, but what I can tell you is that you have taken a tremendous step forward in enhancing and improving the quality of your life and the lives of those close to you by implementing the knowledge that Vinny shares with you in this book. I am extremely proud of him and the effort that he has set forward because he is clearly demonstrating what our organization is all about—committed individuals, realizing their dreams! At the same time, it is highly unlikely that Vinny began his quest with our organization to, one day, write a book called *The Spirituality of Success*. But what he saw was an opportunity to improve the quality of life for himself and the family that he loved so dearly. He embraced that opportunity and then reached the pinnacles of success that our family and team offered. Upon reaching his summit, he, unlike so many others, chose to continue the climb, as opposed to stopping, enjoying the view, and taking a well-deserved rest.

The purpose of his writing is to share and inform that all of us have a spirit inside that allows us to succeed in whatever endeavors we choose. It's about getting up when you fall down, carrying on when you are out of breath, and believing in yourself when you can go no farther. I hope you see the value and wisdom in his thoughts and that they will help you and your family excel in life, much like the Roazzis have. I would like to share with you some of my fondest memories of our competitive climb together.

Please keep in mind as you read some of my memories below that I share them with the utmost respect and admiration for Vinny. He and every single leader in this organization, myself included, started at exactly the same place you are right now. We have laughed together, cried together, fought like brothers and sisters, and ultimately shared success together. You have a tremendous advantage over where we were in the beginning because there has been so much maturity since our birth years ago; that I believe you can soar right away. Regardless of the ups and downs, the good and the bad, you have joined an organization that has grown since 1989 over thirty percent per year! That is an amazing accomplishment in any industry, and we welcome you to our family with extreme pride!

1.   The very first time I saw the name "Vincent M. Roazzi" was in 1990 when we were sorting some stock certificates for field distribution on a sales contest that the company was running at the time. As I sorted through them I couldn't help but notice that this Roazzi fellow had the majority of the distribution with very few other people receiving anything at all. I turned to my only coworker at the time (yes, there were only two of us) and I said, "My friend, we are in some serious trouble. This guy has to be a crook!" Well, I was wrong, he was simply the top salesperson we had.
Score: Vinny 1, David 0

2.   The first time I met Vinny, we were at a meeting in New Rochelle, New York. Being born and bred in the gracious South, I extended my hand to greet him, and he, being a New York City Italian, tried to kiss me! Swift thinking on my part allowed me to turn my head and take the hit on the cheek instead of square on the mouth.
Score: Vinny 1, David 1

3.   When we made the business decision to cease sales in the state of New York, we were able to convince Vinny to take the state of Connecticut and build sales there for the shareholders. The only problem was we had no products approved for Connecticut.
Score: Vinny 1, David 2

4.   As soon as Vinny got product approved and in his hands, he took sales in Connecticut to over $300,000 overnight.

Score: Vinny 2, David 2

5.   I chose Vinny to be part of an elite group to film a new recruitment video in California. While at an outdoor restaurant in the seaside town of Capitola, Vinny got so amused at the script (it was really bad) that he disrupted the shoot, making it nearly impossible to get the scene finished. After many more hours than expected, and at a much higher cost, I got it done, but Vinny put on a great show for the paying patrons.

Score: Vinny 2, David 3

6.   In Clearwater Beach, Florida on a beautiful Saturday evening, Vinny, the rest of our senior leadership team, and I gathered at a local beach bar for a few drinks before dinner. Dinner never happened, the beers turned into shots, and the cap to the evening was Vinny and I slow dancing with no one else on the dance floor. As the crowd cheered, we cut a rug that left them roaring. Vinny wins this one, as he is a much better dancer, and he got to lead.

Score: Vinny 3, David 3

7.   One day, Vinny and I got into a disagreement on the phone at around 8:00 A.M. The disagreement went on for four straight hours when we agreed to take a break for lunch and to call each other back. We resumed our argument around 1:00 P.M., and it continued well into the evening. The only problem is neither one of us can remember what the argument was about or if either one of us won! This is a draw and the score remains 3 to 3.

8.   In May of 1995, I was at home, in bed, extremely sick with the flu, when I got a call from my office that Vinny had decided to step down because he and I were experiencing "philosophical and business differences." I promptly called him, as bad as I felt, and said, from my view "you can either step up or step out but not down." That may sound harsh, but it was the best thing I feel I ever did for Vinny and his family. If I had accepted it, we wouldn't be sharing this with you today!

Score: Vinny 3, David 4

9.   On June 27, 1997, Vinny, Richard Pertile and I met in Washington D.C. to discuss the feasibility of taking one of our products in a totally new direction for our sales organization. The idea was one that Vinny had brought to me a few years earlier, and I hadn't felt the time was right for us to tackle it then. So I asked Vinny if he still thought he could pull it together, and he said, "Absolutely, I just need eighteen months." I said, "My friend, you have six months, and we have to be ready to roll on January 5, 1998." He picked himself up off of the floor, and said, "I'll get it done." He did, in fact, get it done, and yes, it had problems, but it saved the day and gave our sales representatives the continued opportunity to grow the business.

Score: Vinny 4, David 4

10.   In December 1999, Vinny and I were in Monterey, California hosting a small awards trip for some of our top sales representatives, when I had an allergic reaction to some medication and had to be rushed to the emergency room. Vinny was there for me and remained calm throughout the entire event, as well as keeping my family and friends updated on my progress. While I was lying there trying to make sense of what was going on, he said, "You and I will never argue again." We never have, and I will never forget how kind he was.

Score: Vinny 5, David 4

11.   After being with this organization for over a decade, Vinny is once again "getting out front" and taking the lead in our continued quest to positively effect the lives of individuals we touch. When it comes to the salesperson in the street, he has always fought for what he believed was right (even when he was clearly wrong). He has never lost sight of the bigger picture, when others around him were being small. I believe he will take his last breath attempting to help someone be or do better. Being a witness to and a participant of Vinny's actions has led me to believe that some people can be taken for face value.

Score: Vinny 5, David 5

I could go on and on with stories and memories that may or may not touch your soul. The point that I hope I have made to you is quite simple: no matter what the score is now, if you are doing the right things, with the right people, with the right intentions, the score will always end up tied.

Welcome to our family; thank you for becoming a part of our team; and God Bless America!

Sincerely,

David W. Keeler
President
Cornerstone Marketing of America

xviii   The Spirituality of Success

·   PREFACE

For over a decade as a sales manager, I recruited and trained thousands of individuals into what I consider to be the greatest opportunity in the marketplace today. What amazed me was how few individuals took advantage of this opportunity to change their lives. In my rapid ascension up the corporate ladder, my position changed from salesman to sales trainer to recruiter to regional manager, and then finally to one of national influence.

As I progressed, I was innocent and naïve with regard to the number of individuals who were not achieving success. When I reached the middle management level, it then became quite obvious to me. At the top level, my position was better defined as that of an advisor or mentor than as a manager. I was responsible for a hierarchy of people, some of whom had already produced a certain degree of achievement but still had not achieved long-lasting success. To help them all realize their dreams I had to become better educated about the science of success. So, I read every book and listened to every tape that I could find, and studied the people that succeeded and those who failed. I learned more from the failures than I did from the successes! What follows in this book is what I have learned while attempting to help them.

You will discover that my findings refute some of the generally accepted beliefs about the achievement of success. Initially, I was concerned about this. For years, I always had this nagging question in the back of my mind—why did some of my conclusions not match those of other trainers and authors in the success-training world? Why the discrepancies? I realized the answer as a result of a question that a gentleman named Aric Caplan asked me, "Why do you say that failure is a learned trait?" In answering that question, I realized that most of the other trainers and authors invariably did their research by studying success. They took their findings and, consciously or unconsciously, but I believe unwittingly, attempted to explain them by using today's generally accepted societal and business logic. That's where the error was made—on two counts. That's why, as you will soon learn, success is not logical. To use different terms from another subject to dramatize this, they each chose the upper torso of the human body to explain how and why the body works the way it does. Then they took their limited findings and tried to fit them into the generally accepted belief structure to explain the operation of the whole.

I, on the other hand, studied both the successes and the failures. As a corporate success trainer, I was presented with both of them every day. I studied the failures first because it intrigued me that a person with all the necessary tools was not assured of success. There were many of them, and with 93% of people failing (that too you will soon learn), I had much material to work with. But I wasn't plagued with trying to make it fit into a generally accepted belief structure. There was a reason "why" for everything that happened to these people. I just had to find it. It was simply a study of cause and effect. I also studied the successes, and uncovered a few nuggets of knowledge from that perspective, but they often just confirmed my findings with those who did not succeed. This is the classical scientific method employed by science to arrive at the truth. I just acted like a reporter. *Rich Dad, Poor Dad* did the same thing and revealed some discrepancies in the finance world, the most noteworthy of which is that a house is not an asset, it's a liability, and therefore it's not an investment.

So, I studied the yin AND the yang of the success world, the success and the failure. For, to use another example, how can you ever expect to know what female is, if you don't know what male is? They each have the reason for their being and existence contained within each other. You can't truly know either of them by only studying one of them, because they exist only in relationship to each other. The same is true of up and down, left and right, and success and failure. This all will become crystal clear as you continue to read this book.

It is my fondest wish that this book will help you to change your life, and bring to you the prosperity that you desire. But there is a responsibility connected to the prosperity you seek. If it were not for the successful people of this world, many charities and good works would not exist. I trust you will continue this tradition. After all, your success will not be for you alone to enjoy, nor does anybody become successful by themselves. As you will see, this is a recurring theme in the book. Some call it the secret of success! You be the judge! The secret of success is clearly noted often throughout this book. See if you can uncover the secret, which is the key that unlocks the door to success.

You will notice that the book is presented as a number of short lessons in essay form. I wrote the book in this way because I know that people who are in the process of achieving success have a limited amount of free time. These bits of available time are usually not adequate for reading a normal book chapter. I tried to keep that in mind while writing this book. Various ideas, key words, and sayings are repeated often throughout the book. My experience has been that people learn better through repetition and retain the information for longer periods of time.

So my intention is that you read a chapter a day and ponder the few choice ideas that are highlighted at the end of each chapter. Use the day to absorb these ideas into your belief system and achieve the success of your dreams!

Vinny

The Journey

**He who proposes to be an author,
should first be a student.**
— John Dryden

Like many others who grew up on the tenement streets of Brooklyn, I had dreams of breaking out and becoming a millionaire by the age of 35. At 36, I found myself in a drug rehab, on welfare, with over $100,000 of debts.

Today I am a millionaire.

Living in poverty was like being in prison, except you couldn't see the bars. It's hard to become different when everything around you is the same. The prison of drug addiction made escaping poverty seem like child's play.

I committed myself to treatment because I hated who I had become. I found in recovery not only the answers to a successful life, but also the answers to financial success. After treatment, I accomplished in a year and a half what most people don't accomplish in a lifetime—financial independence.

In my meteoric rise from zero to hero, I attracted the attention of top management in the large public company where I worked. They asked me if I would teach my success skills to their salespeople, which I've been doing for more than a decade. In order to be a trainer, I had to gather as much knowledge as I could about the subject of success. It was important to be able to put into words the steps I had taken in order to enable others to duplicate them. For this reason, I began a series of interviews and studies of successful businesspeople, both entrepreneurs and corporate team players, many of whose stories and experiences you will read about in the following chapters. My discoveries were very interesting and, as you will soon learn, challenge many of today's common beliefs about success.

In the following chapters I will reveal to you what works and what doesn't work. More important, you will learn how to make your success permanent because the success principles being taught are founded in scientific and spiritual truth and follow natural laws. I will *not* teach you how to manipulate others, use mind control, or take advantage of anyone or anything. Success is not about dogs eating dogs or only the strong surviving. That's not real success. It doesn't last. And it doesn't feel good. I will teach you what I call quantum success—authentic, deep, and lasting success based on natural laws. These laws have nothing to do with pushing, controlling, twisting, or hurting. This success is natural. It has a flow. It feels good and it is genuine.

The basis of every concept I will teach you is this: Success is not in what you do, but in who you are. *Success is not in the doing, it's in the being.* Therefore, it's not only physical and mental. It is also spiritual. Authentic success on the outside is simply a reflection of success on the inside. In order for a person to be whole, he must be whole physically, mentally, and spiritually. If any of those is lacking, then the person is not complete, and that has its consequences. Since authentic success is simply a reflection of the person, it too must be whole—physically, mentally, and spiritually. If it isn't, it won't feel good. It won't be authentic. It won't last!

If I were in front of you right now, I'd begin your training by saying, "So you want to become successful? You want to change your life? Are you sure?" The reason why I'd ask you this question is because one of the most remarkable observations I've made in training thousands of people over the past decades is this: *People want to change their lives, but they don't want to change (their lives)!* Oh, I know it sounds ridiculous, but it's ridiculously true. You hear people say it all the time. "If only I had more money, my life would be different." "If only I worked for myself, I'd get paid what I'm worth." "If only I had a different job, different spouse, different environment, if, if, if. . . ." People think that an exterior change will change their lives. If that were true, then 75% to 85% of lottery winners would not be broke again after 5 or 10 years. These lottery winners didn't win true, long-lasting success; they only won money. That's why their affluence is a short-lived experience. Success is not achieved through exterior changes.

Your life today, where you are today, is a result of the decisions you made yesterday. People experience results based upon what they do, or what they fail to do. You may not like to hear it, but you are exactly where you are supposed to be, exactly where you decided to be. After all, you're the one who made the decisions. And as unappetizing as that may sound, it is certainly better to be responsible for where you are than to be a victim with no choice.

The fact that I always have a choice was one of the most illuminating and liberating concepts that I have ever learned. I realized that I may not always like the choices, but I always have a choice. Before this realization, I would often see myself as a victim of the winds and tides of life. A little sailboat trying to stay afloat, explaining the unexplained as luck, and waiting for my big break in life so that it could be different. I had to learn the hard way that nothing in life will be different for you unless you become different. We humans make our life's decisions based upon what we know. From the time we are born, we are programmed and conditioned to believe certain things. As we grow older, we formulate our own opinions (beliefs) and take action based upon this knowledge, which is often tainted with the conditioning and programming we acquired along the way. This is how we each gain our knowledge to make our life's decisions, but too many people go through life never questioning what they think they know. That's one of the reasons why success is difficult for most people to achieve, and why they look to someone else for the answers.

The tin man sang, "If I only had a heart…" The lion wanted courage, the scarecrow—a brain, and Dorothy just wanted to go home. So they spent a lot of time and energy seeking the Wizard and found that what they wanted so badly was always in their possession. They also found that there was no Wizard. There are no gurus, genies, or fairy godmothers that can touch you with a wand and change your life. There is no magic that I, or anyone else, can perform that will give you the success you desire. *The Wizard of Oz* is a metaphor for those of us "searching" for success. Like Dorothy, we all engage in elaborate searches for something that was under our noses all the time. Becoming successful is like coming home. That which you seek has been in your possession all the while. You are the magic! You are success!

Now before you start denying it, let me ask you a few questions. Deep down in the hidden recesses of your being, haven't you felt that your life was meant to be something more? Don't you believe that somehow you were destined for greatness…if you could only find the way or catch that break? Aren't you one of those weary seekers searching for success? You need to understand that, like Dorothy, you have had the power all the time—you only lack the knowledge of that power, but it's there. It's hidden under all the layers of conditioning and programming that you've accumulated over the years.

The following pages will reveal to you the knowledge of your inherent power that lies within and is reflected in the physical and metaphysical laws of the universe. I will use the laws of science to demonstrate the physical and mental aspects of success, and the tenets of Eastern spiritual philosophy as well as the Christian and Jewish traditions to demonstrate the spiritual dimensions of success. These truths have been in effect since time began and are natural and universal. I will explain them using everyday language because their truths are simple. I'm not attempting to get you to be interested, nor does it matter if you ever become interested, in the sciences, spirituality, or religion. The truths they are based upon operate no matter what you think or what you believe. You can be aware of them, or you can be a victim of them. Ignorance of the law of gravity does not change it one bit. The uninformed call it good luck or bad luck. The informed realize it's the difference between knowledge and lack of knowledge. It's the difference between authentic success and lack of success.

These same laws, these simple truths, are what have allowed the universe to operate successfully since the beginning of time. They are tried and true, and they will change your life. They are the blueprints that point the way to *lasting* success, to *authentic* success, to *quantum* success!

POINTS TO PONDER

Success is not in the doing, it's in the being!

People want to change their lives, but they don't want to change (their lives)!

2

THE TRUTH IS OUT

**If a thousand old beliefs were ruined
in our march to truth, we must still march on.**
— Stopford Augustus Brooke

By their sixty-fifth birthday, 93 percent of people are either dead or dead broke and require the good-natured financial support of family and friends or social security just to provide for the basic necessities. Here, in the greatest country in the world for opportunity, and after forty to fifty years of hard work, 93 percent of Americans achieve—POVERTY! This fact is provided by a study of the 1980 U.S. Department of Labor Statistics and Mortality Tables as to what happened to people between their twenty-fifth and sixty-fifth birthdays. The study found that only seven percent became financially secure enough to maintain a comfortable retirement lifestyle.

I don't know about you, but I was told a completely different story. It was impressed upon me in many ways, that the key to becoming successful was to get a good education and open a small business, or work for a good company, be a loyal hardworker, and climb the corporate ladder. In the end, I would receive a pension, or have enough savings to live a comfortable retirement. Obviously that story isn't true or why would so many people be barely surviving in retirement?

As if barely surviving isn't bad enough, consider these facts

1. Fewer men are worth $100 at age 68 after fifty years of hard work than at age 18. (Denby's Economic Tables, 1990.)

2. Eighty-five out of 100 people do not have $250 in cash at retirement. (Social Security Administration, 1990.)

3. Over one-third of all senior citizens live below the poverty level as established by the federal government. (U.S. Census, 1990.)

4. Two and a quarter million senior citizens forfeit their social security because they have to work.
(Social Security Administration, 1990.)

Is it true? Yes, it is, and the sources are, unfortunately, highly respected. The results are in. You have a 93 percent chance of being dead or dead broke if you follow what I, and probably you, were taught. At one time I thought it was a master hoax perpetrated by big business to keep people at the worker level to fulfill its need for personnel in the office and on the assembly line. That was my "Big Brother" period, and it is no longer what I believe. But you have to admit that it's mind-boggling that people still believe that this commonly believed formula will lead to success when the results of this plan unmistakably deny its validity.

Unfortunately if we have the hope that the rising stock market and the lowest unemployment rate in history could change these results, we only have to look at these recent statistics to realize the truth:

1. Between 1996 and 1997, median household income in the U.S. [for all age groups] increased 1.9 percent, the third consecutive year that real (inflation adjusted) income increased significantly. With this increase in income, overall household median income has *almost* returned to its 1989 level. (October 1998 study by Ke Bin Wu, Economist—Source: U.S. Department of Commerce.)

2. For those 65 years or older, the total mean income in 1999 was $21,417 per year, of which $9,129 was from social security. (Bureau of Labor Statistics & Bureau of the Census—Study of Source Income in 1999.)

3. Nine percent of aged Social Security beneficiaries are living below the poverty level and 39 percent are kept out of poverty by their social security benefits—so that the total poverty rate without social security would be 48 percent! (Social Security Administration, 1998.)

4. For those approaching retirement (55 to 64 years of age), median family net worth increased from $124,600 in 1989 to only $127,500 in 1998.

A total increase in net worth of *only* $2900! (*Federal Reserve Bulletin*, January 2000, Authored by A. Kennickell.)

5. Social security is the major source of income (50 percent or more) for 63 percent of those aged 65 or older. It contributes 90 percent or more of income for almost one-third of the beneficiaries and is the only source of income for 18 percent of them. (Social Security Administration, 1998.)

6. The financial assets held by the typical boomer [born 1946-1964] are worth only about $1000 and only one-fifth [20 percent] of boomers have more than $25,000 in financial assets. Even the top ten percent of the boomers have only modest financial assets [$66,000] and the lowest one-quarter have negative financial assets, i.e. their liabilities exceed their financial assets. (1993 Wealth Module tabulated by AARP Public Policy Institute.)

The importance of these facts is sobering in the realization that the more things change the more they stay the same. The measurement of assets is important because, upon retirement, one's assets determine one's source of income, which determines a person's ability to live a comfortable lifestyle. And even if we use the average assets of the top 10 percent of boomers (statistic #6), those who, one would think have the best handle on their retirement, and use an average safe return (5 percent) we find that their current assets would provide a return of only $3300 per year in income—hardly the good life! Add to that the possible disappearance of social security and the future looks bleak.

The truth is that this isn't about 1980, 1990, 1998 or 2010. At any given point in time these statistics are either a little less true or a little more true, but they are always true! The point is that the average person never achieves financial independence, and therefore has the wrong formula for success, which we keep unwittingly passing down from generation to generation. Even if you were born just yesterday, these statistics point to the ineffectiveness of the success formulas of the teachers whom you will encounter in your lifetime.

The good news is now that you know the results; you do not have to become a victim. You can change your life and its outcome by changing what you "know."

Unfortunately, many people go through life never questioning what they think they know. From the time we are born, our minds, which operate all too much like a computer, are programmed to believe certain things. As we get older, we formulate our beliefs and actions based on what we "know." Just like a computer, our minds can only feed back the information that was originally fed into it. And if the initial input is wrong, the results will be disastrous!

By the statistics we already know, *93 percent of people have the wrong formula for success*, and the odds are that these are the people who provided your knowledge, beliefs, and programming. Our parents, teachers, associates, etc., taught us as best they could, but little did they know that the formula for success, as they knew it, was inaccurate. If you need further proof, just look at where they are financially. Is that what you dream of achieving? If it is, go no further, forget this book, and ask for a refund. The basic premise that escapes the multitude is that if you want to be successful, seek the advice of a successful person. If you want to learn how to play tennis well, you can't ask someone who has never played and expect to get the right results. People can't teach you what they don't know! They may love you, have the greatest of intentions, and do the best they can, but they can't teach you what they don't know!

Much of the reason why 93 percent of people have the wrong formula for success is that many of today's popular beliefs are based upon the military style of management and achievement. For much of the twentieth century, the world, including the United States, was engaged in military conflict. Since it was news, it commanded much media attention. And in our part of the world, that attention was centered on the numerous American victories: our success in battle. Military conflict was so prevalent that it became embedded in our culture through the media, and along with that military conflict came military thinking. The world was so convinced of the success achieved through utilizing military strategy that many of the high-ranking military officers secured high-profile management positions in corporate America after their term of service in the armed forces. But military success is not authentic, long-lasting financial success! These two types of success operate according to diametrically different principles, primarily because one works through aggression and the other through attraction— they're opposites!

So the people (our teachers) that the prior statistics spoke about were the people who were indoctrinated into believing that the military principles of achievement could be applied to financial achievement to create financial independence and its corresponding peace of mind, but the results of their lives tell us otherwise. For the most part, the world has learned that there is nothing good about war. Military victory is a short-lived experience and there are no true winners in a military conflict. But the residual subconscious programming of achievement through military principles is still there, forever corrupting what we believe is necessary to achieve financial success and peace of mind. Except for a few prehistoric-thinking organizations, this military approach to management has long since been abandoned by much of corporate America, but its resultant aggressive thinking and belief about financial achievement are much more deeply embedded in our society. The military style of management and achievement is based on fighting, deception, competition, secrecy, retribution, power, fear, and selfishness. Corporate America found out the hard way that when you fight to gain something, you also have to fight to keep it, and so much time and energy are consumed in fighting to keep it that it saps your ability to gain further progress. In other words, the militaristic approach can only bring you so far and then no further, because the very nature of its operation is self-consuming. There comes a point with the military approach when all available time and energy are consumed in simply maintaining and fighting to keep what has already been accomplished.

The same is true of financial success that is achieved by using military principles. If you fight to achieve financial success, then it naturally follows that you have to fight to keep it. Financial success achieved in this way brings enough worries that the happiness and peace of mind that success is supposed to bring is fleeting at best. The worries of "Who is trying to take my money?" "Who's just being my friend because of my money?" "What if I lose my money?" plague your mind. Where is the happiness in that? If your time and energy is spent on trying to keep it, where's the peace of mind? That's why people who do achieve financial success in this way aren't happy no matter how successful they become. If you watch them, you see that when they discover that having six figures doesn't make them happy, they push to become millionaires. And when they discover that becoming a millionaire isn't enough, they fight to become multi-millionaires. They keep buying things in their subconscious hope that maybe the "things" will bring them the peace and happiness that they so greatly desire. So their cars are Mercedes, Jaguar, or the like, and depending on how much wealth they accumulate, they have boats and planes that keep being replaced with larger versions. They have the large jewelry, the expensive furs, the latest contraptions, the best of this and the best of that, but it's all for naught. It's important to point out that the "things" themselves are not the problem. It's why they buy the "things" that's the problem. You should always ask yourself, "Why do I want that new Mercedes?" or "Why do I want that Rolex?" After all, they are just a car and a watch! If you need them to feel successful or to feel better about yourself, then you're buying them for the wrong reasons.

The book, *The Millionaire Next Door*, displayed this point artfully. The true rich do not display their wealth. They don't have to appear rich. They are rich. The book reveals that a truly rich person could be your next-door neighbor and you'd never know it. For example, Warren Buffet lives in the first house that he and his wife ever bought before they became wealthy. And all of the successful people that I have interviewed fit the same mold. They are subtle, humble, and just downright nice people to be with. They aren't flashy or famous and they don't use their possessions to broadcast their success to the world. That's not to say that they don't have some of the trappings of success. They have them and that's the point. The wealthy don't buy a Mercedes or a Rolex for the same reasons that the average person buys them. The difference is that if they buy them, they buy them for performance over the long term, and because the difference between $15,000 and $50,000 to a wealthy person is inconsequential. They own their possessions; their possessions don't own them.

In the following chapters, we will uncover how to achieve true financial success and peace of mind by examining some of the self-limiting beliefs that are a part of society's knowledge. Since childhood, these self-limiting beliefs have formed the basis of many a person's belief structure, but sabotage their efforts to achieve prosperity. The evidence that these self-defeating beliefs are embedded in our society is demonstrated by the colloquialisms that we use.

A popular belief that I've heard many times is, "Don't burn your bridges behind you" and another less popular version is "Always leave the door open." Another well-intentioned success-killer is "Become a good loser." How about "Be careful" or "I'm not negative, I'm being realistic." Every one of these "truths" teaches us to play it safe. They teach us to play the game "not to lose" as opposed to "playing to win." People are so careful that success is not possible. Financial success is winning. There is no other way to accomplish it. But it's different from the military idea of winning where there has to be a loser. With financial success, everyone can win. In fact, most truly successful people are the source of financial independence for many others. That is one of the trademarks of authentic financial success. However, since these colloquialisms are part of your belief structure, and there's a 93 percent chance that they are, how can you ever experience your financial dreams? In the next chapter, we will begin the process that will change your life!

POINT TO PONDER

Ninety-three percent of people have the wrong formula for success!

3

Success Is Not Logical

Man is not the creature of circumstances;
circumstances are the creates of man.
— Benjamin Disraeli

When people hear the phrase, "success is not logical" for the first time, they get a puzzled look and ask me what I mean. To fully comprehend its meaning, we must first understand what it means to be "logical." "Logical" is the opinion of the majority. It's what most people think makes sense, but in truth it is a subjective viewpoint based on time and place. Here in America, the vast majority end up broke, which makes their "logic" illogical, or at least, illogical to those who are successful.

The most amazing thing I've noticed about the successful people I've met is that they've done some things that the average person (the 93 percent) would determine to be foolish. They've taken risks and made decisions that defy all "reason." Their choices were illogical and sometimes appeared to be downright irresponsible. In fact, it's so prevalent in the stories of successful people that I suspect it qualifies as a requirement for success. *You'll know you're on the right track if at least 93 percent of people disagree with you!*

Let's examine why. Since childhood, we've been trained to try to be right, to be correct. Heaven forbid we should make a mistake and be wrong! That brings negative consequences, right? Wrong! The only way to find out what is truly right is by risking the possibility of being wrong. Errors are training experiences. The fact that we need to constantly keep in mind is that every action produces a result. Unfortunately, inaction also produces a result, a fact of which most people are unaware. Like an experimental scientist, a successful person keeps trying different combinations, in whatever area he chooses, until he finds one that works. He tries something and records the results, both positive and negative. Then he makes adjustments to enhance the positive and eliminate the negative. He keeps performing and refining until he gets the outcome he desires, and then he repeats it to build wealth.

Upon closer inspection, you will note that in the course of the refining process, every time the experimenter did not achieve his final optimum result, he could be said, in the world's terms, to have failed. However, without the initial failures and subsequent refining, the eventual success would not have been possible. That is because success is born of failure. It has its roots in failure, so that those who will not chance failure cannot experience success. It may sound crazy to you, but you need to celebrate failure. You need to revel in its presence. You need to invite it into your life.

Now, I know you were taught differently, but take a good look at who taught you. You need to understand that the world will not give up its wealth in exchange for something that is easily accomplished or readily found. The most expensive things you can buy are among the rarest available, like gold and diamonds. Likewise, the world's wealth goes to those rare people who have the stomach for failure; those who celebrate it and revel in it because they know each failure brings them one step closer to their eventual success. It's a law of nature that works every time. *Nothing in this world can resist a person on a mission.*

You've already experienced this in your life on a smaller scale. Some of you may remember experiencing this when you bought your first car. Remember how determined you were, how it dominated almost all of your waking thoughts? Nothing could stop you. You wouldn't let it! And although buying your first car is usually plagued with challenges, buying a car is relatively easy. Becoming wealthy is somewhat more difficult, but the process is the same. It requires unwavering focus on your objective, which we will discuss later in greater detail.

Another example, which everyone has experienced, occurred when you were young, before your full programming was complete. You may not remember your own experience, but you'll understand because it's a common experience for humans. It was when you learned to walk. When all you could do was crawl, you had a driving desire to stand up and walk upright because you wanted to be like everyone else. You risked life and limb to achieve your desired result.

Did you do it on your first try? How about your second attempt? The answer to both questions is no. In fact, you failed many times in the process of learning to walk. But that didn't stop you; nothing could stop you. You wanted to walk like everyone else, and you wouldn't have it any other way. You were focused. You were too young to realize how potentially dangerous the undertaking was. You could have poked out your eye, cracked open your skull, or experienced a multitude of negative, damaging outcomes. But you were too young to know and unable to comprehend the language if someone would have attempted to inform you of these dangers.

In fact, if you engaged in the same behavior and risk as an adult, people would call you stupid. Little do you know that being called stupid in the pursuit of success is the highest compliment anyone can pay you. Yes, to be successful requires that you be stupid—stupid enough to do the things that unsuccessful people refuse to do, and take the risks that they refuse to take! I call this "intelligent stupidity."

Another illogical characteristic of success is the ease with which it can be duplicated. If what you want to accomplish has already been done, then seek out a person who has achieved your desired result, duplicate his or her process, and you will get the same result. This is called modeling, but it's more difficult than it sounds because we are naturally predisposed and programmed to do everything with the least effort possible. This is something we often do unconsciously or with very little thought. And because we were taught that accomplishing something with less effort was a desirable result called "being efficient," we often try to accomplish this result whenever possible. When you are modeling someone else's process, this predisposition toward efficiency is deadly. It causes you to get a different result. We will cover this predisposition toward efficiency in greater detail later on, but for now you must realize that modeling is copying a person's process exactly as you observed or as you were instructed.

Modeling does not require thinking; it only requires doing. This is where laziness becomes an asset. If someone else has already achieved your desired result, be lazy enough to do it exactly as he or she did and you will achieve the same result. This is "intelligent laziness." Once you have done that, then you can experiment on refining the process to achieve a greater result. But you can only do that once you have achieved the initial positive result, not before. The reason is that once you've already accomplished it, you will understand and comprehend the essential parts of the success formula. Then if you experience a less than desirable result, you'll know why.

I hope you can appreciate why success is not logical. To sum up what was said in this entire section, *in order to be successful, you have to be stupid and lazy*. I'll bet you never heard it expressed that way before!

POINTS TO PONDER

You'll know you're on the right track if
at least 93 percent of people disagree with you.

Nothing in this world can resist a person on a mission.

In order to be successful, you have to be stupid and lazy!

Success is not logical!

4

The Ego and Failure

**I have more trouble with D.L. Moody
than any other man I know.**

— D. L. Moody, religious leader (1837-1899)

I'm thoroughly convinced that what truly plagues mankind is ego. If it were not for ego, we wouldn't separate things by good or bad, positive or negative, success or failure, etc. There would just be what is. As far as I can determine, man is the only living creature that has this handicap. It comes included with the gift of free will or choice. Depending on how it's used, the ego not only determines a person's destiny, but also the destiny of the world. Unbridled ego has been the cause of every war, every injustice in the annals of history. If you do not control your ego, your ego will control you. If you do not have a plan for your ego, your ego will have a plan for you. You can be the master of your ego, or you can be its slave. It's your choice.

One facet of our ego is our perception of who we are. It's not who we really are; it's who we think we should be as a result of who we were programmed to be. I remember vividly, during my childhood, being constantly called "lazy" or "slow." I grew up believing that, and would subconsciously and consciously beat myself up because I was lazy. I believed it. Today, I know it's not true. It was never true. The truth was that I was bored, but nobody bothered to find that out. They chose instead to label me lazy. Part of the problem is that when you start believing the labels, you start exhibiting the behavior. I actually started to become lazy, except I didn't do a very good job of it. I'm the type who always has to be doing something, so for me, being lazy is hard work.

Another label I was saddled with until my first year in college had to do with my appearance, specifically my appeal to the opposite sex. I was led to believe that I was unattractive and very close to ugly. When I left those labelers and their surroundings to enter college life, I discovered the opposite was true. Not immediately, though. It took many years to undo what it took years to do. And it took that long because I was not consciously active in the process. I was still allowing life to happen to me instead of through me.

In the beginning, I thought that the college girls who were attracted to me were blind. I became suspicious. It couldn't be my looks, so what were they after? Eventually, when I realized there was nothing I had that they could want to exploit, I slowly started to believe I was attractive. I enjoyed the ride. But I always had the shadow of the program hanging over me—the pang of disbelief deep in my gut that it might not be true. It wasn't until my mid-thirties that I finally realized that I really do have attractive qualities.

A byproduct of this belief of being unattractive was that I also became shy. People who know me today find this impossible to believe, but it's true. I felt unwanted and different. I felt inferior. Thinking of myself as uninteresting, I found it hard to get to know people, especially the opposite sex. To compensate, I would gravitate to friends who were outgoing and very sociable. How else would I be able to meet girls? I couldn't do it myself.

My shyness was shattered when I was elected to student government. I was elected on the coattails of the social butterfly on campus—he knew everybody. Being on the same party ticket, I won the election because he won the election. But now I had a problem: I had to perform. I found myself thrust in front of the student population, expected to speak. It was a time of crisis in the New York City University system, and I found myself presenting our case to the chancellor and the school board. Before I knew it, I was speaking to the senate and the assembly of New York State in Albany. It was baptism by fire. My shyness was annihilated. I unlearned it almost as quickly as I had learned it. That may have been who I had thought I was, but it was true no more. The shyness was part of me that I didn't like, but I didn't know I had the power to change it. Circumstances forced me to change it. Today I know I can change anything about myself at will.

All these insights into who I formerly was I offer to you to help in your understanding of yourself. Is there something about you that you don't like, that you would like to change? What is it about you that you like that you wouldn't want to change? If you decrease your dislikes about yourself and accentuate what you like, then you'll be well on the way to becoming who you want to be, not whom everyone else wants or wanted you to be. You already know what you like and dislike about yourself. That nagging little voice in the back of your head has been trying to tell you for years. Maybe now you're ready to listen!

Your ego is the source of all your pain. Periodically, your ego may help you to achieve something because someone challenges your picture of yourself. Unfortunately, the achievement doesn't last very long. It withers away and dies because it doesn't have its roots in a firm foundation. Your ego is not reality, and therefore cannot sustain anything worthwhile for any length of time. It's one of the reasons why certain people experience initial or periodic success but just can't seem to hold on to it. Your ego is a block to your full potential. Whenever the ego is present, disappointment will surely follow.

One of my greatest challenges in writing this book is my ego. Every day I have to wrestle with it, beat it down, and put it away. It's necessary in order to have this book written for you and not me. I will not tell you anything that you don't know. None of it is new, although it might seem that way. No knowledge is ever new, just unrealized. The moment I believe that the insights I share are my doing will mark the beginning of the end. I am merely the observer, the reporter commissioned to clarify what already is. My job is to take the difficult and try to make it simple. As soon as I begin to believe that any of the wisdom in these words flows from me instead of through me, I become of no value to you, and you deserve better.

So you see, the ego never disappears. We all, always, have a picture of ourselves that we try to live up to. The decisive point is being aware that our ego is always on duty. It's always there, but your awareness gives you power over it. It is imperative, however, to ensure that the ego you carry around is at least yours. Not everybody's picture of you that you were conditioned to accept, but *your* picture of *yourself*. To quote Polonius in *Hamlet*, "This above all: to thine own self be true." Your picture of yourself should at least be yours; it should be true, for better or for worse. Then and only then, when you have to wrestle with it, at least you'll know what you're dealing with. As GI Joe says, "Knowing is half the battle." The sign over the entrance door of Socrates' school in ancient Greece read, "Know thyself." I will tell you that you must first *"Be thyself."* It begins with the question "Who am I?"

POINTS TO PONDER

Your ego is the source of all your pain!

Be thyself!

5

WHO AM I?

As a man-of-war that sails through the sea, so this earth
that sails through the air. We mortals are all on board a fast-sailing,
never-sinking world-frigate, of which God was the ship-wright.
Thus sailing with sealed orders, we ourselves are the repositories
of the secret packet, whose mysterious contents we long to learn.
There are no mysteries out of ourselves.
— Herman Melville in *Moby Dick*

The Atman [the real self] is permanent, eternal,
and therefore existence itself.
— Hindu Philosophy

The question "Who am I?" to an individual is synonymous
with the magic words, "Open, Sesame." But it's not the question that's important, it's the process. In order for you to change or reprogram what you know,
you first have to find out who you are, because you are what you know. You
are the sum total of all your years of accumulated knowledge. Your knowledge
determines where you live, how you dress, whom you marry, and where you
work. We pride ourselves as logical beings who do things for a reason. The
logic and reasoning of what we do is based on our knowledge and beliefs,
which, for the most part, are a result of our conditioning and programming.
People with different programming or those who have chosen to reprogram
themselves have different logic and different reasoning. In our culture, these
are the people who become successful. That's why examining your programming is so important. If you're going to have any possibility at all to change
your financial future, it must begin with a realization of the self-limiting
beliefs that cause you to unconsciously self-destruct.

For the thousands of people I've come in contact with over the years, this truly was the major reason for their lack of success. As their trainer, I could see how their unexamined programming gave rise to their beliefs and behavior that unwittingly violated the natural universal laws that govern success. And most of the laws they violated concerned the spiritual aspects of success, the spirituality of success. This is the same reason why the 93 percent, that we spoke of earlier, do not achieve financial independence. They do not know that success is the result of conscious *and* unconscious (automatic) behavior. Their automatic responses, their reactions, are almost always the main culprit. Without examination of this programmed belief structure, their reactions will always be the same, which we already know did not and will not result in success. No matter how gifted, skilled, or determined a person might be, any and all attempts to become permanently successful will fail eventually until they examine their programming and its resultant self-destructive behavior and make the necessary changes.

In order to begin the process, you need to find a quiet place to be alone for a while. I'm not giving you a definitive time period because it's the start of a lifelong process. The one thing about success you should know is that it's addictive. In order to constantly continue to grow, you have to constantly reexamine what you know. Once you get your first taste of success, you'll want to continue the improvement process throughout your life. That's the only way to get the kind of success that lasts. Many of us know people who were once successful, but then they ran into some "bad luck." Luck plays no role either way in the formulation of success. When you are finished reading this book, you will know that. People experience results based upon what they do or fail to do. Everybody is exactly where he or she decided to be, for better or for worse. And as we already discussed, people make decisions based on what they know. So the only way to change where you are is to change who you are. And you are what you know. Knowledge is power.

Once you get yourself in a quiet place with no distractions, contemplate for a moment what you are about to do. As soon as you begin, your whole life from that moment on will be different. Your life will improve. You are making a conscious decision to change your life for the better. Not like the many countless souls who will go through this life and in their later years reflect back, saying, "I should have..." or "If only I..." or "I could have...."

You are about to take full responsibility for the prosperity that will occur in your life. You are about to exercise your free will, quite possibly for the first time! It's a very exciting moment and yet a fearful one. You may feel apprehension, as many people often do. They are afraid of what they will find if they look deeply. You see, the exercise "Who am I?" is not a résumé of your life. It is not where you were born, where you received your education, how many children you have, or what you've done. Believe it or not, these were predestined based on your programming. The "Who am I?" is an examination of that programming. It goes way beyond a résumé. It's about honesty. It's about the you that only you really know. It's about all your strengths and weaknesses, and usually the weaknesses are what people are afraid to discover. They see them as inadequacies instead of areas for improvement. If they see themselves as lacking, usually their self-image can't handle it. Their ego wants no part of that pain. You must keep in mind, though, that for the most part, *who you are today is not your doing.* Who you are today is who you decided to be based on what you know. And what you know today is based on what you were taught from an early age. You are your program!

The real shame in all of this is that few people really are who they decided to be. They are who other people programmed or decided for them to be, like an electronic robot that can think, but when it does, it can only think the way it was programmed to think. It can only think *what* it was programmed to think. But as I am transferring this information to you, I am also transferring the responsibility to you, from now on, for all that you are or are not. The good news is that up until this point, you were not responsible for the results of your life because those were predestined by your programming. The bad news is that from this point on, you are!

Very often, it is extremely difficult for people to get to the bottom of who they are. The answer lies in why we do the things that we do. We decide what we do or how we react based on who we are, which is what we know. For this reason, until you really progress in the process of changing your inner program, you would be better off to ignore your first response to anything regarding success or at least seriously question it before taking action. The odds are that your first response will be a programmed response, the same response as the 93 percent we spoke of earlier who do not achieve financial independence. This programmed response may or may not be the response of the real you, the part of you that innately already knows how to be successful. Ultimately, the trouble with most people is that they just don't think. They can't understand why their lives don't change when they do nothing to change their lives. They continually keep doing the same things, thinking the same thoughts, and reacting the same way, time and time again. And then they wonder why they keep getting the same results! A little gem of street knowledge says, "If you keep doing what you're doing, you'll keep getting what you're getting!" It's so simple and so fundamental, and yet the simplest things are sometimes the most difficult to grasp.

If you are not yet convinced that you're living a life that was charted by other people through programming, then let me give you an example. There have been many times while walking with different friends when I would come in contact with an animal, usually a dog. I would immediately freeze and feel apprehension and fear while the other person would smile, walk over, and pet the animal. I would think that my friend was acting foolishly and taking too much of a risk. Of course, this thinking was a product of my fear, which was usually in direct proportion to the size of the animal. But no matter how small the dog may have been, I still felt fear. I remember catching myself in the midst of one of these episodes once and thinking that my reaction was strange. I've never been bitten or attacked by a dog or any other animal. It didn't make any sense. So I examined my past to find out why I reacted in this way.

What I remember is my mother cautioning me many times, at an early age, about trusting animals, especially dogs. I also remember being scolded for doing the same thing my friend did. It was indelibly etched in my mind that a strange animal would harm me, and I should be careful. Of course, watching my friend pet and hug the strange dog and watching the dog wag its tail and lick with appreciation should have dispelled my fear, but it didn't. I still believed that it would hurt me. What's important about this incident is the question, who was really afraid of the dog? Was it me or my mother? Or my mother living through me? These programs are so strong that even today I feel apprehension when a dog is in sight, even though I know about this program and have no real reason to fear it. However, the knowledge of myself keeps me from taking action based on that fear because it really isn't my fear. It's just my programming.

I will use another example directly related to success. In my present company, the new salespeople must pay for their own license, which is required in our business. In return, they receive a higher than usual commission rate and the opportunity to earn what they are truly worth. It is an unlimited, performance-based opportunity, which is what many people voice that they yearn for. Since most of the prospective salespeople have contacted us in response to a classified ad, they are basically in a job-seeking mode. This mind-set and the programmed beliefs attached to it make it impossible for them to make the couple hundred dollars' investment to get themselves into a position to take advantage of the opportunity, which could yield hundred of thousands of dollars.

Why? Because they won't "pay for a job," as they put it. They get excited about the position and its earning potential, but they can't get past paying for their own license. Why? Because it's not normal. What they don't know is that when you don't pay for your own license, you usually pay for it dearly in lower commissions and less residual income. These prospective salespeople really want financial success—they want a better than normal result—but they want it to be the result of normal actions. Not possible! If it were possible, then all normal people, the majority, would be successful. In order to be successful, you have to learn how to go beyond being normal. The programming of the prospective salespeople does not allow them the ability to make an investment for success as long as they perceive that they are in a "job" situation. What dictates this? Memory. The memory program of a negative experience for themselves or someone they know who wasted money in a similar situation. They are living out their programming of playing "not to lose," instead of playing to win, as if success doesn't involve risk. A few hundred dollars keeps them from fulfilling the dreams of a lifetime. It doesn't make much sense when you look at it from a different perspective.

Being conscious of why you do the things you do, or knowing why you react in a certain way to a specific stimulus, will help to define who you are. Armed with this knowledge, you no longer have to be a victim of your conditioning or your programming. You will know immediately when the program surfaces exactly what is happening. This will give you the freedom to choose your action or reaction intelligently, and change the course of your life.

Before I go any further, I want to clarify something. The "you" that the "Who am I?" exercise reveals is not really you. It is the person you were conditioned to be. The real you lies waiting to be discovered deep inside. In fact, let's do that first. Let's uncover the real you so that when we eventually do the "Who am I?" exercise, you will be better able to understand the point I am trying to make. This exercise is designed to reveal some of the beauty the real you possesses.

For this exercise, take five minutes of quiet time and spend it on nothing but yourself. Take a clean sheet of paper and list all the people you admire. They don't have to be living people. You can use people from your past, historical figures, and even characters from mythology. **Do this before you read any further.**

Next, put a one-word adjective next to each name as the reason for your admiration. For instance, if you admire somebody for the ability to make good decisions, you might use the term "very smart," but instead of using "very smart," use one descriptive word such as "intelligent," "wise," or "smart." To describe someone whom you may admire for being a "good mother," you might use the word "maternal." Make sure it's a descriptive adjective, so instead of using the word "wisdom," you would use the word "wise." You can use more than one admirable quality; in fact, it's preferable that you do, but it's important that you use just one-word descriptions of why you admire them. **Do this before you go to the next step.**

The next thing I would like for you to do is combine the list on the bottom of your page so that all these admirable qualities each appear only once. So if you listed "wise" for your Uncle Harry and Abraham Lincoln, you would list "wise" once at the bottom of your page. **Do this now.**

Now that you have completed that task, take a look at your final list before you go any further.

What I am about to reveal to you now is foolproof. Your list represents the values that you admire in other people. You chose specific values from a vast assortment of possible values, because they are the ones that are important to you. The revelation here comes in response to the question "Why are they important to you?" The answer is that they are important to you because this is a list of your core values. What you have listed is a description of the "real you." Your list is you! Now before you start to shake your head and deny it, think for a second. Doesn't your list represent who you would like to be? The problem is, for every one of them, you probably can remember a time when you weren't "wise," "honest," or "loyal."

One of the problems with being human is that each of us is our own worst critic. We tend to see ourselves in absolute terms. So if you were honest 99 times out of 100, and you can remember the one time you were dishonest, which you will if it's one of your core values, then you won't judge yourself to be honest because you can remember that one time. Notice I use the word "judge" because that's exactly what we do—pass sentence on ourselves. It's best in this case to remember that life (and success) is about growing through mistakes. It's also wise to remember these words of wisdom whenever you judge yourself or anyone else: Even God, in His infinite wisdom, waits until a man has completed his life before He passes judgment.

Still, the mistakes you made don't negate the importance of these values for you. What mistakes represent are the times that you faltered, the times when you failed to portray the "real" you. That has its consequences, as we will discuss shortly, but for now, you cannot deny that the reason you admire these qualities in other people is because they represent the values that are important to you. This is a list of your values. Your values define who you are, even though we are all human and make the mistake of going against ourselves from time to time. Take another good look. This is a list of your core values, the core of who you are. *Your core values reveal your intrinsic perfection.* This list is the *real you!*

The importance of this list is not to pat yourself on the back for the fine human being that you genuinely are, although I don't deny that you should take a few minutes to revel in this realization. The greatest value I have found in this list is the result of what happens when I exhibit behavior that goes against one of the core values I have listed. For instance, I listed honesty as one of the reasons why I admire my brother-in-law, Ricky. When I do something dishonest and go against my value, I pay for it dearly, no matter how much my ego might try to rationalize my actions. When I go against myself and deny one of my core values, I feel hollow inside. I feel guilty, injured, and betrayed, as if someone did something to me. But it was I who did it to myself! I feel a loss of spirit because I've denied the person who I really am. I feel guilty because I know better.

All of this results in an "off" mood. Interestingly enough, even though I've done this exercise and know what happens when I go against myself, I'm not *always* conscious of what I'm doing while I'm doing it. However, I always feel the result. You see, all this takes place whether you're conscious of it or not. All this happens to you, even if you've never made a list. It's one of those laws of the universe that works every time, even if you have no knowledge of it. If you don't know you're going against yourself while you're going against yourself, you will be able to tell it happened because you just won't feel right. Something will be bothering you, even if you can't recall what it might be.

Let me give you another example. One of my core values is to be selfless. It's important to me that I find value in myself by helping other people to realize their dreams. When I work with other people in mind, when I confirm my core values, I am able to accomplish unbelievable things. When my performance is for self-centered reasons, nothing seems to go right. If I receive something because I've helped others, that's okay. But when I work with only myself in mind, it just never seems to go smoothly. When I feel the familiar emptiness that lets me know that I went wrong, I finally become conscious of it. This knowledge allows me to change my mind-set and resume focusing on helping other people. I get back on track by confirming my value, which puts me into the flow where I am again accomplishing unbelievable things. *Your life's continual confirmation of your core values is elemental to long-lasting success.*

The next exercise is designed to help you to realize that besides having a set of core values, you also have values that you were programmed to have. I very simply call these my "conditioned values." For instance, in the next chapter I talk about efficiency as being one of my values, but I didn't mention it when I did my list. I didn't mention it because it wasn't one of my core values. I was taught that being efficient should be important to me and not surprisingly, it was something I strove to become. That was until I realized it wasn't my value, but someone else's value. Consequently, I no longer strive to become efficient, although I am, but for different reasons. What I mean is that, today, I use my energy in pursuing my core values, in confirming and reconfirming who I am and what's important to me. In other words, I spend my life being the "real" me!

Uncovering your conditioned values is more challenging than uncovering your core values. I wish there were a way I could trick you into doing it, like I did with your core values, but that would probably be antiproductive. It was necessary for me to trick you in the last exercise for a number of reasons. First, if I simply asked you to list what was important to you. I would get a mixture of core and conditioned values. In that there would be no revelation because that confusion is the part of the reason why success has eluded you thus far. Second, if you were insightful enough to somehow come up with all of your core values, your poor self-image, which is the affliction of the masses, would begin eliminating them one by one. You would end up with ego-distorted results that would put you right back where you started. One of the purposes of these exercises is to eliminate the ego's overpowering influence. Third, by tricking you in the first exercise, I've already brought you to the point of no return. The truth about you has already been revealed, and the rest of the exercises are all based on this truth. From now on, we'll be looking for the examples in your life that deny that truth. (Message from me to your ego—your goose is cooked! I know that you're not going to just "lay down" and let all this happen, but unfortunately for you, you've lost your grip. Or should I say your stranglehold. It's just a matter of time now!)

Even though this exercise will be more challenging, I can give you an insight to help you to discover your programmed values. The clue lies in the fact that they will seem important to you, but they don't appear on your list of core values. I say "seem" important because we already know that they aren't important to the real you. If they were, they'd be on your list. The reason they seem important is because somebody conditioned you to believe it. The fact that somebody conditioned you to believe a certain value is important does not make it good or bad. The determining factor is the effect it has in your life. So, to use my conditioned value of efficiency again, when I continually could not experience high achievement in all the multiple tasks I was trying to perform, I would berate myself. "What is wrong with me?" The results of these scenarios were negative, unproductive, and had residual effects, even though efficiency is a worthwhile value in and of itself.

I think it's wise to note also that values are not the only things that are important in one's life. When you do this exercise, be careful not to think of some of your objectives such as, to be respected or to be loved. Those may be important to you too, but they are not values because they involve what someone else must do in order for you to realize them. They are objective. Values are subjective. Values consist of what is important for you to be or do. To use the same two examples, if it's important for you to be respectful or to be lovable, then you've expressed values. So, with your core value list in hand, begin to itemize the other values in your life, the other things that are important for you to be that haven't already been mentioned. List them on a separate piece of paper. **Do this now!**

Now put these two lists in front of you, and you will have almost a complete verbal picture of who you are. On the one hand, you have the real you defined by your core values, and on the other hand, you have the person you were taught to be, the person who you think you should be, defined by your conditioned values. The more complementary the two lists are, the better your life will be. However, you may notice that one or more of your conditioned values contradicts one or more of your core values. This causes inner personal conflict, and the more numerous those contradictions are, the more serious the personal conflict will be, even to the point of needing psychological therapy. These contradictions are also the cause of your inability to experience prolonged success!

I can give you an example. Three of my core values were to be honest, selfless, and loving. When I made a list of the other things that were important to me I listed "getting over" as one of them. It's a street value. It's two words that function as one, and it means to get ahead, to end up on top, to win. It was an important value in the streets of Brooklyn, which is where it was taught to me. You can "get over" on the system, or you can "get over" on a specific person or group. Most people who have this conditioned value use it against the system. It's more impersonal that way, which is attested to by their oft-quoted defense, "...but I'm not hurting anyone." What they mean is anyone they can specifically name. People who "get over" on the system do so in varied ways. They take office supplies from work, buy "hot" (stolen) merchandise, take towels, ashtrays, etc., from hotels they visit, cheat on their taxes, work as little as possible while trying to give an impression to the contrary, or just generally look for the easy score, the shortcut, or the easy money. As an offshoot of this mentality, they also play the lottery, bet on sports, horses, and the numbers, and crowd the casinos. On the street, a buck made in this way is more valuable than a dollar.

And while they are in the minority, there are those who try to "get over" on specific people or groups. They simply try to get ahead of everyone, which is socially acceptable on the street, or taken further, try to "beat" people out of their money or valuables, real and perceived, at every opportunity. (This creates a kind of "jungle" mentality where only the strong survive, which is what makes the streets so tough.) So they "cut" the line to get ahead of you, borrow money they never pay back, or jockey around to get one space further ahead in a traffic jam. They also renege on agreements, cut in front of you while driving, "welch" on wages, "borrow" your valuables, or make promises they don't keep.

Some of them even strive to become professionals at "getting over." They are called "hustlers." They range from the kid dressed in jeans running a three-card monte game on the street to the guy in the $1,000 suit and a winter tan trying to sell you an investment in a stock or commodity that he knows deep down inside isn't worthwhile. The people they hustle, the "marks," they refer to as "chumps." After they "get over" on you, they brag about it and tell people how stupid you were. Little do they know that people who try to "get over" never get anywhere. They can't, because to "get over," you have to break many of the universal laws that govern one's ability to become successful. In order to engage in this behavior, you have to rationalize shading the truth.

And when you "get over" there is always a winner and always a loser. In other words, you have to learn how to hurt people, and in order to do that, you have to learn how to shut down your emotions. You can't feel. You have to operate like a machine. This machine mentality pulls you away from your spiritual core, your humanity, the very thing responsible for producing your success destiny.

My conditioned value to "get over" was one of my greatest challenges to becoming successful. You can easily see how it violated my core values of being honest, selfless, and loving. Until I exposed this dichotomy in values, this conditioned value kept popping up often and tempting me whenever the opportunity presented itself. In retrospect, every time I took the bait, the result was to dilute and dissolve whatever success I had achieved. It had to. I violated the universal laws. Thank goodness I wasn't very good at "getting over." When someone gave me the wrong change or charged me too little and I didn't tell them, I wouldn't feel like I made a score—I'd feel guilty. I felt guilty because I was going against my core values. I was denying my true self. I would get that hollow, empty feeling, only I didn't know then what it was.

Growing up on the streets of Brooklyn, I pursued this conditioned value for so many years that I came dangerously close to shutting down my feelings about others altogether. If that had happened, I would have been doomed to a lifetime of unsuccessful attempts to achieve my dreams because I would have violated the spirituality of success. If you were conditioned to have this value of "getting over" as I was, then I challenge you to redirect that ability and *test your own limits, not those of the world!*

Besides the obvious difference between your core values and conditioned values, namely, that one is the real you and the other isn't, there are also many other differences that can help you to separate them and overcome the possible negative effects that your conditioned values can have in your life. I have alluded to the first major difference, but now I will define it more fully. Your core values come from the center of your being. They involve your whole being. Your conditioned values reside in your mind and only in your mind. One is spiritual, the other is mental. Your core values are what you *know* is the truth, and your conditioned values are what you were *taught* is the truth. When you judge that you've violated a value, your judgment about violating a core value will surface first as a feeling, which you then think about. Your conscience "talks" to you.

Your judgment about violating a conditioned value will conversely emerge first as a thought about which you then have feelings. The feelings and subsequent judgment that produce the thoughts you have about denying a core value are genuine and produce positive results by making you a better person. The thoughts and resulting judgments that produce feelings when you have violated a conditioned value are fabricated because they are not really your values. They produce negative results. You feel and judge yourself as less because you can't measure up to who you think you should be, who someone else taught you that (you think) you should be. This repeated experience results in a poor self-image and self-doubt and is the source of all of your feelings of inadequacy.

Everything you judge negatively about yourself, your weaknesses and shortcomings, is the result of having conditioned values. This repeated experience produces a self-defeating, self-fulfilling downward spiral that, without enlightened intervention, results in a lifetime of lack of success. Not only in the financial area, but also in every area of your life. This is the "suffering" that the Buddha spoke about. The Buddha's enlightenment was his realization of the illusions created by the conditioned self, the ego. He realized that who he thought he should be, who he was taught to be, who he was conditioned to be, had no substance, no basis, no form, and no continuity. The Buddha realized that his conditioned self kept him from the truth about himself and life in general. Part of the Eastern concept of enlightenment is to become aware of, to wake up to, this realization. The next step is to do something about it.

The next exercise is designed to help you to do that in the form of an essay. The purpose of this "Who am I?" exercise is to uncover the ways that we've been conditioned and programmed to believe, feel, or act in a certain way. For many of us, there is this truth—that we've been doing, thinking, and feeling a certain way for so long, that we haven't bothered to ask the question "Why?" The question "Why?" has the amazing power to enlighten and is the key to unlocking the door to your potential for success. *Use it often.* In writing the answer to this question "Why?" I want you to step out of your life and look at it from the perspective of an observer—not defending, not judging, but simply as an unbiased reporter detailing all that you see. I want you to take a look at that image of yourself that has been created to determine if it is who you truly want to be. I want you to learn to self-image yourself objectively.

As a trainer, getting trainees to do this exercise was always a challenge. People don't like to write essays, especially about themselves, but this is where we start to bump up against reality. If you feel resistance, I am prompted to ask you one question: "Do you *really* want to be successful?" Many people say they do, but when it comes to performing the necessary steps, your desire and enthusiasm to do them will be very revealing. Maybe the truth is that you were programmed to believe that successful is something you should strive to be, but the real you has no such desire. There's nothing wrong with that. In fact, it's wonderful! If this is your scenario, then you should be ecstatic because you don't have to spend the rest of your life trying to be something you don't really want to be and beating yourself up because you haven't achieved it. The realization that you don't really want financial success is success for you, and my objective with you will have been accomplished. That revelation is good enough for me and should be pleasing also to you! But even if you fit that scenario, this essay will help you in all areas of your life. Success in any part of your life will, for the most part, follow the same principles that are necessary to become financially successful. Universal success is universal success!

So this "Who am I?" exercise is a two- to three-page essay written by you, the observer, about you. Look at the behavior of this individual, you, and document your strengths and weaknesses. First, document all of your strengths, the things you like about yourself, but beware of your poor self-image immediately negating them as we discussed earlier. For instance, I saw myself as a patient person, but then remembered losing my patience with my daughter Daria a few days earlier. Again, this is because we are our own worst critics. No one would chastise us as badly as we chastise ourselves. The truth is it is not possible to be completely one way or another. That's part of being human, part of the quantum complementary relationship between both ends of the spectrum, the yin and yang of the universe. After all, if a person doesn't have the possibility of losing his patience, can he really be said to be a patient person? Finally, what we're looking for here is how you behave generally, your dominant traits. Documenting your positive dominant traits will help you to achieve success sooner because you will be able to capitalize on them to your utmost advantage.

The next step is to document the things you would like to improve. Don't look at them as inadequacies. Remember, they're probably the result of trying to be the person you think you should be, the person you were programmed to be, not the real you. If you can be truthful with yourself about these, then success will be sure and swift. If not, then you will be destined to repeat the self-destructive behavior that has caused success to elude you in the past. Those who do not learn from the mistakes of the past are destined to repeat them. Enough said!

Before you actually begin this essay, this exposé, I would like to caution you about some common errors committed by those who have done this exercise in the past. The first one was already briefly mentioned. Often, people make the error of writing this self-examination defensively, just in case someone might read it. If you do that, you will be wasting the time you put into it because it will reveal nothing to help you to change your life. And remember, your weaknesses are the result of false, conditioned values, not the real you.

Second, people will often negate their observations in the same exercise. We also touched on this briefly. For instance, one trainee wrote in the beginning of his self-examination that he was an introvert and shy. Two paragraphs later he said that he especially preferred being with people and interacting with them. These two observations are exact opposites, and although I've already said that no one is completely one way or another, there is a dominant slant to our behavior. That dominance is what you want to uncover. The truth about this trainee that he alluded to with the words "shy" and "introvert" was the fact that he was lonely. A fact that was too painful for him to admit to himself. So even though he loved to be around people and interact with them, inside, deep inside, he was a lonely man. This revelation helped him to change his life, but initially his ego would not allow him to see the truth. The possible experience of pain caused the ego to go into the survival mode and massage the truth so that it was easier to digest. We will go into this in greater detail in a later chapter but I want you to understand how your ego can be your worst enemy while doing this exercise. Be very conscious of its tricks. After all, if you're like most people, your ego has been in control all of your life. It will not give up easily and allow you to take your life back. All it knows is that it wants what it wants when it wants it, regardless of the truth.

A mundane existence is what the ego, in the survival mode, strives for, i.e., no pain. But you want more and you know "no pain, no gain." This is the dichotomy of what we experience through the different parts of ourselves. Even though we've only discussed two levels thus far, this realization can be an eye-opening experience—to realize that we have different levels of mind and conscious, and that they all want something, often the direct opposite of what another level wants. This is the cause of personal conflict. What magnifies this conflict is that usually one of these levels is in dominant control without the person realizing it.

The level of dominant control for most people is the ego in the survival mode operating with conditioned values. It's like being possessed! (By the way, possessed people don't know that they're possessed.) But this level is only one aspect of who you are, not the real you, but the person you think you should be. If you don't realize what's happening, then you'll go through life like a puppet doing the dance that your ego wants you to do. You'll live your life in automatic pilot and never experience your dreams. You need to be in control of all aspects and levels that comprise you and not let any one of them be in control. It's like being the CEO with a Board of Directors. Their input is valuable, but no matter how domineering any one of these directors might be, ultimately the final decision should rest with you. The answer to being in control lies in the successful performance of this exercise, "Who am I?" **Write this essay now!**

POINTS TO PONDER

Test your own limits, not those of the world.

Your conditioned values are the source of your feelings of inadequacy.

Your core values reveal your intrinsic perfection!

Your life's continual confirmation of your core values is elemental to long-lasting success.

Who you are today is not your doing.

6

THE EASY WAY — THE PARADOX

There is an easy solution to every human
problem—neat, plausible, and wrong.
— H. L. Mencken

Ever since I can remember, finding the shortcut always had value to me. I don't remember exactly when or how I got this conditioned value, but in examining my life, I know it exists. Also, although I can't remember who did it, I do remember being taught the following lessons:

"You're doing it the hard way (wrong way)."

"Why do you have to learn everything the hard way?"

"Be efficient!"

The "who" in the teaching is not important, but the "what" that was being taught is all-important. Add to that having grown up in the streets of Brooklyn, where "getting over" was constantly being taught, and you have the perfect formula for failure.

One thing successful people will tell you is that success is not easy. Consciously or unconsciously, they are telling you the literal truth. They are not saying it's difficult, because it really isn't. What they're saying is that it doesn't come naturally. You have to think about it. If it came naturally, then everyone would be successful, and it wouldn't be such a valued treasure. The reason it doesn't come naturally, although it should, is because *you* are no longer natural. The programming and conditioning over the years has changed your nature, your natural state. The natural state of success, as experienced by everything else in the universe, has become unnatural for you. We'll further discuss this idea later in the book.

We said that in order to become successful, you have to think about it. So what is it that you're supposed to think about? It's not so much what you think about, like positive thinking or visualization, as it is that you think at all. By now, you should be thoroughly confused and that's good. That's exactly where I want you to be. Your confusion tells you that you have no realization of what I'm saying, but you need this knowledge to materialize your dreams. Man is predisposed and conditioned to do things in the easiest way possible. It is so ingrained in our being that it's automatic. In order for us to perform any action in other than the easiest way, we have to first think about it. I'll give you an example. Suppose there's a coin on the floor. If I tell you to pick it up, you will naturally just bend over and pick it up. You won't get down on one knee or both knees to pick it up, nor will you do a handstand and pick it up with your teeth. That's the hard way and seems absurd. Our action in this example is automatic and is reflective of how we live our lives.

In training thousands of salespeople over the years in how to be successful, I was always perplexed by their "seeming" inability to follow directions. It wasn't that they couldn't perform the task or that it was difficult to perform, but they were always able to find an "easier" way to do it. There was only one problem—they didn't get the same results. They saved themselves some work by finding a simpler way, but they cost themselves success. Let me give you an example. We supplied sales leads of interested prospective clients to our salespeople. Through trial and error, we found that there was a sixty percent greater chance of actually getting an appointment with the prospects if you met them face to face as opposed to any other form of contact. In training, we would stress this "truth" enthusiastically to drive the point into their minds because it was so important. And after all this effort, what did many of them do? They called the customer on the phone! Why? This was their answer: "Because it is easier to contact more customers on the phone than by making personal appearances; especially if the contact is not available; you won't waste your time." Sounds reasonable, right? The logic is almost unarguable, except for one thing—success is not logical! If it were, everyone would be successful. To successful people, not getting the right results is illogical.

Even more astounding were the salespeople who did go out and meet the prospective clients. Not surprisingly, most of them got off to a great start, making many sales. Then, after a while, their sales would begin to drop. Investigation revealed that they stopped going out to meet clients and stopped doing what worked, in favor of getting on the phone and doing what was not working. Why? Because it was easier.

And that's not the worst part. What's worse is that when they began to see poorer results, you'd think it would occur to them to go back to what did work. They didn't! We had to tell them the mistake they made. Why couldn't they see it for themselves? The answer lies in the programming of our "automatic-easy" predisposition. Unless you are aware of what you are doing, you can't change what you're doing. *To be aware is to be alive!* You have to think! You cannot go through life on automatic pilot with the wrong course settings and arrive at the right destination!

The paradox of these "easy" actions is that they make everything more difficult. Life becomes harder. I have experienced failure in my life, and I've experienced success. Believe me when I tell you that failure involves more work than success. Initially, failure is easier, but for a long time afterward, it's more difficult. *The easy way is the hard way!* That's the paradox. That's what people don't understand. If you could start today by not doing anything the easy way, you would see your life change dramatically, almost overnight. Don't look to operate in the easy way, the way of least work. Instead, focus on performing in the most productive way.

You will find that rarely will the easiest way be the most productive way. In fact, as a rule, I always eliminate the first thought, reaction, or idea that enters my mind. Why? Because it's the same one that everyone else would think of, and if 93 percent of them fail, why would I want to do what they would do? Besides, it's probably not even my thought, reaction, or idea. It's probably someone else's that was programmed into me at an early age. There's a pretty good chance. One thing's for sure: if I don't think about it, if I don't control my thoughts, then in the end my thoughts control me. I become the product of my programming, of someone else's thoughts, and instead of the victor, I become the victim!

POINTS TO PONDER

To be aware is to be alive.

The easy way is the hard way!

EXPECTATIONS ARE EXCUSES

When a man points a finger at someone else, he should remember
that three of his fingers are pointing at himself.

—Louis Nizer, lawyer

Whenever I did an initial introductory training session, I would ask the trainees to share with the group their expectations of training. What did they expect would be covered during the training sessions? What did they need to learn about in order to become successful? The first few answers came rather easily, but I kept asking until I would have at least ten answers. Of the hundreds of training sessions I conducted, the list of training expectations were always basically the same:

1. The Company
2. The Product
3. The Sales Leads
4. The Competition
5. The Customers
6. Pricing
7. Paperwork
8. Management
9. Sales Techniques
10. Underwriting (We sold an insurance product.)

As the group said each item, I would list them on a white board in the front of the room. I was always amazed that no one ever included themselves, the salesperson, on the list! The salesperson, according to studies, is 85 percent of the sale, and yet no one referred to the 85 percent as what they needed or expected to learn about.

One day, as I was standing in the back of the room, I looked at the list and realized that all their expectations were also the excuses they would give if they failed. Now the fact that they never mentioned themselves and what that meant was even more amazing. I would distribute to each trainee a copy of a study entitled "The Six Primary Factors That Result in a Purchase From a Sales Presentation" by Stephan Schiffman. The first five items refer to the salesperson, i.e., tone of voice, posture, appearance, handshake, and attitude (personal enthusiasm). The sixth item was all those things they listed on the board taken together. The company, the product, and its incidentals were not why the customer bought. They bought the salesperson! And yet none of them saw the need to concentrate on what the customer was really buying.

The sales profession, like success, is merely a reflection of life itself. When a sale is made, you will hear the salesperson, with flowering exultation, explain that he or she was the reason for the success. When a sale isn't made, salespeople often point to everything outside of themselves as the cause of their failure. This second observation is especially true of those striving for success.

The fact that "a person's expectations became his excuses" had me puzzled. Why did what we think we needed, or hoped for, come to be the source of our escape from reality? The realization I came to is that expectations are setups to protect our egos. We construct our failure scenario, our rationalization of failure, even before it happens. This is the proper functioning of our ego's survival instinct. Since we see our ego as who we really are, we make preparations to preserve it at all costs, consciously or unconsciously, even at the expense of the truth! Expectations are not to be confused with objectives. Objectives are where we would like to end up eventually. Expectations are what we expect others to supply in order for us to accomplish our objectives, to be a success! Under those conditions, expectations take the control, and therefore the responsibility, out of our hands. Expectations put others, supposedly, in control of our destiny. Now *if* you fail, (and you already have), you can point to something or someone outside of yourself as the cause of your failure.

Listen up, people! Everything you need to be successful you already possess. You just need to realize that fact. As soon as you do, your expectations have no value, and you see them for what they are—excuses. It is written in Scripture that God created us in His own image and likeness. However you interpret God, do you think He has the ability to be successful, or does He need other people to fulfill His expectations for success to be realized? The answer is obvious. It is also just as obvious that if we are created in His image and likeness, we possess that same ability. Man is the only creature with the god-like quality of being able to create. It's called "progress." Success and failure are two abilities you already possess. You've been well taught, by people with experience, how to fail. In fact, you've become so good at it, you can do it time and time again. You are very successful at failing! Now you need to learn how to be successful at succeeding.

There is a flow to success, much like that of a river, and once you step into it, it will carry you effortlessly to whatever point you wish. You can step in at any time, and you can step out at any time. Failure, too, has a flow, just like a river, but it travels in the opposite direction from the flow of success. This flow also gives you the choice of stepping in or out at will. How do I know this to be true? The most puzzling question that successful people wonder about is why another person, in exactly the same business, selling the same product, under exactly the same market conditions, can wind up with drastically opposite results. What perplexes them is, "How is this possible?" The answer is because everyone is capable of both success and failure. Which one you choose to experience will be related to your knowledge of each and your conscious effort to experience it. You know a lot about failure, that's easy. But believe it or not, it's not so easy for successful people to fail. Things just always "seem" to work out for them. They "seem" to have the golden touch. The uninformed call it "luck."

Do you think that you have within you, right now, the ability to fly an airplane? You may not know how, or you may have a fear of flying, but if someone taught you everything you needed to know, and you had no fear, do you think you would be able to do it? The answer is, of course you would. The ability to fly a plane has always been within you; the only thing you really lack is the knowledge. The same is true with your ability to be financially successful. The same was also true with your ability to drive a car or to ride a bicycle. You always had the ability, and when someone finally taught you how, you did it. It may have been difficult when you initially learned the principles, but the more you exercised them, the easier it became until it became effortless. Today, you don't even think about driving the car or riding the bicycle; you just do it, effortlessly. Success works in the same way. Once you become familiar with the principles, through repetition, it becomes effortless. And then you begin to wonder how other people can fail, because, as with learning to drive a car, once you learn how to drive effortlessly, not being able to drive is something you have to try hard to do. That's why it's difficult for successful people to fail. They are as experienced and second-natured about success as you are about failure. They have to try hard not to succeed!

Successful people have no expectations, i.e., they have no excuses for failure, therefore, they don't fail. I'll never forget the wisdom imparted to me by a car mechanic about twenty years ago. I pushed my car into a service station, and the mechanic asked me what was the problem. I replied, "I don't know, but all of a sudden it wouldn't start." The mechanic replied, "There is no all-of-a-sudden with a car!" Either you exercise your control over the maintenance of the car or it will exercise its control over you! Having expectations of a car leaves the door open for mishaps to occur all of a sudden.

Likewise, *you either plan your success, or you plan your failure*. Either way, you exercise your control. Having no plan is a plan. Not a very good one, but a plan nevertheless. *Not exercising control is within your control*. An expectation of what others must do in order for you to be successful is you unconsciously putting your destiny in the hands of others. You do it every time; this is what you were taught. It's so well-learned it's automatic. Somewhere along the line of your life you were taught that, alone, you are not enough. This, too, is not true. God doesn't make junk! Created in His image and likeness, you are capable of all things, including success!

POINTS TO PONDER

Your expectations become your excuses.

You either plan your success, or you plan your failure.

Not exercising control is within your control.

8

Success Is In What You "See"

People see only what they are prepared to see.

— Ralph Waldo Emerson

Over the years many people have asked me, "What do I have to do to be successful?" My answer has always been the same: "Nothing." From an early age, we've all learned the equation that states the relationship between hard work and success. But it isn't true. It's just another one of those false principles that everyone walks around with until they find the truth. At one time in the history of man, everyone thought the world to be flat—except for a few "nuts." What do we believe today? We thought the universe revolved around the Earth. What do we know now? In the development of man, a principle is true until it isn't. Open your mind to the possibilities.

Success is not in what you do, it's in what you see. *Those who are successful see things differently than most people. They create their own reality.* One of the ideas the behavioral sciences have come to realize is that reality is subjective. Two people seeing the same event can have two completely different interpretations of what they saw. That's because every event is both positive and negative—good and bad. There is nothing that occurs in this world that is ever entirely positive or entirely negative. It is always both. And you get to choose which side you will see. Successful people, most of the time, choose to see the positive. To them, everyone and everything is conspiring to make them successful. It's like some divine plan unfolding. They see how everything that happens prepares and brings them effortlessly closer to their dreams of success. And consequently, it does!

What you see is a direct result of what you know, and what you know is a result of what you see. It's a confusing, self-fulfilling, and self-generating cycle that is impossible to break out of unconsciously. What you see is called your perception, your interpretation. You interpret events based on the facts that you have at your disposal. These facts are stored in your memory, and this is why most people cannot break out of their failure cycle. Unless people consciously make an effort to experience otherwise, their past produces their present and their future. Their past "reproduces" in their present and in their future. The failure cycle is self-generating and self-reinforcing, so that failure *is* their reality—past, present, and future!

Again, you interpret events based on the *facts* you have at your disposal. "Facts," also, are often subjective. Many facts are true until they become invalid. What makes them invalid? Questioning and examination. In order to change the way you see things, you have to change the person doing the seeing. All the skill, techniques, hard work, long hours, etc., will do you no good if you're missing this piece of the puzzle. It's like the recipe for a cake. If you have all the ingredients you need except flour, what kind of cake will you create? Questioning what you "know" is the flour in the recipe for success. *True prosperity and wisdom lie in the questions, not the answers.* Knowing the answers confines you, by acceptance, to a certain specific level of knowledge and understanding. Consider this: For the most part, mankind doesn't know yet what it doesn't know. According to statistics, the past couple of decades have seen man double his knowledge over that of the past hundreds of centuries. And in the next ten to fifteen years, because of all the technological breakthroughs, man's knowledge will double once more, and then double again in five to ten years after that, and so on. So in the next twenty-five years, man's knowledge will quadruple over what it is now. That means that today we don't know 75 percent of what we will know twenty-five years from now! Twenty-five years from now, man will see things differently.

You can choose to wait, or you can begin the process now. This book is meant to inspire you to take action—now! You have to entertain the possibility that the knowledge you have might be incorrect. If you are not successful yet, there is a 93 percent chance that this is true *for you*. A new, mechanically perfect clock initially set with the wrong time will be wrong tomorrow, ten years from now, and fifty years from now. What's your setting? Do you have the courage to find out? If you're not successful yet, I would think that the possibility of having the wrong directions or recipe would come as a great relief to you. What this means is that it's not *you* that is wrong, only the setting of the course that you were put on. If you're driving a car following directions to a destination and fail to get there, when do you begin to question the directions? When do you begin to question the programming? Happiness is your destiny, and financial success is part of that happiness. It will be true, however, only for those who are aware that their course, for better or worse, has been preset. If it's not working—change it!

This brings us back to the question "why?" Why do I do the things that I do? Why do I feel disappointed when a certain event happens or when certain words are said? Why did I react in the way I did to that particular set of circumstances? Try to "see" things differently. There are always three sides to every story—what are the other sides? (The third side is always the truth.) I know how I feel and react to certain circumstances; how would someone with different, or opposite, programming react to the same circumstances? In other words, who am I? But it takes honesty. The worst sin a man can commit is to fool himself. Remember, it's not you that's wrong; it's your setting, your course, that's incorrect. However your life turns out, wouldn't you rather it be as a result of your own doing?

Once you complete this exercise, and it may take some time, (the older you are, the more you have to undo) success is relatively easy. Like the failure cycle, the success cycle is also self-generating and self-reinforcing. It will come naturally and fluidly. You may find that you will have to do very little (physical) work. And if "doing" is required, depending on your choice of endeavors, it's usually not for very long. In fact, it won't feel like work. You'll enjoy the process because you'll know where you're going. Successful people, and those soon to be successful, don't go to work; they go to play! Have fun; enjoy the process with the anticipation you felt as a child on the way to the amusement park. Just knowing where you were going made you feel happy and excited. Being there, arriving there, was often less satisfying than the anticipation along the way. So, enjoy the process, the road to success. You deserve it, and it's your destiny. You were born to be happy!

POINTS TO PONDER

Those who are successful see things differently.
They create their own reality.

True prosperity and wisdom lie in the questions,
not the answers.

9

BEING IN THE FLOW

**I don't know what your destiny will be, but one thing I know;
the only ones among you who will be really happy
are those who have sought and found how to serve.**

— Albert Schweitzer

Did you ever have the kind of day when you could do nothing wrong? Maybe it wasn't for a whole day, it may have only lasted for an hour, but no matter what you did, everything you touched turned to gold. Even your supposed mistakes turned out to be strokes of genius! If you've ever had this experience, then you know what it's like to be "in the flow." Flow is an indication and example of the perfection of the universe. It seems as if you've tapped into the source of divine wisdom. You don't know how you did it, you just experience the result. I believe these moments are of divine inspiration and give you a picture of what can be, but most people don't get the message. They chalk it up to luck.

If you've ever seen the movie *Let It Ride* with Richard Dreyfus, you'll recall that he portrayed a racetrack addict who has one of these "flow" days. Normally he's a big loser when it comes to picking a winning horse, and his addiction puts a serious strain on his marriage and his job. He is in danger of losing both. The movie shows that no matter what he does on this "flow" day, he just can't lose. He wins every bet he makes, gets propositioned by beautiful women, is admired by everyone around him, and even when he makes the wrong choice, he still wins. For instance, in one race, he picked the wrong horse but got shut out at the betting window. He realized that he still won because he wasn't able to make the bet. As the day progressed, his positive attitude grew and grew until it had become contagious and creative. It changed life around him, which ultimately changed his life. The movie had a very happy ending. He became rich, his marriage improved, and he lived happily ever after.

I've experienced these same "flow" days. I've done it at racetracks, casinos, as a salesman, as a sales manager, and while playing sports. There have been those days when I was seemingly infallible. But in that sentence lies the problem of why, for most people, it only lasts for a short time. They think that they are the source of the infallibility. Their ego becomes inflated until it overshadows and overpowers everything else, and all they are left with is how good they think they are. The next day when they wake up, they find their infallibility is gone and they return to normal, no longer god-like.

"Why can't the next day be the same as the day before?" you might ask. And you're right, it can be. As long as the ego is in the way, however, you cannot duplicate the experience. There are people who can, though. They are called successful. Maybe you know one of them, someone who is successful at just about anything he or she gets involved with. People for whom "everything they touch turns to gold." Most people dismiss their performance as luck, because otherwise it would be a call to action. But it's not luck, it's being "in the flow" and staying there. They are not always conscious of this. They do it because it works, even though they do not know about the laws of the universe that are being engaged.

As I stated earlier, one of the blocks to this "flow" state is the ego. The more the ego is in control, the less the possibility of experiencing this state of infallibility. The reason for this is that to entertain the ego, you have to turn your attention inward. The more your energy or attention is concentrated inward, the more you withdraw yourself, isolate yourself, from the rest of the world. *You cannot be successful by yourself.* Nobody ever was, and nobody ever will be. All the successful people I have ever met know this to be true. True success, the kind that lasts, comes to those who know the truth. Whether they knew it before or learned it along the way is immaterial. *The only way to get success is to give success. Success is only possible through other people.*

As you direct your energy and attention outward, it will be reflected back to you. And the more you project, the more you'll receive. This is the state of flow, and it is within your control. If your energy and attention are other-centered, then you will find that you will prosper. Everything you touch will turn to gold. So-called coincidences will increase dramatically. What you want will find you!

I know this must sound strange and different to you. It's supposed to! If I were to teach you something that felt familiar and comfortable, it would be because I wasn't really teaching you anything. It would feel familiar and comfortable because you already know it. If you already knew these truths, you would already be successful! *My job is to help you. Your job is to try to be helped.* I don't necessarily expect you to buy into these ideas and understandings immediately. Just consider that they may be true, and enlightenment will take its natural course. The truth can no longer be hidden from you once you know what it looks like. Remember that the teachers in your life could only teach you what they themselves knew and no more. What I am trying to help you learn is what they didn't know. There are universal laws, like the law of gravity, which work all the time whether you know about them or not.

If you search deeply, you will know that this law of success is true—that the only way to get success is to give success. Why? Because anything in life that is worth having only comes to you after you give it away. Find someone to love and you become loved. Make someone happy and you receive happiness. Help others become successful, and you achieve success. Is it now beginning to feel right and beginning to ring true?

I will tell you the story of when this became vividly clear to me. When I began working as a salesman, the first product I sold was health insurance. The program was special in that it combined the buying power of self-employed people in order to get them better coverage and rates. Having been previously self-employed, I realized the value of this concept and the product. The price was competitive and the coverage was comprehensive. It took me six weeks to get licensed, and during those six weeks my anticipation grew and grew. I couldn't wait to get in front of the customers and tell them how great this product was.

My sales manager taught us that to be successful in this business it was necessary to get fifteen appointments per week. However, even though I had fifteen appointments every week for the first month, I was able to make only one sale per week while other salespeople were making four or five sales. I became discouraged and thought about quitting. Why didn't the customers see what a great product I was selling? I started to think that maybe it was me. I asked the top salesman in the office if I could accompany him on a presentation. He agreed, and five minutes into the presentation, it hit me like a ton of bricks. It was obvious that this person was there to help the customers, not himself. That's what I was missing.

You see, I went into sales because of the ability in that profession to make lots of money. I obviously communicated that to every customer. I was there to make money, and, as a result, I made very little. When I put the commission aside and started caring about the customer, I not only made lots of sales, I became the top agent in the country! In the final analysis though, what changed? The product, the price, the competition, and everything else were the same. The only thing that was different was me. And that made all the difference in the world. When I do sales training today, I jokingly tell the trainees that the only customers I sold in those first four weeks were the ones I couldn't talk out of it. But that incident vividly taught me a lesson—you can only become successful through other people. Every successful person is surrounded by others who benefit from their success. Successful people are the heroes of many. By bringing success into the lives of others, you can create a flow of success for yourself.

POINTS TO PONDER

My job is to help you. Your job is to try to be helped.

The only way to get success is to give success.

Success is only possible through other people.

You cannot be successful by yourself.

10

Focus

To do two things at once is to do neither.

— Bits & Pieces, January, 1999

Being able to focus is probably the most misunderstood essential of success. The reason is, I believe, the paradoxical nature of definitions associated with the same word, "focus." Focus can be defined as the point from which all your energy emanates outward and whose field of effect widens as it gets further from you. This is called *virtual focus*. At the same time, focus is defined as the point upon which you concentrate all of your energies, and the field of effect narrows as it gets further from you. This is called *real focus*. Deciding which focus is necessary for success is not too difficult because they are so aptly named. Would you prefer real success or virtual success?

Besides the paradoxical definitions, another factor that interferes with successful focus is our programming. All of those wise sayings we grew up with take their toll when it comes to focus. These are sayings like "Don't put all your eggs in one basket," or "Don't burn your bridges behind you," or "Always leave the door open," and other such success killers. In fact, in order to truly be successful you must do exactly the opposite of what people using these "wise" sayings profess that you should do. If you don't burn your bridges and close all the doors you will leave yourself with an alternative to your objective. The problem with that is the alternative is already comfortable and familiar. When the difficulties begin to pile up, the old open door and the precrossed bridge will become too enticing. They will represent safety and virtual success, and they will be easy. Real success is not easy, nor is it safe! These are the safety nets we construct for ourselves so that we can play the game "not to lose."

In order to obtain real success, you need real focus. You need to focus on one positive outcome, which also means eliminating any negative outcomes as well as other so-called positive "safe" outcomes. Remember the example of you as a child wanting to stand up and walk. The possibility of not walking was not even an option. You were determined, if not hell-bent, on achieving your objective. You focused all of your energy and attention on getting the job done. It wasn't a question of "if" you would walk, it was a question of "when" you would walk! In addition, the safety of continuing to crawl was not an option. You mentally burned that bridge when you irrevocably decided that walking was the only outcome you would accept.

Another misconception that is programmed into us early in life is the ability to perform multiple tasks simultaneously. It is impressed upon us that this is desirable behavior. Those who could not "walk and chew gum at the same time" were ridiculed and considered to be failures. For forty-four years, I saw myself as less than I was because I judged myself by this "truth." I was already on the road to success. I just chalked up my inability to focus on more than one thing at a time as a shortcoming. Then the day of enlightenment occurred in my life, and I realized this fallacy for what it was—a conditioned value. I read an article informing me that most people do not have the discipline to do just one thing, to stick with one thing, day in and day out, until its completion and keep it as the focus of their lives. The ability to do only one thing at a time, the article said, is a gift. But in reality, it is not a gift, although the thought was very comforting to me at the time. It's a discipline. Anyone can learn to focus, but it's an acquired skill that is honed through experience and repetition.

Finally, how do you know when your focus is correct? When your objective, when that item that you're focusing on, consumes most of your thoughts and actions of your waking hours. A man will always accomplish his primary objective. This is another law of nature that works every time. Whatever it is that a person truly wants, they will get. What you want also wants you! Unfortunately, most people are often unaware of their main focus. Consciously they may say they want one thing, while unconsciously, deep down, they really want something else. For instance, did you ever wonder why people continue to stay in a damaging relationship week after week, month after month, year after year? Consider the spouses of drug addicts, alcoholics, wife beaters, or child molesters. Why do they continue to stay in the relationships after it has become obvious that their partners have no intention of changing? It's done because it's comfortable and it's safe. They will complain, moan, cry, and tell you how fed up they are, and then do nothing to change it. Why? You would think that people in that position would want to change their lives immediately. Talk about living in hell! And yet the devil you know is better than the devil you don't know.

The fear of the unknown in breaking free is so great that it far overshadows the pain of addiction and cruelty. People stay in torturous situations, willing to see themselves as victims. The reality, of course, is that it's a choice they make every day. It may sound cold and cruel, but these people are exactly where they want to be. It satisfies their need for the safety of the familiar and, as twisted as it may sound, it's true.

Another example of incorrect focus is the story of a businessman named Lou. Lou took advantage of an opportunity to build his own business. He was excited, motivated, and talented enough to get the job done. For a year and a half he would show up at work every day and do what was required and expected, but in the end, he failed. His business failed for the same reason that most businesses fail—lack of capital or at least that's the way it seemed. Upon closer inspection, after answering a few key questions, the truth was revealed. In answer to one of the questions, Lou replied that he at least had been able to save a nice little sum of money from his business venture. What a revelation! Lou did not fail; he succeeded. Unknown to him consciously, saving money was his primary objective, his primary focus. *A man will always accomplish his primary objective—even if it is unknown to him.*

If Lou had been truly committed to building a successful business, he would not have been able to save a penny until it was successful. Money is a tool in building a new business. Lou held back on committing all of his resources to his fledgling business. The extra capital would have made the difference, not only from the commitment of the capital but because of what it meant. Along with the capital would have gone a commitment to purpose. Instead, Lou chose the safety of playing the game "not to lose." Further research showed that prior to the new business venture, Lou had been heavily involved in gambling. He was responsible for creating a very negative financial atmosphere in the home. It almost wrecked his marriage and most of his other relationships. To Lou, saving money was proof that he was a good father, a good husband, and a good person. It also proved that he was no longer trapped by his gambling habit. Lou won, but he did so at the expense of his new business. Victory over the beast called gambling was his true hidden primary objective. If he had known this consciously, he might have postponed his business venture or adjusted his focus.

The cold, hard truth is that the focus you need to be successful, or to accomplish anything for that matter, must supercede everything else in your life. You must commit all of your waking energy to the accomplishment of your objective. We will go into this in greater detail in Chapter Eleven, Personal Energy Limitations, but for now, know that your objective must come before everything else. It must be primary in your life. I can't count how often I've seen people fail because they didn't give enough time and energy, initially, to the accomplishment of their objective! They would talk about spending time with their children, their spouse, their parents, their volunteer work, their hobbies, etc., as the reason why they couldn't commit more to their endeavor. In other words, they wanted to continue the same life as before, exactly as before, and just add being successful. Impossible!

If you are not successful already, there's a good chance that your lifestyle is not conducive to becoming successful. *You can't change your life (become successful) without changing your life*—so it *needs* to be changed! However, it is not necessary to ignore those other important aspects of your life. Once you're well on your way to accomplishing your objective, you can then reallocate your time and energy to address those needs in your life that you also deem important. Only now, you'll have the added ability of being able to focus effectively.

This essential component of focus, namely high concentration, is the one that is most often overlooked by people, and it is usually because they are wrestling with a poor self-image. They need to see themselves, and have others see them, as a good father, a good wife, a good son, a good citizen, a good religious person, etc. This is another reason why the exercise "Who am I?" is so important. If, subconsciously, you believe that you are deficient in any of these areas, then the best thing you can do for yourself is to bring it to the surface, identify it by realizing that it's because of one of your conditioned values, and deal with it. In this way, it won't ruin your chances for success unconsciously. Once you're well on your way, you can address other important issues with better focus. And because you'll be somewhat successful, you'll very likely have the added advantage of having the money and security you need to help you to achieve them better and faster than you could have done before.

In conclusion, focus for a person is as important as a compass is for a ship or a plane. When ships and planes set out for their destinations, they constantly find themselves off course and have to adjust and readjust their direction, often hundreds of times in a voyage or flight. Constant vigilance over the compass ensures that only slight changes need to be made in order to guarantee their arrival. Without this constant vigilance and flexibility, dramatic directional change will need to occur, and at some point the cost of such dramatic change may be judged to not be worth the effort. Finally, everyone is always successful! People may not be successful at what they thought was their primary objective, but they always accomplish their real primary objective, even if it is unknown to them. The lesson here is—know your true objective! Know thyself!

POINTS TO PONDER

A man will always accomplish his primary objective, —even if it is unknown to him!

You can't change your life without changing your life!

11

Personal Energy Limitations

*The energy that could be used to focus on complex goals,
to provide for enjoyable growth, is squandered
on patterns of simulation that only mimic reality.*

— Mihaly Csikszentmihalyi in *Flow*

One of the things you notice when you become much more aware of yourself is that during the course of a day, you spend a specific amount of energy. You know this to be true because at some point you become tired and need to retire to replenish your "strength." Our strength lies in our energy level. Did you ever notice that when you're full of energy you feel strong and vibrant? And conversely, when your energy level is low you feel weak and deflated. These aren't just feelings. They're indications of your energy level. They are a true barometer of your effectiveness to expend energy in order to accomplish and create. In any one day, you have a limited amount of this creative energy at your disposal, and your success will depend on how wisely you use it.

Energy consciousness is not easy, but it is essential. Did you ever notice that when you are in the presence of certain people or are doing certain things, you feel more energized, or conversely, drained? The people and things that boost our energy are important, but more important are the energy drains that we encounter. These sap us of the creative juices that we can use to create affluence in our lives. Negative people are often a serious energy drain when you're trying to improve your life. It seems that as soon as you stand up for yourself and stick your head up above the crowd because you want a better life, you begin to attract negativity.

It's almost like life's test to see if you are truly serious. It's similar to what happens when you put a bunch of crabs into a bushel. As one of them begins to climb up the side of the bushel to escape, the other crabs latch on to him to also get out, which keeps him from gaining his freedom. The same thing happens with a group of people. When one person begins to climb to success, the other people around him "latch" on to him and inhibit his progress. Often, the result is that he falls back into the same rut (bushel) with everyone else.

The people around us have their own reasons why they would or wouldn't like to see us succeed. *It may be your success, but everyone else has a stake in it also.* The ones who will hurt you the most are those who will be threatened by your success. I'm convinced that most of the people who will undermine you will do so because you represent a threat to their comfort. If you make it, if you do become successful, then you will be a glaring and constant reminder of what they could be if they weren't so afraid. You will bring to the surface all the negative things they think about themselves whenever they are in your presence. What they should see is an example of how you or anyone else can change their life for the better. But instead of seeing it as motivation, they see it as a threat. Instead of seeing the positive, they see the negative, which is why they are where they are in the first place!

You will be able to identify these people by the precautions they advise you to take. They will tell you, "Be careful, you're taking too much of a risk." They'll tell you, "Don't burn your bridges," "Leave the door open," and other seemingly wise and logical advice. Whenever people give you advice, the very first thing you should do is examine where their thinking has brought them. Is that where you want to be? Remember, unless they've achieved the result you want to achieve, then they have no direct knowledge for you to draw upon. Search out someone who does! Remember, everyone in your life has a vested interest in seeing you succeed or watching you fail. Their advice will always be tainted by their vested interests, and that imperfection in their advice could make all the difference in its effectiveness, no matter how well intentioned they might be.

I believe that's why many gurus of success caution you to keep your objectives (dreams) to yourself. They advise you not to share them with other people because then people begin to jockey for position based on whether your objective represents a possible positive or negative to them. It's like a mobile above a child's crib. When one person (you) moves, then all the others change their positions based on the person who initially moved (you), and people hate change! It's also important to note that the people around you are not aware of what they're doing, so you really can't hold them responsible for their lack of support or their tainted advice. If they were aware of themselves, they would be some of the successful people whom you could tap for knowledge to help you in your quest. Understanding this, you should not become angry toward them or feel slighted or hurt. That would be a commitment of energy to something other than what you are trying to achieve.

Another area where the use of limited energy becomes important is in focusing on only one thing or objective. During the course of any day, your life is full of energy drains which are necessary just for survival and responsible living. The bare necessities by themselves demand a good portion of your energy. There is no escaping these outputs of energy. However, there are many activities we engage in that are really unnecessary and waste our energy. They are unnecessary because they do not provide a bare necessity or bring us closer to our dream.

For instance, when I began my sales career, I initially worked from home where I would set up my appointments. If you've ever prospected by phone, you know that the first phone call is the most difficult. Even though the phone is right in front of you, it seems a mile away, out of reach. And when you finally do pick it up, it weighs about 500 pounds. I would sit in front of the telephone for at least fifteen minutes trying to work up the courage and motivation to begin. Once I got started, each call became easier to make.

Being at home though, left me open to certain distractions and energy drains. My wife, for instance, would ask me if I could do her a favor and pick up the dry cleaning. She was swamped with the care of the house and our five children. It would help her out a lot, and it would only take fifteen minutes or so, she would say. Of course I wanted to be a good husband and a good father, so I would consent to help her out. Sound familiar? Every day that I worked at home, the opportunity would arise for me to demonstrate my being a good father and husband, and I would jump at the chance. Who wouldn't? Besides, it was only a little thing. When I began to take a good look at what it was costing me to pick up the dry cleaning, I began to look at it differently.

By the time I got back into the rhythm of effectively prospecting on the phone, the fifteen minutes had stretched into an hour. In that hour, I would have been able to set at least one appointment. When I divided my average number of appointments into my average weekly commission, I found that each appointment was worth fifty dollars. Since I didn't use the hour setting an appointment, it cost my family and me fifty dollars to pick up the dry cleaning. If I lost an hour once every day of the week, I would have $250 less income at the end of the week. After I realized this fact, when my wife asked me to do something that would take me away from my work, I would inform her that she would have to pay me fifty dollars. At first she looked at me as if I was crazy, but when I showed her how it cost us that much, she eventually agreed to let me work uninterrupted and to go on with her daily activities as if I was working in an office away from home. Needless to say, my performance improved appreciably, and the closer I looked, the more I noticed and eliminated the drains on my energy and my time.

As a sales manager, I've witnessed time and again the adverse results of new salespeople trying to be successful and, at the same time, being their own worst enemy. Because the salespeople I trained worked on straight commission, people were often reluctant to take the risk. We've always been taught, consciously and sometimes subtly, that if you work, you should get paid. And although I believe in this statement, somewhere along the line it was inferred that we should be "guaranteed" that we would get paid, regardless of production. The lack of a guaranteed weekly paycheck was a scary proposition to many people.

As a result, they would try to create safe situations to subdue their fears. This safety cost them dearly. Often people would get "night jobs" or sell other products or have another form of income that required what they thought was minimal attention. The only problem was that any time or energy they allocated to provide their safety net was time and energy that was not available to them to help accomplish their dream of success. Since this goes against everything we discussed about focus, it always has fatal results.

Remember, a person will always accomplish his or her primary objective. If safety is most important to you, you will accomplish it, usually at the expense of everything else. This also applies to any hobbies or other activities we might have. And as I said earlier, it even applies to what we think it is to be a good father or mother, a good husband, wife, son, or daughter. Yes, these titles are important to us, just as our hobbies or other activities might be. But if we put them before success, if they are most important to us, then they will drain from us the energy and time that must be committed to any attempt at success. Success must be first, foremost, and *the most* important thing in your life, where you initially commit all your time and energy that you have beyond that needed for survival.

This may sound unappetizing to you at first, but the good news is that once you commit to this scenario, success comes very quickly, and you then can accomplish those other things in life. Not only will success come quickly, but also you will be amazed at how easily you are able to accomplish those other things that you would like in your life. That's because *success in anything teaches you about success in everything*. Once you get beyond the fears, the hype, and the flawed programming, success is simple and guaranteed!

Personal energy limitations or personal energy use not only refers to our physical energy, but also applies to our mental and spiritual energy. Thomas Edison was once ridiculed for not being able to remember his own phone number. His reply was why should he clutter his mind with facts that could easily be accessed in a book. For our purpose, I would like to expand that answer to why should a person use his mental energy to remember an unimportant fact when he can use that mental energy to think. We can choose to use our mind as a storehouse of knowledge, or we can use it to think.

Napoleon Hill wrote the first major breakthrough to success in a book entitled *Think and Grow Rich*. He didn't say "Work hard and grow rich" or "Do and grow rich." He specifically chose the word "think" because it's what most people don't do. They spend their mental energy engaging in activities that don't help to bring them closer to their dreams. Worry, fear, other people's opinions, and a host of other mind drains rob them of success, rob them of the creative energy their mind can use to ensure success. What are the drains on your mental energy? How do you rationalize not being focused on your dream? How do you or the people around you undermine your attempts at becoming successful, whether purposely or unconsciously? When will you be ready to commit all of your energy to your dream? These are the questions that result in success.

POINTS TO PONDER

It may be your success, but everyone else has a stake in it also.

Success in anything teaches you about success in everything.

12

What Is Success?

What is done for another is done for oneself.

— Paulus

The question of what is success has been debated for centuries. I think we can agree that success, for the most part, is subjective. There are also many different types of success, just as there are many different areas in our lives in which we can be successful. The purpose of this book is to help you to achieve financial success—affluence. In that context, there are some axioms upon which we can build. First and foremost, *success is happiness*. In its most diluted form, success is our desire to realize peace in our lives. It's that feeling of security, the ability to withstand the future unknown, which allows us to live today with a smile. The pursuit of happiness is the basic drive that motivates us to achieve success. After that, the picture gets cloudy. The cloudiness is caused by the entrance of the ego, the person who you think you are. The ego, the self, takes this heavenly goal of happiness through affluence and either supports it or negates it through the thought process it develops.

Some people mistakenly perceive success to be the accumulation of money. This is usually the result of the ego being a blind filter. Unbridled, the ego is self-serving and blind to the awareness of the world around it. Without conscious direction, the ego becomes a bull in a china shop, commanding everything in its path, and at the same time it is the source of ultimate destruction. Lack of continued consciousness of the ego relegates us to being its slave and, as a result, we also become a slave of what it produces. That is why people who see the accumulation of money as success are usually consumed with all the fears surrounding money. They become the slaves of money.

Who is trying to take your money from you? Who is your friend only because of your money? Whom can you trust? These fears negate the very basis of the pursuit of success, namely happiness. How can anyone be happy with these fears constantly plaguing their mind? Success, affluence, is not the accumulation of money. The main reason it's not is the motivation behind the accumulation of money. The motivation is self-centered. The only way to become truly successful is through the cooperative effort of others. Ideally, you want a mass conspiracy to make you successful. This is how you accomplish that: *give as many people as you can a vested interest in your success.* When they personally have something to gain by your success, they will take an active role in helping you get there. The money that results from your success is merely a by-product of the process.

Many successful people have said that money "is only a way of keeping score" because it's the process, the act of becoming successful that brings happiness, not the money. The resultant affluence is the way you reward those who have conspired to help make you successful. Around every successful man and woman are droves of recipients who share in their success. The more you share your wealth with others, the more they strive to help you become even more successful. That's why whatever successful people touch turns to gold; that's why the rich get richer. If done properly, you'll have the entire cosmos collaborating for your success.

Probably the most misunderstood law of lasting success is that it's not done alone, and it is not accomplished just for you. The successful people of this world are the most generous of contributors to causes alleviating the ills of mankind. I truly believe that the Higher Power, the universe, etc., gives lasting affluence to those who know what to do with it. This point was made glaringly clear to me by a colleague named Jerri Lynne, with whom I've worked for many years and who knows me better than most. One day she commented, "I finally figured out why money just keeps flowing to you; it's because you keep giving it away!"

This giving away of money is comparable to planting seeds for future harvests. They're investments. I don't see it that way when I'm in the process of giving it, but in retrospect, what else do you call the placement of funds that return to you tenfold and a hundredfold? I find worthy, well-deserving people and things to contribute to, and the law of compensation takes over from there. *The law of compensation states that no action goes unrewarded.* Good actions reap good results, and bad actions reap bad results. It always works, so be aware of the seeds that you sow today. They will determine the harvests you reap tomorrow!

I would be remiss if I concluded this chapter without addressing the most elusive characteristic of financial success. This elusiveness is the result of one of those universal laws that works every time whether you're aware of it or not. Very simply stated, *the pursuit of affluence will drive it away!* This is difficult to grasp at first when we think of all the conditioning we've experienced with regard to goals and focus of intention. But if you allow your mind to expand a bit, you'll realize that everything worthwhile in life is subject to this same universal law.

Take love, for instance. How many people make the mistake of feeling sorry for themselves because they are not in a love relationship with someone? They can't find someone to love them. Those of us who have "found" love realize that it only came to us as a result of our loving someone else first. Through the act of giving, we received. The love we valued so dearly was always right at hand, within us. It didn't materialize in our lives until we brought it out into the world, but it was there all the time. We went crazy looking for and thirsting for what we already had. If you haven't had the experience of being loved by someone, then these words sound crazy. They're incomprehensible. But your lack of comprehension doesn't change the law. Once you've experienced love in your life, then you know the truth. In fact, the only thing that then becomes incomprehensible is that people don't understand how simple it really is. This is the spirituality of love.

The same thing is true of another condition upon which we place a high value—happiness. Ever since grade school, we've learned about "the pursuit of happiness." It's even a part of our Declaration of Independence. The paradox, however, is that its pursuit negates its experience. We hear people say, "If I only had the right job, I'd be happy." "If I could only find the right person, I'd be happy." Because of their programming, they place conditions on happiness and their expectations become excuses. This is the "pursuit" in "the pursuit of happiness," but they have it all backwards. Happiness is not the by-product of all these conditions, it is the source! People put their attention on the wrong things and that's why happiness eludes them. Those who are happy know this. If you are happy, the right person will find you. Money will find you, and the right job will find you. The happiness comes first, and you experience it by giving it away. It is already within you, waiting for the moment of experience. This is the spirituality of happiness. That which is given is received!

Another highly valued experience is the gaining of knowledge. We have learned that "knowledge is power." And it is. But there is nothing that is unknown, just unexperienced. The invention of the light bulb did not create electricity. Electrical power was in existence since the beginning of time, waiting to be acknowledged, waiting to be discovered. Being part of the infinite universe gives us immediate access to all its knowledge. The Bible tells us that we are created in the image and likeness of God. In that image and likeness is included all the components thereof, including knowledge. Hidden in the roots of the word "education" lies the truth of this awareness. The word educate means to draw from. When someone is educated, the knowledge is drawn from them. It cannot be drawn unless it is already there! The formal act of education allows the "experience" of what is already known. The operation of a fax machine is a mystery, if not a miracle, until we "experience" its operation. After that, it just becomes another labor-saving device.

To experience the knowledge you already have, teach. That is, give it away. The age-old parable about the teacher learning more than the pupil contains the validity of this course of action. So, too, lies the wisdom in the saying "When the pupil is ready, the teacher will appear." The truth is that the teacher is always present; it is the pupil who is not. I am not speaking of physical presence, but of the presence of awareness. When the awareness of the laws that govern knowledge and the universe become present, the pupil becomes his own teacher. The pursuit of knowledge is a fallacy. All you wish to know you already know. If you wish to learn—teach! This is the spirituality of knowledge.

As with all the rest of the valued treasures of life, the same holds true for affluence. The more you concentrate and focus on money and wealth, the more it eludes you. Oscar Wilde once said, "There is only one class of people that thinks more about money than the rich, and that is the poor. In fact, the poor can think of nothing else." And what do they think about in regard to money? The lack of it. And guess what they experience. The lack of it. The thoughts we hold in our mind become reality. You've heard this from every researcher of success who ever lived. Napoleon Hill, Earl Nightingale, the list is endless. They all knew the same truth. However, it is also true that dwelling on the receiving of affluence (possession of wealth) drives it away. If you wish to experience affluence in your life, make it appear in the lives of others. In the act of giving comes the receiving. Thus it is written in the Bible, "To him that has, even more shall be given until he becomes rich, but the person who has nothing will have taken away from him even the little he has."

I've paraphrased a bit, but you get the message. The rich get richer and the poor get poorer. *Success is not a condition of life, it is a state of mind.* That's why a successful person can be successful at most anything, if not everything. That's why a truly successful person who loses his wealth regains it so quickly. It's not the money that makes a person successful. It's who the person is. This is the spirituality of success. You are first a success on the inside, and then it shows on the outside. To experience the wonders and the treasures of the world, look within.

POINTS TO PONDER

Success is happiness.

Success is not a condition of life, it is a state of mind.

Give as many people as you can a vested interest in your success.

The law of compensation states that no act goes unrewarded.

The pursuit of affluence will drive it away.

13

SUCCESS IS YOUR DESTINY

*When one is identified with the One, all things
will be complete with him. When he reaches the point of having
no subjective feelings, spiritual beings will submit to him.*

— Chuang Tzu

Success is happiness. In fact, all forms of success are a person's attempt to achieve happiness. Financial success is no different. It's not the money, the fame, or the respect that they're after. It's the happiness that money, fame, and respect can bring them. That's the basic motivation to endure whatever is necessary to be truly successful—happiness. When you focus on the money, fame, or respect, success is usually short-lived. Acquiring them gives birth to the fear of losing them, which becomes a self-fulfilling prophecy.

As a child of God, as a part of the universal consciousness, whatever you believe in, happiness is your birthright. I heard one of my managers, Victor, speaking to a group of rookie salespeople, and what he said impressed me regarding the validity of this truth. He said to them, "Do you know how special you are? At the moment of your conception, there were millions of possibilities, because there were at least 200 million sperm that could have possibly made contact with the egg. But you were the one that succeeded. You overcame unbelievable odds just to be born. Do you think that was for nothing? Do you think, perhaps, that you overcame those unbelievable odds for a reason? You were born to achieve greatness. Your birth is proof of that, but so many people live their lives in mediocrity just barely making it. Nothing you will face in life will ever come close to being as difficult as what you've already achieved. You are greatness!"

Part of the problem with realizing that success is your destiny is that you see yourself as separate from everything else around you. This is the result of the ego. When we see ourselves as separate from the rest of nature, the simplicity of our destiny escapes us. Think about it. How do you see yourself? Do you think in terms of you and the world? Do you think in terms of you and me? Do you think in terms of you and nature? Are you separate from everything that occurs around you, like an observer? Or, are we all necessarily essentially entwined in what is? No two people experience the world in the same exact way because we create our own reality. Reality is subjective.

You've heard the expression, "Life is what you make it." Well, it's absolutely true. What we see and the way we see it (our perception) creates what we believe to be true (our reality). Therefore, the world, your world, is a product of you. You cannot be separated from your experience of what is because you create it. If you take the "you" out of the world, it does not exist. You and the world (your world) are inseparable. When you die, so does the world, or at least the world and the reality of it that is exclusively yours. Your world, your interpretation of the world, cannot exist without you. There is no you and the world. You *are* the world!

If you can grasp this concept, then success is simple. Let me tell you why. When you see yourself as separate from everything around you, you see everything else around you as a whole, as one unit. Do you know why you do this? Because it is a whole! When you look at a tree, you have to concentrate and focus on seeing the tree separate from the other trees and the rest of the landscape. Why does it take concentration? Because it's not separate and apart from everything else. When you look out, you see everything together because it is together. In order to separate anything we see from all that we see, we need to concentrate on the separation. The paradox is that because of our ego, in order to see *ourselves* as part of everything we see and not separate from it, it requires concentration. We need to concentrate on seeing ourselves in combination with all that we see. If the tree had eyes, and had the fortune and the misfortune of having an ego, do you think the tree would see us as part of everything else, part of the world? Of course it would, the same way as we see it. Now look at that tree again…how tall can a tree grow? There is no limit. It grows as tall as it can. It is destined to achieve its full potential.

All that we see of the world that is not man-made is already perfect. *Nature is perfection in action. The universe is perfection in action.* And how much effort does it take nature and the universe to achieve this perfection? No effort at all; they just are. How much conscious effort does a tree take to grow? It doesn't make an effort to grow; it just grows. That is its destiny, and because it doesn't have an ego, it fulfills that destiny. As a part of the whole, we, too, have a destiny. Just as the tree grows as tall as it can, we are destined to be all we can be. So who sets the limits on what you can be? Only you.

Inside a mighty oak tree is an acorn. And inside that acorn is not only the promise of another mighty oak tree, but the promise of a forest of mighty oak trees. The promise in each seed is limitless. Inside each of us lies the seed of happiness, of limitless happiness, financially but also emotionally, physically, spiritually, and completely. It's our birthright. It's what we were born to do. It is our destiny!

The realization that it is our birthright to succeed, carried to its optimum, results in effortless success. Did you ever wonder why successful people make it look so easy? Because it is easy. And the better they are at it, the easier they make it look. *Just as everything in the universe is already perfect, so are you.* You just need to get out of your own way! The gift we have that separates us from every other living thing is our ability to choose. It's our greatest gift and our worst handicap. Everything in life is paradoxically so, because if it weren't for choice, we would naturally achieve the same perfection as experienced by the rest of the universe.

Unfortunately, our choice gives us an alternative to perfection. To be aware of this alternative makes all the difference in the world. It's what people talk about when they refer to "letting go." It's the curse of the ego. Who we think we are or who we think we should be (in other words, the ego) keeps us from becoming who we can be! The programming, the conditioning, the memories of what happened to us, and what was taught to us before we could discern for ourselves, forever affects everything we do and every decision we make. We will forever be the victims of our programming. It will forever have power over us until we make possible (cause to happen) that day of reckoning when we begin to take an honest evaluation of who we are and why we do the things we do. When that day comes, our conditioning begins to lose its power over us. And the more we reveal to ourselves about ourselves, the weaker the grip of that power becomes until it reverses direction and we gain power over it. The more power over our conditioning that we gain, the more successful we become.

When we are born, we are already perfect. Except for a few basic needs, happiness is a way of life. That's why the happiness in the smile on a baby's face is so genuine. That's also why you feel the uncontrollable urge to smile too. The baby touches one of your memories. The memory of how you felt when you were a baby. Pure bliss! No worries! Then the world began to condition you, to create the person that today, you think you should be. But you were perfect to begin with, and the more you conquer and eliminate this conditioning, the more you return to that state of perfection. What is a baby afraid to do? Almost nothing! What could you accomplish if you had no fear? Anything! Therein lies the perfection!

The innocence and the sublime happiness inherent in innocence you had when you were born were taken from you. But it is your birthright. It is your destiny. It wasn't all part of a diabolical plan to ruin your life. We've been doing this to each other as far back as anyone can remember. We are creatures of habit. We do and pass on what we know—the conditioning. Where it all began is unimportant. Where it ends is all-important. And you have to make a conscious decision not to allow the conditioning to dictate your life anymore.

That brings to mind one of my favorite movie lines. At one point in the movie *Network*, all the characters were sticking their heads out of their apartment windows and screaming, "I'm mad as hell. And I'm not going to take it anymore!" When will you get mad as hell? When will you realize what happened to you and finally take control of your life? The day you do will mark the beginning of your success.

POINTS TO PONDER

Nature is perfection in action. The universe is perfection in action.

Just as everything in the universe is already perfect, so are you.

Success is your destiny!

14

GUILT AND ENVIRONMENT

A smooth sea never made a successful sailor.

— Herman Melville

The most valuable thing I have learned from life is to regret nothing.

— Somerset Maugham

One of the major obstacles that I've seen hold people back from becoming successful is guilt. Guilt for what they have done, haven't done, are doing now, or are not doing now. Somewhere along the line we picked up the idea that we needed to be punished, incessantly, for our misdoings. And who better to inflict that punishment than ourselves, our own worst critic? I've seen many a promising new superstar sabotage his own success. Because of what we have or haven't done, we believe we don't deserve to be successful (happy). I know from whence I speak because guilt not only kept me from achieving what I was capable of, but it also caused me to create an unmanageable life.

I grew up on the streets of Brooklyn, N.Y., in a rough area called Fort Greene. I remember getting pushed around a lot in my early childhood. I was the favorite target of the neighborhood bully. I didn't like fighting—it hurt. But the more I backed down, the more bullies I seemed to accumulate. I was often the object of practical jokes and as a result was laughed at and ridiculed. I was a loner; I had no choice. I wasn't cool and the only friends I had were those who suffered the same fate of being bullied. I was close to no one and often played by myself. I was physically weak in comparison to many of the other boys, and that only made things worse. I didn't play sports. I didn't know how. When it came to choosing up for a game of baseball, I usually played the position of "left out." I can't blame them; I couldn't catch or hit the ball. In sports, I was a liability to whatever team I was on.

My mom and dad had difficulty showing their love. Today, I know that they loved me deeply. Back then I judged myself to be unlovable and unworthy. Who could blame them, though? I didn't love myself. Who could love a weak, shy coward who was always being chased home by somebody? About the only bright spot in my childhood was in school. I was a good student, mostly straight A's through grammar school. My parents were proud of that, but before long it became expected. If I received a 98 on a test, my father would ask me why I didn't get a 100. I screwed up. Getting good grades, though, only made the situation with the bullies worse. They hated me for making them feel stupid. I paid for it. Not only did I get nerd-like marks, I also looked the part. Big horn-rimmed glasses to match my big nose, and a hairstyle constructed by Mother every morning. Where the opposite sex was concerned, I wasn't cool enough. Not many girls wanted to be seen with a nerdy coward at whom people were always laughing. I judged myself to be ugly. Why else weren't the girls attracted to me?

My dad, my role model, was a very interesting character. I say that in retrospect, because as a child I saw very little of him. He was a plumber in the days when plumbing didn't pay well. He would usually be up and gone before I woke up, and would usually come home after I was asleep. I used to think he worked a lot of hours. My parents were the type who wouldn't talk about problems in front of the children. They felt we needed to be protected from the difficulties of life. But the older I became, and the more drastic the situation became, the more I began to learn. My dad was a gambler. Those nights I thought he was working, he was either playing cards or playing the ponies. Like most gamblers, he would usually lose, but when he won, you would think it was Christmas. When my dad won, everybody won. He was a very generous man, but the winnings were too few and far between.

I can't blame him, though. Gambling was my father's attempt at becoming successful. That's what the street teaches you. Success in the streets is hitting the number, winning the lottery, or catching the triple in the ninth race at Aqueduct. Being a dad wasn't one of my father's strong points either. His expectations were very high and sometimes unrealistic. He never said it, but I think he secretly wanted to make sure I didn't wind up like him. But the pressure didn't make me better. I became worse than he was because the constant reassurance of not being good enough in my own mind would drag me further and further down.

The male figure who was most present in my early years was my grandfather. He was a simple man with simple pleasures. He loved to cook, he loved his garden, and he loved his family. He communicated these simple pleasures to me by his actions. Today, I'm grateful for the lesson, but he couldn't keep me from the experiences I would have to encounter on the road that I had chosen to travel.

As my early years became my teenage years, my lack of confidence and poor self-image took its toll. Wanting to change my life, I looked for the alternatives in my environment. I joined a street gang, the Juvenile Gents. Little did we know that the "juvenile" part fit very well. We hung out in "our" park. We drank, gambled, shoplifted, stole cars, took drugs and flunked high school. We were cool! I was cool! I even had a girlfriend, Julie. She was the first girl with whom I went steady. She wasn't very popular, but that was the best that I could do. I bought her an ankle bracelet. The relationship didn't last very long.

I cut school often to play pool, to hang out, or to do other important things like that. I went from A's to F's and was proud of it. I was in a very competitive school, Brooklyn Technical High School. It was full of nerdy types. Brainy people who had no clue how important it was to be cool. Yes, it was a competitive school, but I chose not to compete. When I was in school, I was usually in detention. At least I could meet some "normal" people there.

This downward spiral seemed to gather momentum, and I kept getting worse and worse. The gang became more active. We wanted to increase our "turf." There was only one problem. To increase our turf, we would have to take over someone else's turf. For this we needed a "warlord." This was the guy who would lead the gang into battle. He was usually the toughest in the group and often would fight it out with the other gang's warlord in front of both groups before the gang fight would start. The council met to decide. One guy, Ronnie, said, "Vinny should be the warlord." I couldn't believe my ears. Up until now I was able to hide my cowardice quite well. I was able to avoid any confrontations with a well-constructed stare and a threatening bop when I walked, which said, "Don't mess with me."

But now I would actually have to fight. I would have to hurt someone, but more important, I could get hurt. My life flashed before me. Had Ronnie lost his mind? I wasn't the only one who thought so; some of the other guys actually asked if he had gone crazy. Some in the gang were the bullies of my youth, and they remembered what an easy mark I was.

Ronnie told them a story I had completely forgotten. Ronnie was tough; nobody messed with him. One day, when we were younger, he and his friends chased me home. I could usually outrun my trouble, but Ronnie was as fast as I was. I couldn't make the turn to run up the stairs to our third-floor apartment without getting caught, so I raced straight into the backyard where I was cornered.

I was able to avoid getting caught for a while with my running ability, but eventually I found myself running straight into Ronnie. Instinctively, I raised my fist and knocked him to the ground. I jumped on top of him, picked up a brick, and was about to smash him in the face when my mother yelled at me from our apartment window to stop. Ronnie said that nobody else had ever knocked him down, and that if it were not for my mother, he wouldn't look the same. His reasoning was, I should be the warlord because nobody else in the gang had ever come that close to beating him. I got instant respect. I felt great and terrible at the same time because eventually they would all find out what I already knew. I was a coward. And when they finally found out for sure, no amount of staring or bopping could save me. This was my first experience with the exercise called "act as if," which is a crude, street version of visualization.

I acted as if I was courageous, as if I was a warlord, and eventually I became one. Even the other gangs respected me as a warlord, a feat not easily accomplished. My fear motivated me to become what I was not. The "act as if" eventually became reality, because if you act as if something is true, and you don't need the cooperation of others for its realization, then eventually it becomes true. I was a warlord! Not exactly the pursuit of a successful person, but on the street it was a position of honor and respect.

I transferred out of Brooklyn Tech in my senior year because I would not graduate if I stayed there. I went to a private school to complete the minimum requirements to be able to fulfill my parents' dream of a lifetime. I would be the first child on either side of the family to go to college. I would become an accountant or maybe even a lawyer. College changed my view of life.

In college, I was a square peg in a round hole. I stood out like a sore thumb. These weren't street people. They were educated, intelligent, mature, and socially adept. I was intelligent, somewhat educated, immature, and socially crippled. I was shy—painfully so. Not only could I not initiate a conversation, I couldn't keep one going if someone else started it. My answers were short and abrupt. I always let everyone else do the talking. What I had to say wasn't important. I would pick my friends by their ability to speak. Since I could not get myself to meet people, I would do it through somebody else.

One such person was Tony. Tony knew everybody, especially the girls. His nickname was "motor mouth." Boy, could he talk. Just the prescription I needed to balance my shyness and lack of confidence. At least I'd finally have a chance of meeting a woman because Tony was bold and very sociable.

They were holding elections for student government, and Tony asked me if I'd like to be in student government with him. Tony had a way of getting people to agree. Even though I didn't know much about it because I was still struggling to fit in, I reluctantly agreed. I forgot about it until they published the various party tickets for the election. I saw my name listed as a candidate for president and a slew of others in various positions. "There has to be a mistake," I thought. "Either that or Tony has gone completely out of his mind. I can't be president. I can't even talk!" I searched for Tony and questioned what was obviously a mistake. Tony said it was no mistake. "You're the president. Don't worry. It'll be all right." "It'll be all right," I thought. "Boy, am I in trouble! Now everyone will find out how shy and insecure I really am."

I remember my campaign speech. It was a terrible example of public speaking, but somehow I won! "These people are nuts," I thought. "They want me to lead them and I can't even get out of my own way." But lead them I did. It was baptism by fire, similar to my warlord story. Sometimes people rise to meet the occasion. Before I knew it, I was speaking in front of multi-college assemblies and demonstrations. I spoke in front of teachers' groups, negotiated with the chancellor of the City University, and addressed the state assembly in Albany. I had no choice. People were relying on me. That was my motivation. I didn't have time for fear and insecurity.

During my second year of college, I met Marlene. She was the woman of my dreams. I fell in love with her the first moment I saw her. God, was she beautiful! By this time, I had become very popular. I was BMOC (big man on campus). I went out with dozens of girls, but Marlene was out of my league. Still, I couldn't deny what my heart was telling me. I was in love. I had to have her. It wasn't easy. I wanted what every other guy in school wanted—Marlene. She became my wife six years later, and even today brings me the same joy as when I first saw her. She was the first thing in life that I really wanted with all my being. She was also an example of what a person can accomplish if they want something badly enough. She could make any man's life into heaven, but my hell still lay before me, waiting.

Being drafted into the army interrupted my college years. I had lost my college deferment by being laid up in a hospital in Puerto Rico, the result of a motor scooter accident. I dreaded the thought of going into the Vietnam War. You can't stare down a bullet! Besides, if I had to be in the service, I wanted to be a Marine. My ego made a lot of decisions in those days. The Marines made me a man, but only put off the inevitable crash for a few more years.

I got injured in boot camp, which wasn't bad because I got a medical discharge. I came home to finish college at night while working on Wall Street as an accountant during the day. I found out that I hated accounting. Today, I'm almost thoroughly convinced that people pick a major in college so they know what they're *not* going to do for the rest of their lives. I started my own business. It was something I always wanted to do. In the beginning, I was a partner with my father and brother in a hardware store, but the store couldn't withstand the assault of all of our gambling habits. As a result, I went off on my own. I started a small wholesaling business out of a rented garage.

I dreamt of one day having a million dollars in sales, and I did it. But instead of marking an achievement, it was the beginning of my decline. It was a self-centered objective, the kind that doesn't last, and since I neglected to set a higher, other-centered objective, I floundered aimlessly. I had no direction and became bored.

That's when I found cocaine. For four years I watched myself degenerate into what everyone fears they might become. Morally, spiritually, emotionally, and physically, I amounted to zero. I destroyed all the lives around me. The guilt was unbearable. I even thought of suicide to spare people the pain of what I represented for them. When I hit bottom, when things couldn't get any worse, I hated myself and sought help. I put myself into treatment and prayed for recovery.

While in treatment, I realized that by all accounts, I should be dead. I realized that cocaine was my attempt at suicide, but it became obvious that God had other plans. Countless people have died for a lot less than what I had done to myself, but I didn't die. Why? I began to realize that it must be for a reason. A reason larger than I was, and that started my road to recovery. I realized my life must have a purpose. Why else was I spared? I also realized that to accomplish this purpose, I must already have the necessary gifts. That prompted the question "Who am I?" It wasn't easy to get beyond the hate, disgust, and remorse I had for myself and what I had done. I didn't know then about my conditioned values being the cause of my inadequacies, which were really just areas for possible improvement. But taking them head on and looking them dead in the eye made them less and less horrible. Eventually, I was finally able to start looking for my good points, my gifts. I realized I was good with people; I could bond with them quickly. People trusted me and I could see through the defenses that they put up to protect themselves.

I also realized I was very intuitive. I used these gifts to help others with whom I was in treatment, to find their own recovery. My life finally meant something, and I found value through helping other people. It took me thirty-six years, but I finally began to live. When I was ready to reenter the world, I answered an ad in the newspaper and chose sales as my career. I figured with all the convincing I had done to maintain a successful habit, I must be pretty good in sales. With what I had learned about myself, I achieved in a year and a half what most people don't achieve in a lifetime— financial security. I flew up the corporate ladder, always trying to remember that success and happiness come through helping other people find success and happiness.

Today, I'm wealthy, happy, and successful. I have recounted my story, not to boast about how far I've come, but rather to make it clear that no matter how far down you are, you can still wind up on top. No matter how low your opinion of yourself, no matter how disgusted you are with who you are, you don't have to stay that way. It all starts, though, with the question "Who am I—really?" If you find something you don't like about yourself, like I did, change it. It's that simple. I guarantee you that whatever you dislike about yourself is not usually the result of heredity. It's what you became as you developed. I wasn't born a coward or a cocaine abuser. I became those things. I *changed* to become those things, and I could change into whatever else I wanted to be, including becoming a success. Whatever you've done in life that you are ashamed of can be changed, and you have the power. I sank about as low as anyone can go, but I still found my way to the top, and you can too!

As crazy as it may sound, I am grateful for all the negative experiences in my life. I am very happy with my life right now, and if you are happy with where you are, you cannot deny the road that got you there! I am grateful for the bullies, the gambling, the gangs, and especially the addiction to cocaine. I realize, in retrospect, that it was all part of the training that made me who

I am today. The lesson here, I think, is not to regret your shortcomings and shortfalls, but to rejoice in them.

I know this is something different from anything you've ever heard. Thank God for your misfortunes, because unless iron is put to the fire, it can never become steel. As Napoleon Hill said in his great book *Think and Grow Rich*, "Every adversity carries within it the seed of an equivalent or greater benefit." *Let your adversities, your weaknesses, teach you, instead of using them as a source of guilt and remorse!* As I said earlier, remember these wise words, which were said to me when I needed them most—Even God, in His infinite wisdom, waits until a man has completed his life before He passes judgment. Give yourself the same break, and attaining success will be a much easier proposition!

POINT TO PONDER

Let your adversities, your weaknesses, teach you instead of using them as a source of guilt and remorse!

15

The Goal Myth

**For an idea that does not at first seem insane,
there is no hope.**

— Albert Einstein

This is another one of those times when I am going to tell you something directly opposite of what the world has taught you. Goals, and more precisely, today's goal-setting strategies, keep you from achieving success! Of all the concepts I've related to you so far, this is probably the most surprising, because most success formulas today make goal setting a major part of their program. Up until now, you've been following their teachings and wondering what's wrong with you because you're not getting the results. It's because they have you focusing on the wrong things.

Goal setting in the success training world has become so accepted that nobody has bothered to question its validity. I'm not saying that a person shouldn't know where he's going; that would be suicidal. What I am saying, though, is that concentration and fixation on what you want will cause you to not get it. I've read success books that suggest that you do everything possible to keep your goal in front of you at all times. From pasting a picture of your goal on your bathroom mirror or the dashboard of your car to carrying an 8 1/2" by 11" picture around with you all day on your key chain. I don't know of people who have achieved their goals in this manner, although I'm sure some exist. The real trick to success is not getting it, it's keeping it. Sometimes people stumble onto success, but staying successful is a completely different story. That's why so many lottery winners wind up right back where they started before they bought the winning lottery ticket. They didn't win success. They only won money! Ask any successful person you know if it was as hard to get to the top as it is to stay on top. Without true success consciousness, achieving a specific outcome becomes a short-lived experience.

The success law of detachment states that one becomes detached from the outcome, which is exactly what is wrong with the goal-setting techniques that are taught today. Focusing on your goal for its own importance is so lethal that *goal setting should come with a warning label.* Just as Norman Vincent Peale wrote about the many different examples of *The Power of Positive Thinking,* it is infinitely more important that we acknowledge the power of negative thinking. Napoleon Hill and Earl Nightingale expressed the same complementary principle: the thoughts you hold in your mind become your reality, for better or for worse. Every time you think about your goal, as many trainings prescribe today, you come face to face with the fact that you *don't* have it. The result is that you inadvertently conjure up all the power of negative thinking, and the thought that you constantly hold and reinforce in your mind is one of lack. Your focus is on failure!

Additionally, constant focus on a self-centered goal flirts with the danger of it becoming part of your ego. Until you examine your conditioning and exert control over it through the "Who am I?" your ego is your worst enemy. Until you gain power over it, it has power over you. As long as that statement is true, it will cause you to make foolish and unproductive decisions. The ego causes us to be self-centered, and since success is achieved through others, this practice is usually self-defeating.

I remember once deciding that I wanted to have the number-one sales force in the country. Why? So I could receive all the recognition and the glory that went with it. It wasn't surprising that I couldn't get anyone else to buy into my "goal," and of course without them, there was no way I could achieve it. Not surprisingly, nothing happened. Realizing my objective was selfish and self-centered, I rethought my desire. From the start, as a salesman and throughout my sales management career, I always received what I wanted by helping other people to get what they wanted. Zig Ziglar says, "You can get everything you want in life if you can help enough other people get what they want." His words are worth their weight in gold.

I started thinking of my sales team and what a fine group of individuals they were, and how they deserved national recognition for the hard work they did. Three-quarters of the year had already passed and we were in third place, impossibly behind. Impossible, that is, for a mechanical goal, but not impossible for a dream! When I began to focus on getting them the recognition they deserved, everything fell into place. I knew it would. The team didn't think it was possible—nobody did. It didn't even make sense to consider making up that much ground. But success isn't logical. I set the objective and then focused on the path. I forgot about number one for me and focused on recognition for them. The rest is history.

Focusing on what your ego wants, on your goal, creates fear—the fear of not achieving it. Before you know it, negative programming steps in and you begin to hedge on your goal. You start to invent the excuses (expectations) that you'll use when it doesn't materialize. *Your focus on an ego-centered goal causes you not to achieve it.*

As an example, when I began writing this book I felt fear. I feared not doing it right, and that fear indicated the overwhelming presence of my ego. As a result, I had great difficulty writing and I realized that I was attempting to write for the wrong reasons. So in order to write this book properly, I had to suppress my ego. I had to suppress the way I wanted the book to turn out. I had to forget about it becoming a best-seller or even getting it published. My *objective* was to write a book, not to become a famous writer of a best-seller. That *goal* would be ego-based, which proved to be the block in my attempt to write. When I focused on who I was writing the book for, the words began to flow. That taught me an important lesson: *It's not so important where you want to go as why you want to get there!* If this book can help change just one person's life, then it was worth writing. You can be that one person.

The race to become the number-one sales team and my writing experience congealed for me the reason why today's goal-setting strategies do not work. When trying to accomplish a goal, the ego is engaged and the focus is on "I." If there are more people than "I" involved, then one must employ a different strategy. It's not so much having a goal that is the problem, but the problem is the meaning that today's goal-setting strategies have given to the word "goal." I don't think anyone would argue about having a vision of a possible final outcome. All people need to have an idea of where they're going if they have any hope of getting there, but Columbus setting out to discover new worlds didn't stubbornly decide where he would land his ships. He didn't define an exact course to a well-defined destination. He went with the flow of the winds and the currents and had a general idea of where he wanted to end up. If he was looking for India, he missed it by a few miles! He did, however, make one of the most amazing discoveries of his time! Many of the successful people whom I've interviewed for this book will quickly tell you that you don't always end up exactly where you had planned. Sometimes the universe knows better than you do. You have to be flexible, and many of today's goal-setting strategies do not allow for flexibility.

Instead of setting goals, I propose that you establish objectives. Objectives allow for flexibility, while goals are more rigid. However, that is not the greatest difference between setting a goal and establishing an objective. The major difference between them is how they're formulated. The goal-setting strategies today teach that when a person sets a goal, he or she should begin by deciding what they want (desire), and then figure out how to get it (thought). That strategy and the resulting goal has its roots in emotion (desire) and is followed up by a thought process. Using that process, the goals are usually self-centered, egotistical, and sometimes just plain selfish.

Establishing an objective is different. In formulating an objective, the thought comes first, and then you back it up with emotion (desire). It's exactly the opposite way that people are instructed to formulate their goals. The thoughts by which you establish your objective begin with the good you can bring to other people, the world, or the marketplace. You can set a goal to start a business so that you can become rich, and you'll probably fail (nine out of ten do), or you can start a business to help people by delivering the best (product) to the marketplace, and as a result, have a much better chance of becoming wealthy.

It may seem like a fine point, but it makes all the difference in the world. Take my example of having the number-one sales team in the country. When I began, I wanted the top sales team for egotistical reasons. I wanted to be number one and made a plan to get the job done. The plan did not allow for anyone else to become number one, just me. No wonder no one else would buy into my plan. But as soon as I focused on the thought of the team being number one, they and the entire universe conspired to get the job done. We backed up the thought with emotion, and achieving it was almost effortless. In the end, they gave me an award for being the number-one area manager in the country, but by this time, I knew who deserved the real credit, and I made sure everyone else knew it when I gave my acceptance speech. The lesson is simple—*have an end result that helps people, and in the end you will be helped!*

A goal that has its origin in desire is usually destined to fail because desire is an expression of the ego. Since the untamed ego is a person's worst enemy and, for most of us, is negatively conditioned from birth by the 93 percent rule, it is futile to even consider having a goal whose roots are based in desire (ego). The goal has no choice other than to follow its program of failure. And yet this is the way most success formulas will suggest that you formulate your goals. They tell you to ask yourself, "What do you want?" which is the worst thing you can do! "What you want" taps into the negative failure program of your unexamined and untamed ego, so that *what you want keeps you from what you want!* Your goal, because it has its roots in the desire of the unbridled ego, keeps you from achieving your goal. Desire-thought goals are a self-defeating process.

It is imperative that you conquer the ego because, as already stated, until you gain power over it, it has power over you. Moreover, anything that has its roots in the ego will exert that same power over you. The reason for this is that part of that negative programming is the fear upon which so many people have "learned" what they know. A fear-based ego will produce fear-based desires, which produce fear-based goals. Anything that has its roots in fear exerts power over you. The fear runs the show. How can you accomplish anything under those circumstances? And even if you do, what will naturally continue is the fear. The fear of losing it. Not a very rewarding proposition, is it? You finally achieve something, and now you can't even enjoy it because you're afraid of losing it.

It is better to bypass your ego and its traps until you have conquered it. The way to do this is to have your objective originate in your mind, and then back it up with desire (emotion). The desire under this process is completely different from the desire in desire-thought goals. When you formulate your objectives based on thought, be careful to keep your self-centeredness in check. Remember, no one is successful by himself. The more your objective helps others to be successful, the greater chance you have of materializing that objective. The more you are in service to others, the more others will be in service to you. "As ye sow, so shall ye reap," or as they say in the street, "What goes around, comes around."

Ideally, what you will then have is an other-based objective formulated in your mind, which you support with your beliefs through your emotions. There is nothing in the world that can withstand that combination! In fact, it will be uncanny how all the forces in the universe will muster behind you to propel your objective toward you. You will become success-attractive. It will seem easy, because it is!

Part of what you will notice, once the ego has been conquered, is that your desires, in general, will change. They will change from self-centered to other-centered. This is why so many truly successful people are philanthropic.

To the uneducated, it seems as though the more they give away, the more they receive. It doesn't "seem" to be that way; it *is* that way. That's why the desire in establishing objectives is different than that in setting goals. It's not self-centered desire and emotion, it's other-centered desire and emotion. That's why I recommended in the introduction that you find a cause and back it up. Successful people are the source of much of the good that is done in this world.

Some might say that the difference that I have expressed between a goal and an objective is simply a matter of semantics. I would strongly argue otherwise, even though I will admit that there is a fine line between the two. In sales management, there is a fine line between being a manager and being a leader, but that fine line makes all the difference in the world when you're talking about results. Managers manage what has already happened and leaders make things happen. Need I say more? Goals can be productive when you are dealing with something that is completely physical and mental and doesn't involve anyone else, like setting a goal to eventually run a mile. However, if your objective has a spiritual side to it, which is the case if there are other people involved, then setting a goal will be detrimental to your success. This goes back to the military style of thinking mentioned earlier, specifically to its principles of victory and scarcity, which tap directly into one's ego and selfish emotions. Ego-based goals ultimately fail. Financial success, like all the other prized objectives of life, has a spiritual side to it, and not addressing that truth will have fatal results. Except for man, the universe and everything in it have no need for goals. They simply achieve their ultimate potential. *Your universal destiny is to achieve your ultimate potential.*

I hope the points I have made in this section are clear. They are important to your finally achieving the success that you were born to realize. The goal-setting techniques taught today have their origin in failure, and that's why they haven't worked for you thus far. The scientific facts behind why this is true will be discussed in a later chapter. But another interesting adjunct to what's wrong with the generally accepted idea of goal setting was published in a book entitled *Stop Setting Goals* by Bobb Biehl. In it, he says that many people set goals when they should be solving problems. He relates that many people become unmotivated by setting goals, but they are very motivated by the problem-solving process. Those individuals and companies that are setting goals are striving to achieve greater heights when some of them should be solving the problems within their existing plan. This behavior, he says, is not only irresponsible, but it causes anxiety, conflict, tension, and energy loss.

Spirituality and mysticism also have insights about goals and goal setting. In *Questions to a Zen Master* by Taisen Deshimaru, we read:

> To have a goal, not just in zazen [meditation], but in everyday living, to want to get something or grasp something, is a sickness of the mind. You don't need a goal, if here and now, you are concentrating on what you're doing: on your work when you're working, on your food when you're eating.... Here and now, if you are concentrated, your concentration will follow you to your death and illuminate you unfailingly; but that is not having a goal. On the other hand, you must have an ideal [objective]. But an ideal and a goal are completely different.

The spiritual insights of mysticism, the result of thousands of years of introspection and refinement, have come to the same conclusion, albeit through different methods of discovery. One other important principle that mysticism has discovered in regard to goals is one that was already briefly mentioned: the concept of detachment. Detachment means to let go of the final result and trust that the universe, the Higher Power, etc., will bring to you the best possible scenario which can very well be different from what you envisioned. My experience has been that it is always the best scenario. Thus the wisdom of the words "Be careful what you ask for; you just might get it!" The spiritual concept of detachment works because it provides the flexibility needed to position you to be aware of the alternate solutions, the alternate opportunities. But the reason why it works is in direct conflict with the principles employed by the goal-setting strategies that are taught today. They profess varying degrees of fixation on the final outcome that you desire. Detachment, "letting go," and fixation on your goal are direct opposites, so that goal detachment, which is part of some success formulas I've read, becomes an impossibility. "Goal detachment" is an oxymoron, like jumbo shrimp!

I suggest that you continue to review this section on "the goal myth" after you have finished reading this book. It is imperative that you deprogram yourself with regard to what the popular success formulas have taught you about goals. The goal-setting strategists have their facts and figures, and most of the formulas often quote a now familiar study to validate the importance of goals and goal-setting strategies. In this study, the 1953 Yale graduating class was surveyed as to whether or not they had specific goals, and if they did, did they write them down? A certain percentage said that they had goals, but only three percent of the entire graduating class had goals that were written down somewhere. After twenty years, they contacted these graduates and found some amazing results. The percentage who had goals, had done decidedly better financially than those who didn't. But more shocking, the three percent who wrote down their goals were worth more financially than the other 97 percent *combined!*

There was only one problem with this amazing goal-setting validation study—it never happened! (*Fast Company* magazine, Dec/Jan 1997) Yale University has no record of any such study having been done, and when the researchers were asked to validate their source, they could not. They never verified the story as true. It never could be true, because as you and I have found out the hard way, goal setting doesn't work. Recognize ego-based goals for what they are—a source of frustration and failure. In order to attain success, you must first make room within you for success by minimizing the effect of your ego. Empty yourself of your ego. Your ego is the source of your fear. Fear kills!

POINTS TO PONDER

Goal setting should come with a warning label!

Your focus on an ego-centered goal causes you not to achieve it.

It's not so important where you want to go,
as why you want to get there!

Have an end that helps people, and in the end you will be helped!

What you want keeps you from what you want!

Your universal destiny is to achieve your ultimate potential.

16

To Be Aware Is to Be Alive

The greatest revolution of my life is the discovery
that individuals can change the outer aspects of their lives
by changing the inner attitudes of their minds.

— William James

Lasting success in anything is achieved through conquering the ego. This may be done consciously or unconsciously. However, if it's done unconsciously, then it can be lost as quickly as it was found because the person is unaware of the state of being needed to prolong the experience. The ego is the idea of who we think we are. It's that little voice that talks to us when we are in the process of making a decision, and afterward when we get the results of our decision. In fact, the ego is that little voice we hear most of the time.

When we're born, we come equipped with an ego which gets imprinted or programmed by the various people and experiences of our lives. Initially, it helps us to develop and survive. It shields us from the danger that is constantly bombarding us from birth. When a baby is born, in its own mind, there is nothing that it cannot do. It is almost fearless about doing things because to babies everything is possible. We call this innocent and naïve, and teach the baby about fear for its own protection. We teach it that there are things that it can do, and there are things it cannot do. We teach the baby our accomplishments and our failures so that the child takes over from where we left off. We teach the child who he is by programming his ego. In reality, of course, we have taught the child who we are. We have duplicated ourselves, for better and for worse, and this is the point from which we all begin.

The irony is that we spend the rest of our lives, if we ever wake up, trying to achieve the same innocence, wonder, and ability that we already had when we came into this world as a child. *We search a lifetime to find what was always there!*

The imprinting of the ego is what deftly conceals the reality of who we are and makes it so difficult for us to experience those things in life that have true value. The ego is the mask that hides the true self that was revealed in the core-value exercise—the self that was already perfect from its inception and was created "in the image and likeness" of the Higher Power—the self who, like the universe and nature, is already perfection in action.

I sometimes wonder if life isn't just a challenge or a test that the spirit has accepted. A game of sorts in which our true self comes into this world without memory, and is encased in a mind and body that it uses for sensory perception to experience this "physical" dimension. Further, it is disguised with an ego which gets imprinted from birth and fools us into believing that we are who we think we are. The object of the game is to find out "Who am I—really?" We have thoughts, emotions, and physical and mental experiences, but none of them are us. They are just the experiences we have. But through the ego, we are blinded to this fact. We each spend our entire lives trying to see through this ruse and find our true self. It's a hell of a game, and the solution begins with awareness.

Until we become aware of the role of the ego in our lives, we will forever be its victim. We periodically receive clues, insights, and intuitions into who we really are, but until we become completely conscious of our ego, we are predisposed to live in its make-believe world. *The path to truth, the path to success, begins with awareness.* Once you become aware of your ego, you become aware of the games and the tricks that it plays on you. For instance, the ego creates the polarity of good and bad. Whether you judge an occurrence to be good or bad is determined by whether or not you wanted the result of that occurrence. A desired result is a function of the ego. There is no good or bad, there is only "what is."

How do we know this to be true? Because what is good for one person can be bad for another. Thus the saying "One man's poison is another man's cup of tea." Let's take an extreme case as an example. The death of a loved one is the cause of much pain to many people. In fact, the pain can last a lifetime. But what if the loved ones were suffering with severe pain and they themselves had actually prayed for death? Would they not welcome it? Wouldn't it, for them, be good? In fact, in some religions and cultures, death is a cause for celebration.

Another extreme example might be physical abuse. You would be hard-pressed to find someone who would voice the goodness of physical abuse, but if you come in contact with a masochist, you might get a different story. They not only see physical abuse as good, but for them it is so good that they can have an orgasm as a result of the pain! So what is good or bad? Whatever our ego tells us is. Our ego, then, is the source of most of the pain and suffering that we experience in this world, and until we come to this awareness, we will be its victim. Our awareness, our realization of how much our ego rules us, starts us on the road to gaining power over our ego so that we no longer have to be its slave.

We've already examined one of the ways our ego enslaves us, through the polarity mirage of good and bad. Let's look at some other ways that the untamed ego victimizes us and impedes our attainment of success. It was mentioned earlier that the ego is the little voice that speaks to us. To someone truly unaware, he believes that it is himself speaking or thinking to himself. This is part of the deception that the ego engages in to keep us "asleep." Since people are basically the same, your inner voice probably says to you the same things that mine says to me. For instance, when I know that there is something that I must do, but I don't "feel" like doing it, my ego's voice begins to speak.

Once I was on a road trip visiting the various sales offices throughout my area. The plan was to fly from Philadelphia to Columbus, Ohio, meet one of my division managers, rent a car, and drive to Louisville, Kentucky. The plane was delayed (what a surprise), and I didn't arrive in Columbus until nine o'clock in the evening. Then on the trip to Louisville, we encountered traffic that turned a three-hour trip into four and a half hours. By the time we checked into the hotel, unpacked, and found the pillow, it was two o'clock in the morning. The meeting was scheduled for 7:30 a.m., which meant I would have to wake up at 6:30. The thought of it made me more tired than I already was, and my ego jumped at the opportunity. "You're an area manager. You can do anything you want. Who would dare question you? You work hard and you need your sleep. Anyone can understand that. You're not doing the training, so if you walk in late, it won't matter much." That all sounded good, but my job was to be the role model, and the responsibility of that mission still overshadowed all those good reasons to stay in bed. How would it look if the leader couldn't get there on time? What kind of a message would I be sending if I showed up in any other way than on time, well-dressed, enthusiastic, and with a great attitude?

When all those logical reasons didn't dissuade me from what I knew was the right thing to do, my ego let me have it with both barrels. It pulled out its secret weapon that in the past had always worked. The little voice said, "Sleep eight hours; *you deserve it!*" Despite all of my self-analysis, introspection, and awareness, those words appealed to me and fed into my desire. Then I remembered how many times those words got me into trouble. I remembered the words of my little voice (ego) that followed after I listened to its logical rationalization—"I deserved it." After I took its advice and did what I "deserved," the little voice would then scold, "You're a leader? You're a role model?" "You're the worst example of a leader and a role model I've ever seen! You should be ashamed of yourself, arriving late and taking advantage of your position. You're supposed to teach people how to be successful, not how to fail. *What a loser!*"

After hearing those words, I would get down on myself and become depressed. And what's worse, I would usually take it out on the people around me, scolding them for their lack of responsible behavior. No wonder they failed. What a bunch of losers! In psychological terms, this is called projection, in which you blame or accuse everyone around you for your own guilty acts. A hell of a game, isn't it?

What's important to note here is that the game gets played whether you're conscious of it or not. If you're standing in the middle of a football field and a game is being played, don't be too surprised if you get tackled. Your lack of awareness of the game doesn't protect you from experiencing the consequences of the game. The only safe course is to realize that the game is always in progress. That will enable you to take a defensive posture, especially when you find yourself in the midst of the play called the "you deserve it" play. It will also keep you from being surprisingly tackled so often. And when the opportunity presents itself—and you'll know because you'll be aware and "playing"—then you can go on the offensive and score. This is one of the essential components of success. This is awareness. This is the difference between being consciously awake or consciously asleep. This is living, not just existing!

POINTS TO PONDER

We search a lifetime to find what was always there!

The path to truth, the path to success, begins with awareness.

To be aware is to be alive!

17

Spiritual Images of Success

**All troubles in life come because we refuse to sit quietly
for a while each day in our rooms.**

— Blaise Pascal

As is above, so is below. As is the atom, so is the universe.
As is the microcosm, so is the macrocosm. As is within, so is without. There
are many ways to say it, but they all say the same thing—everything in our
world is undoubtedly and inexplicably intertwined and dependent on everything else in our world. That is why you must be successful on the inside first,
and then success follows on the outside for the entire world to see. It is possible for it to happen in reverse, but it's much more difficult to sustain. The
reason for the difficulty is that we begin to believe our own press clippings
about how wonderful we are. As a result, the untamed ego grows stronger and
wilder to the point where it runs rampant, and we become more and more
self-centered. Lack of success soon follows. That's why some people achieve
what appears to be success, but they just can't seem to hold on to it. Self-
destruction sets in. The unreconciled has its consequences.

Man is said to be basically composed of three major areas—physical,
mental, and spiritual. Unless success is experienced and prevalent in all three,
it cannot last. Of the three, the area that usually escapes people is the spiritual one. This is because it is the least tangible of the three. We have been
programmed so that what is "real" can be experienced through our senses. Our
physical body is obviously real to us because we can experience it through all
of our senses. The mental part we know because we constantly have thoughts.
But the spiritual is quite elusive. It usually operates unconsciously in the realm
beyond our five senses until we become conscious of it and bring it into our
awareness. Then we begin to consciously experience it.

Spirituality is not necessarily religious, although it can be. Whatever form it takes for you, I believe its essence lies in three elemental components. First, each one of us is composed of many levels of physical and nonphysical existence, none of which alone is us, all of which are ours to command. Second, we are all connected to everyone and everything else in this universe. What affects one has an effect on all. And third, there is some power or entity, that is greater than we are. We, each of us, are not the center of the universe, at least not for the reasons that we think we are. We are simply part of the whole and because of that, through us, the whole is experienced or made real. One of the things I've come to realize is the unbelievable number of paradoxes that are reality. Even though we are only part of the whole, a piece of the universe, within us lies the whole. *Within us is the total universe.* Lasting success relies on the comprehension and knowledge of this spiritual principle.

One of the ways to experience this is through meditation. Many people in the Western culture view meditation as hocus-pocus, belonging to the realm of "weirdos." As a result, very few people will openly admit that they meditate, but you would be surprised at how many people actually do, especially the successful ones. They don't really care if it's not socially acceptable. They know only the benefits they receive from it. It's peaceful. It's exhilarating. It feels safe. The amazing effect it has on stress reduction is reason enough to engage in its practice. More important, the insights and intuitions that you can experience in meditation can cause breakthroughs in your life and can save you years of hard work and anguish. But it takes practice.

I wish I could tell you that you sit down and close your eyes and immediately begin to meditate and experience, in great depth, the inner undiscovered world that is you. Unfortunately it's not that easy, but that's how you start. In the beginning, when you close your eyes, you will hear the same inner chatter in your head that you experience when your eyes are open —only worse. When your eyes are open, at least you have things you can see to distract you from the constant chatter. When your eyes are closed, all you seem to experience is constant chatter, the endless stream of thoughts that flows through your mind. It's been said that we think over 150,000 thoughts in a day, and 90 percent are the same thoughts that we thought yesterday. Most of the time these thoughts just happen. They pop in and pop out. It's almost like watching a quick-moving slide presentation. Every once in a while a thought will catch our attention, and we exercise control over our minds and think about it for a while. Without the acquired skill of concentration that we need to prolong this exercise, another idea soon pops into our minds and the mind is off racing again.

Deepak Chopra, a seer whom I respect, talks about the spirit lying in the space between our thoughts. Between each thought lies a moment of silence, and the objective of meditation is to prolong that silence longer than a moment. This enables us to tap in to the level of higher consciousness. In this spirit space lies infinite wisdom and is the field, as Deepak Chopra states, of infinite possibilities. But you don't get there in one day. Gradually, with greater and greater effectiveness, you gain control over your thoughts and begin to control the slide projector.

There are many methods you can use, and what's important is not so much which one you use as the fact that you use one. In meditation, there are many paths to the inner world, but every journey begins with taking the first step. I will relate to you the process that works for me. The first thing that is necessary is that I have the intention. Without making a determined effort to meditate, it's just a waste of time. That means finding the right place and the right time. I have five children, so finding a quiet time and place when they're awake is almost impossible. So I meditate before they get up. I have a comfortable easy chair in the living room that I settle into and close my eyes.

I sit upright with my head bent forward and my chin close to my chest and take three deep, cleansing breaths to mark the beginning of my entrance into my inner world. I concentrate on feeling the air flow into my nostrils and concentrate on my breathing. Then I move my awareness to the soles of my feet and feel them resting on the floor. I imagine roots coming out from my feet and tunneling into the earth below. I imagine them wrapping themselves around a pulsating large crystal that represents the vibratory life of the earth. Science tells us that everything has a vibration and by tapping into that vibration you can experience the object of your attention. I do this to "ground" myself into a spiritual experience of the physical world. This puts me in touch with the earth below. I imagine a flow of positive energy from the pulsating crystal entering my body through my feet and traveling up through my entire body to the top of my head. From here it overflows to coat me with a protective shield, a suit of armor if you will, of positive energy that repels any negative thoughts, energies, or emotions that may be in my area of influence throughout the day.

Then I imagine a pulsating globe of white light radiating down upon me from above with pulsating beams of positive energy washing over me. This white light engulfs my entire body and heals me. It displaces any negative energy I might possess at that moment, and washes it through my feet and into the earth below. Very often the feeling is so peaceful and fulfilling that a smile comes to my face.

Next I realize that the pulsating crystal below and the pulsating globe of white light above are vibrating or pulsating, at the same rate. I then synchronize my own heartbeat, my vibration, with theirs until I, the world above, and the earth below become one. All three are synchronized and pulsating at the same rate. I have consciously realized myself as part of the whole, as an integral part of all that is. With this understanding, I then re-focus on my breathing, feeling the air come in and the air go out, all the while with my eyes closed, trying to quiet my thoughts. I concentrate on my breathing to eliminate the uncontrollable chatter that takes place in my mind. In the beginning, this focus on breathing was almost impossible. As soon as I tried to put my awareness on my breathing, the thoughts kept fighting for their space, for their existence. But every time I lost my concentration, I would bring it back to focus on my inhaling and exhaling. I can't tell you how frustrating it was to try to quiet my mind the first time I attempted it, but it improves with repetition.

That's why the intention to meditate is so important. Your mind and your thoughts will test your resolve. The good news is that every time you do it, it gets easier and easier. It's a matter of practice. Very often teachers prescribe a "mantra" to help you through this difficulty. A mantra is a sound, a word, or series of sounds and words that have no meaning but give your inner voice something to do. It harnesses your inner voice to help create the experience that you are trying to achieve instead of the constant chatter that your inner voice is accustomed to producing, which is antiproductive to your experience of meditation.

It is also said that each of us has a personal mantra which spiritual teachers can help us to discover. My mantra is the word "rithy." I didn't use a spiritual teacher to find it. It just came to me one day while meditating. I don't use it often, but when I do, I synchronize the syllables to my breathing. When I breathe in, my inner voice says "ri" and when I breathe out, it says "thy." The word rithy has no meaning that I know of; it just helps me to focus when the chatter is uncontrollable.

As you're concentrating on breathing and quieting your mind to the point where your mind is as blank as a new chalkboard, you begin to imagine going within yourself to the core of your being. Once your meditative state gets deeper, you will naturally leave behind the awareness of your breathing and you will enter your inner space. You will know that you are there because you will barely be able to feel your body, and the deeper you go, the less physically present you will become. Once you are there, even though your eyes are closed, you can focus your vision to see the spectacle of your inner world. And what a spectacle it is! With enough practice, you will eventually see within you the same vision you see when you look at the midnight sky. The twinkling, dancing flickers of light that you see above are the same sights you can see when you look deep within. The vast expanse of undiscovered worlds lies not only outside of us, but also inside of us.

Just as there is a universe around us, there is a universe within us. At the center of this inner universe lies a bright, pulsating light that grows larger as your meditation gets deeper. At one point the light gets so large that it engulfs you, and what you experience is a peacefulness that is beyond the capability of words to express. The first time this happened to me, I experienced such peace and joy that tears came to my eyes. I felt it throughout my entire body, and it seemed for a split second that my body began to vibrate. I have to admit that it felt so good I became afraid of it and cut it short prematurely. But the memory of the feeling will always stay with me. It was more peaceful, more fulfilling, and more exciting than anything I have ever felt in my life.

I think that it's important to note that although this is my experience of meditation, I'm just a beginner. I certainly have not arrived, and I am just beginning to experience the wonders of my inner world. Many gurus, monks, and others who engage in this spiritual experience achieve much higher states of consciousness. This is just my experience. And as opposed to what some people think, you don't have to shave your head, wear an orange robe, or engage in the life of a hermit in order to meditate. With practice, it's a very easy thing to experience. You don't have to seclude yourself in a monastery or a temple. You can do it right at home.

I think it's important not to set goals for your meditation. I believe that you should have an objective to meditate, but you should also trust that your meditation will unfold as it should and when it should. After I have quieted my mind from the incessant, uncontrollable chatter, I don't try to have any specific thoughts or intentions, but I also no longer stop thoughts from entering my mind. In fact, I have found that the thoughts I have after entering a quiet state usually turn out to be illuminating insights. Many of them you've been reading in this book. When that happens, I make a point to remember it and write it down when I stop meditating. In writing this book, that has happened many times, and often the insights I have written after meditation I didn't immediately comprehend. But it is my mission to take those insights and define them in understandable language so that you can experience the fruit of their teachings.

I have come to realize that I am just a vehicle, a reporter of sorts, who is given the picture or the insight, and whose responsibility it is to put that picture into words so that you can "see" it too. I have also experienced actual dreams while meditating, but it doesn't happen often. I am fully awake but experience a dream state in which I see people, places, and things that I often don't understand, but I trust that I eventually will. One time during one of these dream states, I recall reading a concept I'd written for this book (which is how I know it will be published) and I remember how difficult it was to explain the concept even though I knew it. I wish I could remember which concept it was, but maybe the picture was just to assure me that the book would get published and achieve what it was meant to do—change people's lives. The future will tell.

When you're through meditating, I believe it's important to come out of it slowly, not all at once. I don't know why, but I sense there is a danger in going deep, through process, and then coming back quickly, without process. What I do is simply bring my awareness back to realize that I am in my living room, and then I feel my body as it rests on the chair. With my eyes still closed, I take three cleansing breaths to end the process the way I started it. Then I slowly open my eyes and often have to rub them to focus on my surroundings. One interesting thing is very apparent to me when I open my eyes. Everything seems brighter. I'm sure somebody will have a logical explanation for this, but I'd like to believe that this is how everything really looks until the boredom of constantly seeing dulls the luminosity of the world around us.

This may all seem very foreign to you, and you may perceive meditating as something supernatural. But I assure you it's very natural. In fact, the odds are pretty good that you have already engaged in meditation. Prayer is a form of meditation, and so is daydreaming. I'm sure you've done one of them, and probably both of them. Any state of being that quiets the chatter in your mind, even one continuous thought, is a form of meditation. So since it's something you've already done in one form or another, albeit unconsciously, trying a different form of something you've already done shouldn't be very foreign or uncomfortable. Going into the space between your thoughts on purpose, and stretching that space, is just another form of what you've already accomplished.

The realization that there is something beyond the everyday sensory world opens you up to the kingdom of infinite possibilities. *The greatest frontier of undiscovered worlds lies not in outer space, but in inner space.* The realization that you are the center of the universe and at the same time just a minute part of the universe is wherein lies the paradoxical wisdom. Its simplicity is what makes it so complicated and confusing and yet intriguing.

Since spirituality is so essential to lasting affluence and success, guess who its number-one enemy is? That's right, the ego! The ego thrives on deception and confusion and, like a wild animal, resists being tamed. It likes being in control, and any threat to that control will be met with resistance. That's why it's so hard, initially, in meditation to quiet the constant chatter in your mind.

Many people have compared the behavior of the ego to that of an excited monkey. If you've ever watched an excited monkey at the zoo, you'll see him chatter incessantly while he jumps from tree to tree, much the same as the ego chatters incessantly while it jumps from thought to thought. The monkey picks up a piece of fruit, bites it, throws it up in the air and then grabs a banana, eats half, and throws that in the air. In much the same way, the ego goes halfway into a thought and then jumps to another idea, which it doesn't complete before it's off to yet another one. And you wonder why your life is so confusing and unfulfilled? Take the monkey off your back and look at him for the undisciplined maniac that he is. That part of you, the ego level, is yours to command, and the time to do that is now!

POINTS TO PONDER

Within us is the total universe.

The greatest frontier of undiscovered worlds lies
not in outer space, but in inner space.

18

Emotional Affluence

Self-conquest is the greatest of all victories.

—Plato

**It takes only ten minutes to find in others the faults
we often fail to discover in ourselves in a lifetime.**

— Bits & Pieces, January, 1999

O ver the course of the years, I've seen so many gifted individuals lose the success they deserved because of their emotions. One of the
easiest mistakes to make is arriving at a business decision based primarily on
emotion. In the heat of experiencing the feeling, we invariably make the
wrong decision. It's important to note here that I am not referring to the
"feeling" or intuition that we may get about a business deal or condition. I'm
talking about making a decision while feeling angry, unappreciated, betrayed,
scared, or even happy, confident, or fortunate. I realize that feeling these
emotions may be commonplace at any given point in a day, but it's the intensity of the emotions that govern the feasibility of making important decisions. If your emotions are "in play," if you're experiencing any emotion to
a heightened degree, positive or negative, hold off any important decisions,
business or otherwise, until your emotions are no longer "in play."

If I've heard it once, I've heard it a thousand times—"It's a matter
of principle." To me, that's another way of saying, "It's a matter of satisfying
the spoiled child inside of me!" There aren't too many spoiled children who
have achieved the affluence of success. There is also an immense difference
between doing what you "think" is right or doing what you "feel" is right
when your emotions are in play. In sales, which is the business of emotions to
begin with, you occasionally run into a rude customer, or the company makes
a change that starts your emotions swirling. I've had salespeople come to me
complaining, "It's not fair!" and I say, "Maybe not." They say, "It's not right!"

and I say, "Maybe not." And they say, "It's a matter of principle!" and I say, "Maybe not!"

I often relate to them the story of the pedestrian who was waiting for the light to turn green so that he could cross a busy street. When the light finally changed, he hesitated because the cars didn't stop. Then a little voice told him "It isn't fair. It's a matter of principle. The light is green and you are right." So he began to cross the street anyway, and he turned out to be right—**dead right!** What good is right, fairness, or principle if it costs you the success and happiness that is rightfully yours? Invariably, because of the intensity of your emotions, you're not seeing things very clearly. Better to wait until the storm subsides before making any important decisions lest you be a victim of that little voice, who later on will call you an idiot for making those decisions. Unless your life is in danger, a couple of hours' or a couple of days' delay won't make that much difference. Remember, there are always three sides to a story—your version, their version, and the truth. Search for the truth, then make your decision.

Speaking of the truth, the reality is that every decision we make has emotional and rational components because we are emotional and rational beings. Certain decisions require that you should be more influenced by one than the other. So how do you know when to pay more attention to the emotional side? How do you know when to pay more attention to the rational side? In sales management, we have the same quandary with the fact that sales managers are required to be leaders and managers at the same time. How do you know when to be more of one and less of the other? The rule of thumb is that you lead *people* and you manage *things*. So when dealing with facts and figures and the like, you should lean toward your rational intelligence, and with people, your emotional intelligence, but you'll notice that in all cases you use intelligence. You won't be able to achieve long-lasting success by using just one of them. You will need both. Part of becoming successful will require intelligent business decisions (rational intelligence), and, since no one becomes successful by themselves, the other part of becoming successful will require intelligent decisions about people (emotional intelligence). I wanted to make this point to clear up any misconceptions about whether or not emotions should enter into the decision-making process. The truth is that they always will, because emotions are part of who we are. What I am reflecting on in this chapter is the great number of gifted individuals that I've seen self-destruct because they made decisions during very emotional times in their lives.

One of the glaring examples I've witnessed happened to someone for whom I had a great amount of respect. His name was Jeff. Jeff was about ten years younger than I, earned about $5,000 a week, and was my national sales manager when I was still new in my present company. He was the epitome of a sales manager and a salesman. He was wise beyond his years and had the people skills the likes of which are hard to find. One day, the company decided to beef up our management by transferring some sales managers from another one of its successful divisions. The reason they did so was because we weren't very profitable. The sales were there and climbing, but they just weren't turning into profits. Jeff felt threatened. He felt sure that he'd be replaced or demoted in a short period of time. Many of the other managers felt the same way. They began to feed off each other until, all together, they quit. I was shocked. These were my colleagues. These were my peers and my teachers. I was the only one who stayed. They asked me, "Why are you staying?" To which I replied, "Why are you leaving?" They gave me a lot of expectations as excuses, but none of them made any sense to me. Ironically, something Jeff had taught me made me stay. As I was racing up the company's ladder of success, he took me aside one day and said, "No matter what happens, no one can ever take away from you the ability that you've demonstrated here as a sales manager." I figured if they decided to fire or demote me, then it would obviously be a mistake on their part. Jeff's wisdom is what saved me from making a serious business error, but it couldn't save him. His emotions were in play. It was all very confusing.

Five months after he left, Jeff asked me to help him move because he was losing his house to foreclosure. While helping him, I asked him the question that had been burning inside of me for those past five months. "Jeff, what was the real reason that you decided to leave?" His answer shocked the hell out of me. He said, "I just couldn't support my family on $5,000 a week anymore." Talk about confusion. I was worse off now than before I asked the question that I had hoped would clarify things! One day I finally figured it out. Jeff's answer was so absurd that I knew it's what he decided to believe so that he could live with his decision, his bad decision.

One of the amazing things you learn in sales is that people make their buying decisions based on emotion, and then they look at the features and benefits of the product to rationalize that decision. Jeff had done the same thing, but the decision was so irrational that he grabbed on to anything he could believe to rationalize it. Imagine not being able to support your family on $5,000 a week? Well, so much for the lesson, but it taught me a lot about myself. Today I refuse to make a decision while in the heat of battle. Invariably, I make decisions that I regret.

Another reason not to make decisions while under the influence of heightened emotions is the fact that it's never really your decision. What do I mean by that? Whenever you're in a heightened state of emotion, negative or positive, and your mind is racing a mile a minute, the conclusions you come to are very often a result of the emotions you are feeling. When angry, you might want to retaliate. When fearful, you might want to run, and when jubilant, you might feel immortal or omnipotent. What's important to realize is that without awareness the conclusions you arrive at when feeling heightened emotions are not the result of your good sense; they're a result of how you feel. And since they're a result of how you feel, giving in to those conclusions validates the power that your emotions have over you. (I sense the insidious work of the ego lurking in the shadows!) If your emotions have power over you, then your emotions are making the decisions, not you. You have emotions, but you are not your emotions. Emotions are something you *experience*, but they are not who you are!

In addition, very often we feel emotions based on our response to a person, place, or thing. Just the fact that without them (the stimuli) we wouldn't feel the way we do should be reason enough not to make any decisions based on these emotions. When people, places, or things make you feel a certain way, they have power over you. Any decision, therefore, is really their decision! Allowing this to happen is to agree to a form of slavery. It's agreeing to be a victim. It's bowing down to the power that is being exerted over you. I don't think that's your intention. Now that you know, you no longer have to be someone's "patsy." Like the bully who keeps picking on the neighborhood weakling—he does so because he can. Believe it or not, there are people who know that by making you feel a certain way, they are exercising power over you. This is where knowledge goes astray because they manipulate you through your emotions to get you to perform in the way they want you to perform. Like a puppet on a string, they use your emotions against you. They use your emotions to use you!

Your emotions are a result of your beliefs, and your beliefs are not always correct. What you believe is based on what you know—your knowledge. Where did you get your knowledge? Generally, from other people. You have to consider that what they taught you may not be true. If you find that something you "know" turns out to be false, then what you believe changes, and so do your emotions attached to that belief. For instance, as I stated earlier, when I was young I thought I was unattractive to the point of being ugly. So if someone called me ugly, I would feel hurt and depressed because I believed it to be true. Today, now that I realize that I am attractive and not ugly, if someone called me ugly, it would have no effect on me other than to make me wonder what was wrong with their eyesight.

There is an important insight here. When people or things cause you to have a negative emotional response, it's because they have tapped into what you already believe to be true. So feelings of hurt, insult, insecurity, inferiority, etc., are the result of people expressing what you already fear and believe is true. Nobody makes you feel anything. You, through your beliefs, have complete control over what you feel. *Nobody can make you feel anything without your permission.* So if someone says something about you and it hurts you, it is not he or she doing the hurting, it's you. Taking responsibility for your emotions is the first great step to becoming awake. For when you feel a certain way about someone or something, you should immediately look in the mirror and ask yourself, "Why?" Again, the continual use of that three-letter question "Why?" will lead you to conscious awareness and enlightenment.

Building an awareness of self involves the skill of an investigative detective. The clues are your emotions. Since what you believe about yourself is usually so ingrained, it is often very difficult to separate the truth from the programmed "truths," which aren't really true! Your emotions, your reactions to people, places, things, and their interactions, give you an insight to your reality based on what you believe. Verifying that your reality and true reality are one and the same will give you enormous insight and advantage in your business dealings. For that reason, self-discovery is a required prerequisite for anyone who aspires to achieve authentic, long-lasting financial success.

So far, everything I've written in this chapter is based on the supposition that you have given yourself permission to feel in the first place. When investigating your emotions and your beliefs that give birth to their existence, an age-old barrier—the freedom to feel—immediately confronts you. Instead of looking at our emotions as merely evidence of our inner beliefs, we make judgments about them. We judge our feelings to be either good or bad and we've already discussed how that affects our individual reality. But hear this: *feelings are neither right nor wrong; they just are.* Once we take action based on those feelings, then the time for judgment becomes applicable. For instance, a vengeful feeling of wanting to do physical harm to someone has no meaning morally unless we actually take action, and then the *action* is either good or bad.

The emotional barrier to the freedom to feel is especially difficult for men. At an early age, many men are taught to be in control of their feelings. We are told not to "cry like a baby" or "cry like a girl." This programming leads to a suppression of much of our feelings or at least our awareness of them as indicators of our reality. Fortunately, many women have a sensitivity that is permissible. So before we can look to our feelings to uncover our beliefs, we first have to give ourselves permission to feel!

For some people the following may be an unnecessary exercise, but for others it will be absolutely crucial to their progress. To initially understand our feelings, we have to first examine the difference between the way we think we feel and the way we actually feel. There is a very simple exercise to help discern the difference. If your sentence starts with "I feel that..." then you are about to express a thought, not a feeling. If you concentrate on having the word "feel" followed by an adverb of description, then you can *feel safe* that you've expressed a feeling. For instance, "I feel ... good, bad, sad, hurt, happy, motivated, etc." Once you've identified your true feelings, then you are ready to progress to the next step.

The other hurdle we need to clear in order to understand the effect that our feelings have in our lives is to abolish self-judgment. Judge neither your feelings nor your observations of yourself. You must break this habitual way of thinking, of separating everything into opposites of good or bad, right or wrong. There is a third viewpoint from which to observe your feelings, thoughts, and observations of yourself. This third viewpoint is simple awareness, the awareness that that's simply the way it is. When your inner study is viewed with simple awareness, there is no need for justification or categorization. That which is viewed is neither right nor wrong. It just is! Again, we're only referring to the nonjudgment of your thoughts and feelings. When you take an action based on those thoughts and feelings, then judgment becomes applicable.

Our need to categorize by right and wrong creates fear in what we might find if we delve deeper into who we are. Simple awareness eliminates that fear and allows the process to be fruitful. The simplicity of simple awareness is the reason why it escapes most people. We make life too complex, and this complexity of life is one of the subconscious programs that we carry with us. It's one of the reasons why many of the great truths escape most people, even though they are, for the most part, simple truths. Avoid the complexity of judgment, and especially condemnation. See things simply as the way they are. If you can do this, you finally will be able to view reality.

As stated earlier in different words, *wisdom and progress lie in the questions, not the answers.* So what questions can you ask yourself that will give birth to the revelations that will change your life? The first thing you must realize is that there are an infinite number of questions that one can ask oneself. It's a process that takes a lifetime, but each series of questions propels you to a higher awareness of yourself, and you will see your life improve by leaps and bounds. The greater the number of questions, the greater the life progression. Perfection is the ultimate achievement, and although you never finally experience it on an emotional level, each question makes you more and more perfect. The process is to undo all the damage that has been done over the years, albeit unconsciously and accidentally, and return to the perfection of who you were at birth.

Remember that success is in the being, not in the doing. I could tell you all the things you have to be in order to be successful, as many success writers and motivational speakers have already done. But if I don't help you with the process of *becoming* all the things you have to be, then it will be a waste of time. Besides, you already know exactly what it takes to be successful. The problem is that you haven't been able to become those things. To give you an idea of what you're up against, ponder this question: What do you do today that reminds you of your parents in your relationship with your spouse, children, coworkers, etc.? To make it really interesting, what is it that you do that reminds you of your parents which, when you were younger, you thought was wrong, but you do it today, anyway? You may even remember swearing that you would never be like that when you became older! You may have noticed this before but not realized the implications. If while growing up, you were the object of these actions, and because of the resultant feelings swore you would never be like that but yet find that you are, what does that tell you about how powerful these influences are in your life?

Now you have some idea of what you're up against. These programs are powerful in their grip. More powerful than your will, unless your will is focused. That's why desire is so important. Without desire, you will lack the drive to continue the difficult work of self-examination and change. So, before you proceed any further, you have to decide. Do you really want to be successful? Do you really want to change your life? What are you willing to give up to realize your dreams? If your answers to these questions are wishy-washy, then go no further. You'll just waste your time. But if you're determined, if you're willing to change, then the following words will prove most fruitful.

As opposed to all current beliefs, *the worst disease that grips mankind is conscious sleep.* Not knowing why you feel the way you feel, not knowing why you do the things you do—in a nutshell, not knowing who you are—is the disease of conscious sleep. Waking up to the answers to these questions is the decision to trade the life of an automaton or robot, for the life of awareness and enlightenment, a decision to trade a life of scarcity for a life of abundance. Whatever you wish to know about your fellow man, whatever you wish to know about the world, whatever you wish to know about the universe, and whatever you wish to know about success you will find when you finally have this knowledge of yourself. This is what it means to be aware. This is what it means to be awake. This is what it means to be alive!

POINTS TO PONDER

Nobody can make you feel anything without your permission.

Feelings are neither right nor wrong; they just are.

Wisdom and progress are in the questions, not the answers.

The worst disease that grips mankind is conscious sleep.

19

Thoughts Are Alive

**You are today where your thoughts brought you;
you will be tomorrow where your thoughts take you.**
— James Allen

One of the essential realizations necessary for success is that thoughts are things. How can I make such a statement? When I was meditating this morning, this realization made itself known, but in reality, I always "knew" it. We know that many unseen "things" are real, although we have no concrete evidence to support their existence. That's the problem with relying strictly on your senses for your reality. You miss most of what really is.

I think it would be beneficial to perhaps supply an example or two. For instance, we know emotions exist, but you can never find them if you dissect a body. Emotions, to everyone, are as real as the nose on your face, as the hand at the end of your arm, and yet you would be hard pressed to be able to physically produce them for someone else to examine. But people can see the resultant actions that our emotions produce. The ranting and raving of an angry person is about as real as it gets, and because of this physical evidence, we know that the emotion of anger exists. In fact, that's how our feelings become things. We make them come alive through expression. We can feel them inside and are able to physically demonstrate them to those around us, but they physically escape our five senses. Immediately you might think that we can feel an emotion and that fits in with the sense of touch. Feeling an emotion is one thing; touching it is something else.

Other examples of reality that we do not experience with our five senses are the various waves of energy that fill the space in a room—what we call empty space. The space not taken up by "physical" things is full of waves of energy that are completely undetected by our senses. Ultraviolet rays, X-rays, radio waves, sound waves, infrared rays, etc., flood what we call empty space. They are real but, lacking the necessary receptors, we need sophisticated equipment to detect them. Or maybe it's that we have the receptors but have not developed them. Whatever the case, all of these energy waves are real, even though they are "not real."

In the same way, our thoughts are real. Biologists have discovered that when we have a thought, the body transforms it into a molecule called a neuropeptide. I propose that the same is true of an emotion. If it hasn't already been done, one day they will discover that our emotions become molecules. One of the indirect ways we know this to be true is that our thoughts, which science already knows become molecules, produce emotions. Another indirect way we know this to be true is the phenomenon of ESP, or extrasensory perception.

Did you ever know what someone was thinking? Have you ever preceded a statement by saying, "I know what you're thinking..." Have you ever said something and had someone respond by saying, "That's exactly what I was thinking?" Did you ever "know," while listening to someone say something, that he was lying through his teeth? How did you know? My contention is that the mind or body must produce something for us to grab hold of, so that we do "know." Whether it produces a thought molecule or a thought wave is not the point. The point is that it must produce some "thing" for us to receive, which makes all the above phenomena possible.

I bring out this point to lay the groundwork for my belief in the importance of positive thinking in attaining success. Positive thinking has been part of all the success plans that I have read. In fact, there's a best-selling book entitled *The Power of Positive Thinking* by Norman Vincent Peale. I think everyone, deep down, knows the power of positive thinking. But when you're brought up in a negative-thinking world, it's hard to think positive. Negative thinking is, after all, part of your programming (I'm 93 percent sure!). And remember these words: *Negativity kills!* Not only does it kill your spirit, your dreams of success, and your relationships, but also science is beginning to find out that negativity destroys your body. My belief is that negative thinking fills your body with destructive molecules that wreak havoc on your spiritual, mental, and physical systems. Add to that the additional negative neuropeptides that the resultant emotions become and you have the perfect formula for failure in anything. It is because of this "flood" of negative molecules that negative people are so miserable. They actually are miserable in the feeling sense because of the physical presence of these negative molecules. And how can you be successful if you feel miserable? This is why positive thinking is so important. Many success gurus have voiced its importance, but they haven't really told you why. This is why—negativity kills.

Worrying is negative thinking. I don't remember ever experiencing someone worrying that things would turn out well. They always worry about the worst. So many people are so consumed with worrying about tomorrow that today completely escapes them. It's kind of ironic that the only opportunity they have to do something about that which worries them, i.e., what they can do today, slips through their fingers like a lost treasure. Besides the accompanying waste of energy that could be put to better use, worry has been linked to many forms of arthritis as well as other diseases. It is a parasite, a cancer that eats away at your entire being, just like all other forms of negative thinking. Maybe that's where they get the expression "worry wart." It's a parasitic virus.

This is all very easy for me to say and suppose, but I would be remiss if I didn't tell you that I know positive thinking is hard to do. In fact, without a focused conscious awareness, it's impossible to do. Here's why: What you perceive to be true becomes your belief. What you believe gives rise to what you think. What you think gives birth to what you feel. The way you feel gives rise to certain actions and subsequent thoughts. These thoughts, and especially the actions, become your reality. Your reality is another way of saying "the way you see things," which becomes your perception, which in turn, gives birth to your beliefs, etc. It's a vicious, self-reproductive, self-fulfilling circle and, without conscious intervention on your part, it is impossible to overcome. In fact, you don't even know it's happening. It becomes a way of life. That's why negative thinking is so fatal. The way it starts is the way it finishes—with a negative result. This is how you create your own reality, and since the result is not desirable, this is how you are wasting your creative god-like quality. "As ye sow, so shall ye reap." Negative seeds produce a negative harvest!

In addition, the world will mirror back to us whatever form of thinking, positive or negative, that we internally experience. That's why miserable people live miserable lives, why angry people live angry lives, and why happy people live happy lives. The "living" world around us *fulfills* that which we think and believe to be true.

What's amazing is that science is beginning to discover that everything around us is "alive." We already know that plants and animals have life, but quantum physics is uncovering some principles that are suggesting that even inanimate objects have life. We will discuss this in greater detail later, but they are beginning to discover intelligence in subatomic particles that allow them to "think." Some quantum physicists have proposed that an atom has its own life, and the atom is a small integral part of whatever form it is presently in; just as we are an integral part of, and have different functions in, our family, our community, and our world. This makes sense because the atom of calcium that functions one way in a piece of limestone is the same atom of calcium that functions another way when our body uses it to build our bones and teeth. In both applications, the atom "knows" what to do. The ramifications of what this means to people searching for success is mind-boggling. It says that what you think "in here," in your atomic structure, what you believe throughout your whole being, is what you will experience "out there."

I read a story once in which a traveler asked a farmer coming from the direction of the town he was traveling to, "What kind of people live in the next town?" The farmer asked what kind of people lived in the traveler's last town. The traveler said that they were obnoxious, inhospitable, selfish people, and that's why he left. The farmer said that the people in the next town were exactly the same. A few miles later, the farmer met another traveler who asked him the same question. He responded in the same way by asking what the traveler's experience was of the people in the last town. The traveler said that they were very nice, polite and very accommodating. The farmer replied that the people in the next town were the same way. The moral, of course, is evident. *People will reflect back to you your own reality.*

Another interesting example of this principle came to me as a result of doing something I fear—horseback riding. For forty-seven years, every riding experience I had resulted in disaster. I didn't like it. I was afraid of it. One day, one of the handlers told me that the horse can sense fear, and if he does, the horse will take control. If the horse has control, your riding experience will not be pleasurable. On hearing this, I decided to subdue my fear and change my thinking. I thought of it as a pleasurable experience, and tried to feel happy and relaxed. In the first few moments, it was just an "act as if," but the more I acted as if I wasn't afraid, the more I relaxed. I had a great ride. What an eye-opening, mind-expanding experience!

In my sales management career, the young and wise Jeff, of whom I spoke earlier, imparted some similar words of wisdom to me. When I was brand-new in upper management, I would listen to the complaints of the field agents and managers and bring them to my superior, Jeff. After a few of these negative reportings over the span of a few weeks, Jeff very patiently and in a low voice told me, "Always plan for success. No matter what your fears are, no matter how things are, always do what you would do 'as if' you were successful. *Plan for success.*"

As a result of this, I eventually realized that people in general (the 93 percent) will tell you what can't be done or what's wrong with a certain plan or situation. I realized as a responsible leader, my job was to never agree with them, even if I did. My responsibility to them was to show them why it could be done, what the positives were, and to not validate their fears and apprehensions by agreeing with them. As a result, I've helped people do some amazing things. It's kind of hard to hide your true beliefs sometimes, but if your focus is on helping the other person, it gets a lot easier. This, by the way, is the secret of sales management.

These insights taught me that reality is subjective, that *the world will mirror back life the way you "see" it.* If your resulting thoughts of what you "see" are positive, then the world will mirror back to you a positive life. Conversely, negative thinking will deliver to you a negative experience of life. One of my favorite lines from a comedian came from Flip Wilson when he played the role of "Geraldine." Little did he know how prophetic his favorite one-liner would be. With a little play on words, it takes on a whole new meaning. He said, "What you *see* is what you get." When you finally "know" that, everything for you will change.

POINTS TO PONDER

Negativity kills!

People will reflect back to you your own reality.

Plan for success.

The world will mirror back life the way you "see" it.

20

Thinking Differently: Mind Expansion

The impossible: what nobody can do until somebody does.

— Bits & Pieces
30th Anniversary Edition

Habitual thinking leads you to experience life in a rut. A "rut" has been described as an uncovered coffin with the ends kicked out. That says, for all intents and purposes, that habitual thinking leaves you as one of the living dead.

One of the greatest gifts one can give to another is the expansion of the mind because a mind expanded by a new idea can never return to its original shape. With your cooperation, we will accomplish that in this chapter. Expansion of the mind is necessary for success because successful people think differently. They "see" things differently. *Nothing will change for you until you change the way you think.* Enough said, now let's get on with the actual expansion.

In the examples in the succeeding paragraphs, I don't want you to feel that you need to solve anything or strain yourself to any great depth to understand all of the ramifications. This is simply an exercise to mentally open you up to all the alternate possibilities of your reality. *If you see things only one way, as you were programmed to, you have no choices. Life, your life, your reality, has infinite choices.* Know the truth and "The truth shall set you free." Ponder this as your first example of mind expansion: You are totally free the very instant you read this line!

The next example of mind expansion is simpler. Look at a rock, any rock. Is the rock moving? Just about anyone would think that was a stupid question and reply, "Of course it's not moving." But one of the facts we know to be true is that the Earth, and everything on it, is traveling through space at lightning speed. This means the rock is traveling through space at lightning speed. Imagine what would happen if the Earth came to an abrupt stop. Would the inertia send us all hurtling through space?

Biology shows that every cell in your body is completely replaced in two years. Every cell in your body *dies* and is replaced every two years. So why did *you* not die? If you are not your body, then who are you? If all the cells that contain your memory have died in the past two years, how do you still remember? If the hand I have today is a brand-new hand from the one I had two years ago, why do I still have this wart on it? *You have a body, but you are not your body. You have thoughts, but you are not your thoughts. You have emotions, but you are not your emotions. You experience your reality, but you are not your reality.* In the final analysis then, who are you?

Science tells us that the body and life have energy. Spirituality tells us that we have within us a life force, an energy called the spirit. Within us is electrical energy, magnetic energy, light energy, atomic energy, etc., and this energy is closer to the truth of who we are than our body, thoughts, and emotions, which are our experiences. In physics, the first law of thermodynamics states that energy *never* dies. It gets transformed into something else, but it never dies. If this energy is closer to the truth of who we are, then do we ever die? Or, if when we "die," does our energy, being transformed into something else which would still be us, support the theory of reincarnation? Einstein said that mass (matter) and energy are equivalent to each other. When one is destroyed, the other is created. That would lead us to deduce that our entire physical body is energy, presently in the form of matter. Do we constantly, perpetually, live out the dance of transformation between energy and matter as defined by Einstein in his theory of relativity ($E=mc^2$)? If thoughts are energy, and energy can be transformed into matter, can we transform our thoughts into material things? If we are energy, and a star is energy, does the light energy of that star entering our eyes connect us in some way? Interesting questions, aren't they?

The next few examples come from our neighbors in the East. In Zen and Buddhism, they have a series of riddles called koans, which they use to help train the novice. It is proposed that once you solve one of these riddles, given to you by your teacher, then you will reach a higher state of consciousness toward "enlightenment." These koans not only make you think, they make you think differently. The first example you may have already heard, but it's still worth mentioning. "If a tree falls in a forest, and there is no one there to hear it, does it make a sound?" Still another one is "What is the sound of one hand clapping?"

Both of these koans have to do with sound, which is vibration. When a vibration registers in our eardrum, it is converted into sound. We humans have a limited range of vibrations that we can hear. We know that animals can hear lower and higher vibrations than we can. Since everything that exists has a vibration, think about all the sounds that we are not aware of. Does this raise the possibility of other ways of communicating that we presently don't know about? Can we "talk" to a rock? Can we "speak" to the stars?

According to science, a snail can only see one image every four seconds. So three-fourths of what we humans see and experience as reality is completely unavailable to a snail. What we see and experience gives us a bearing for the passage of time. We see the snail as slow, but the truth is that we experience reality four times faster than it does. In its reality, it is moving at a normal pace and we are dashing around like a video in fast-forward. Conversely, a fly can see the black spaces between the picture frames in a movie. They experience reality and time at a much faster pace than we do. This is why it's so hard to catch a fly with your hands. To the fly, we are the snails. Imagine a snail trying to grab hold of a human. The truth is that the snail, the fly, and we all have a different basis for time and reality. In regard to success, what does this say about the properties of time that we can use to our advantage? What does this tell us about reality?

Did you know that the Earth is the center of the cosmos? No, I'm not crazy. I learned the same things you learned in school—that long ago this was believed to be true, but science proved it to be false. But today, many scientists believe that there is no end to the galaxies and universes that make up the cosmos. They believe, as I do, that the cosmos is infinite. What is interesting about infinity, mathematically, is that any point in it can be called the center. Pick any point you wish, and it can be legitimately called the center. This is what science tells us now. I guess the old Greeks weren't so wrong after all! The Earth really is the center of the cosmos. But my guess is that the reason they saw the Earth as the center of the cosmos was due to that egotistical tendency that man has to celebrate his importance.

If it was due to egotistical reasons, where else may that be causing us a problem? The answer to that question lies in another conclusion man has made based, I believe, on the same tendency. Every book I have ever read always speaks of man as the highest developed thing on Earth. As a result, we also maintain that this makes us superior to everything else on the planet. This need to see ourselves as important is expressed by the great effort we make to stand apart from the crowd, to be as visible as possible.

Eastern philosophy contends that one of the characteristics of highly developed individuals is that when they experience true enlightenment, they become so in tune with the cosmos that they blend in perfectly. The objective of enlightenment, that highly developed state, is to disappear, not to stand out. If the true spiritual objective is to become one with "all that is," there must come the realization that "all that is" does not express itself separately. It is one. When you look at "all there is," you see all that is. Through focus, you can separate the seeming parts of the whole, like an individual rock or one individual tree. But release your focus and it again all becomes one. The rocks, the trees, the blades of grass, and the stars in the sky are unnoticeable, or invisible, in their combining with the cosmos. Perhaps they have already achieved that full blending with "all that is." Perhaps the spiritual path is about becoming more like a blade of grass or a drop of water in the ocean. What if those *are* the higher forms of development because they've already achieved this invisibility? Makes you wonder, doesn't it?

In conclusion, I hope this chapter served its purpose. The whole objective was not to confuse you or convince you of anything. The whole purpose was to make you think, to make you "see" things differently. To realize that the truth is not always apparent, and the facts that are apparent aren't always true. If you don't think differently than the 93 percent who ultimately achieve mediocrity, then you will be destined to join their ranks. If you don't consciously plant the seeds of success by thinking differently, you will reap the weeds of failure!

POINTS TO PONDER

Nothing will change for you until you change the way you think.

If you see things only one way, as you were programmed to, you have no choices. Life, your life, your reality, has infinite choices.

You have a body, but you are not your body.
You have thoughts, but you are not your thoughts.
You have emotions, but you are not your emotions.
You experience reality, but you are not your reality.

21

Who's to Blame?

Your last mistake is your best teacher.
—Bits & Pieces
January, 1999
One who makes no mistakes never makes anything.
—Unknown

So far I've been slamming the ego because of all the hurt and disappointment I've seen it produce in my life and in the lives of others. However, the truth is that the ego isn't really to blame. It's not as if the ego made a conscious decision to destroy our lives and shatter our dreams. It merely performs its function for the survival of the species. Through the varied functions of the ego, its ultimate purpose is the preserving and prolonging of life. By not experiencing our free will, our ability to choose, we relegate the ego to instinctively answer every challenge that it perceives endangers the accomplishment of its main purpose—survival. When this happens, it is functioning the same way as an animal's survival instinct functions. To better understand the ramifications this has on our road to success, it is worthwhile to gain insight into the way that the ego functions when in the survival mode. Since survival is the main objective, the ego determines if a certain event or stimulus promotes or impedes life. Psychology tells us that the ego, in this mode, views everything from only two possible outcomes—life or death.

To feel comfortable, the ego constantly tries to fill our lives with life-giving experiences. If it judges an experience to endanger our survival to *any* degree, which it interprets as death, it springs into action with all the defense mechanisms it has at its disposal. The fight-or-flight response is activated. I'm sure that, psychologically, this is a very simplistic description of the ego in the survival mode, but for our purposes it's all we need. Again, the ego views all input from a life-or-death standpoint, not almost life or death, but definitive life and definitive death. Thus a survival-threatening loss of any type isn't evaluated as to how much of a loss it represents; it is evaluated as death. Risk is death!

In reality, we come into this world with nothing materially, and depart with nothing. The possessions we accumulate during our lifetime, physically, psychologically, spiritually, emotionally, and mentally, are all confirmations of living. They confirm to the ego that all is well. So when we are gaining and accumulating, the ego equates that with more life. If we were to lose ground in any of these areas, which the ego sees such loss as a threat, then the ego equates that with death. It's a very complex and intricate system that doesn't lend itself easily to examination, but in our analysis of its ramifications, I trust this description will make more sense. It will explain why the ego's reaction is usually so bold and demonstrative. How would *you* react if faced with a life or death decision?

To begin our analysis, consider that the ego's survival decisions are usually to fulfill the mundane necessities we need to live. For instance, when we are in need of food, the ego tells us to eat. We feel hungry. When we are in need of fluids, the ego tells us to drink. We feel thirsty. It sees hunger and thirst as threats to our existence, which of course they are when taken to the extreme. The ego is very useful and very valuable in meeting these physical needs of our bodies. However, the trouble arises when the ego perceives threats that are emotional, psychological, or mental in nature. To the ego, comfort means life, and anything that threatens our comfort is death, even on these levels. However, on the emotional, psychological, and mental levels, we are supposed to use our freedom of choice to evaluate and make intelligent decisions. By not exercising our free will, we leave the decision up to the ego, which will operate by instinct in its judgment of whether the stimulus is life-giving or life-threatening. Under these conditions, we are in the basic survival mode and we tend to respond primitively, more like an animal without free will than a human being. This condition is easier to see in others than in ourselves.

Have you ever said to someone, "What are you getting so excited about? It was only …." We see it so clearly when others fly off the handle in a fit of rage, when we judge that they've overreacted. Someone cuts you off in the car and you immediately reply with an irreverent word or gesture. Sure, you feel sorry afterward when you think about it, because you judge that this reaction isn't the real you. If you thought before you *reacted*, you would never have done it.

You're right, it wasn't the real you; it was the basic, primitive part of you called the ego. By cutting you off, that other driver threatened your well-being (life), and you probably really felt like ramming him with your car, but instead you replied irreverently. The responsibility for this action does not disappear because it was your ego's response instead of the real you. But that's what happens when we react to situations instead of responding to them. You're the one who gave the ego the freedom to act by not utilizing your free will. You're still responsible for the action, even though it was the result of something you didn't do (exercise your free will).

As if that example isn't bad enough, wait until you see how the ego's actions keep you from achieving success. When it's in the automatic survival instinct mode, the ego will always search for comfort and safety. Remember comfort equals safety equals life. If we look to the animal world, we see that their survival instinct operates in the same way. When a deer is threatened by an oncoming car, its instinct tells it to go back the way it came because up until that point, it experienced comfort and safety. Now, it doesn't matter that the deer could easily make it to the other side of the road; it will turn around and recross the highway, even if it means going back into traffic. That's why there are so many auto accidents involving deer. They can't help it. Their reaction is automatic. Occasionally you'll see a deer actually continue to cross the road, but that's because it didn't feel threatened and its survival instinct was not activated. I've seen other animals react in the same way.

When we neglect to use our freedom of choice and intelligently respond to the changes that life presents to us, we also act in the same way. So when an opportunity arises and because opportunities always involve risk, we automatically feel discomfort. Our tendency is to search for safety, because risk to the ego might result in death (financially). Our tendency is to continue our life the way it was because, so far, it was safe, even though lack of success was part of that way of life. If we even consider taking on the risk, the anxiety begins to build and, unimpeded, it results in fear: fear of the unknown and fear of possible loss, which the ego defines as death. Without focused thinking, the fear will force us to opt for our present way of life because it is comfortable (known). When this happens, our lack of success is prolonged and perpetuated. We recreate our past lack of success in the present and in the future, for "safety's" sake. *That's why success is not comfortable for those who haven't yet achieved it.* As dissatisfied as people are with their present financial situation and as unrewarding as it might be to their hopes and dreams of financial independence, people will unconsciously choose the known, safe path. A man will always accomplish his primary objective, even if it is unknown to him.

To demonstrate this, let us assume that your boss just told you that your services are no longer needed because the company is downsizing and you have the least seniority. If you didn't know it was coming, you might initially be shocked, but oh, how quickly the fear sets in! But why the fear? The reality is that you just lost your job and the newspaper is full of employment opportunities every week. Unemployment is at an all-time low! But the survival instinct of your ego heard something else. If you have no job, then you have no steady stream of income coming in every week. Judging from a life or death standpoint, this means death. The ego heard your boss say, "You're gonna die!"

As ludicrous as it sounds, that is exactly what happens when we are not conscious of what is occurring. The only way to short-circuit this process is through conscious awareness. We must realize that the ego is always in the survival mode. That's its job. Lack of awareness of this fact will result in us reacting automatically to any given stimuli. The other choice is to respond to the stimulus. React or respond, what's the difference? The difference is that when you respond, you utilize your free will, the gift of choice that separates us from the rest of the animal kingdom. By responding, we look at the situation we are presented with, analyze our alternatives, and choose the best course of action. To do otherwise, to react, makes us no better than an animal.

In reality the loss of your job might be the greatest financial opportunity of your life. It could be the perfect time for you to open that business you've always dreamt about. It might result in being employed by another company where your abilities will be respected and enable you to climb the corporate ladder more rapidly. It might be the perfect chance to write that book or compose that song that is waiting within you to be discovered. If you react, you'll never see these possibilities. *If you respond, you can change your life.*

If you have not achieved financial success, you need to change your life. The only way to accomplish long-lasting success is by responding instead of reacting. Initially, it's not easy. You've spent a lifetime reacting. The ego will not roll over easily so that you can exercise your power of choice. But through repetition, you can gradually gain control of your life. You can take your life back from the ego. The trick to this involves staying in the present moment.

Worrying about the future gives birth to all the possible deadly outcomes you can experience, which will put your emotions into play. Successful people do not make decisions with their emotions. They know that when their emotions are in play, when they're feeling them to a heightened degree, it is the worst time to make a decision about anything.

As if all this damage wasn't enough, the ego is responsible for some other real-life problems and diversions that interfere with our quest for success. In the beginning of the chapter, we noted that the ego uses eating as a life-giving response to the life-threatening need of nourishment. However, that's not the only time that the ego uses eating as a tool. When we are threatened by the loss of something, which the ego equates with death, then eating is one of the possible antidotes because it is life-giving. That's why many people will start eating when under stress. It's so automatic that they don't even realize they're doing it.

This is where awareness becomes important. Without the awareness of what's behind your actions and their consequences, the ego is allowed to run wild and ruin your life. Repetition of this "eating to feel alive" syndrome causes people to become overweight. The degree of being overweight is usually in direct proportion to the ego's experience of life-threatening loss. The result is that the people dislike the way they look and wind up with a poor self-image. *In order to achieve long-lasting success, you need a healthy, positive self-image.*

The same thing is true of shopping. Buying is a life-enhancing experience to the ego because it involves the accumulation of something material. It's another antidote that the ego uses for life-threatening experiences. For instance, you have a fight with your spouse so you go shopping, or you're bored and you go shopping. Shopping, like eating, is not a problem for everyone. Some people hate shopping. It's not the shopping itself that's the problem, except when it is the response that your ego chooses to address the negativity that enters your life. Without awareness, it causes us to buy things that we never use or don't need. Taken really far, it becomes a sickness, just like anything else taken to extremes. Again, the sin is not in the shopping; the sin is in not knowing why you're shopping. The money and time spent could be put to better use materializing your dreams.

Still another favorite tool of the ego, especially for men, is sports. Watching them, playing them, following them, it's all the same when the ego uses them to make us feel more alive. Again, there's nothing wrong with sports unless we subconsciously use them to feel alive. The same is true for soap operas, television, action films, and the list goes on and on. If you add up all the time and money you spend satisfying the ego's need for life-enhancing experiences, you will be surprised to find out how much energy and resources you are wasting to satisfy that primitive part of yourself that has a distorted view of life. Put these resources to work to become successful, and you'll experience real life. The realization of success is one of the most happy, joyful, and invigorating endeavors a person could ever experience.

Your conditioning and your programmed ego are to blame for the lack of success in your life. Unfortunately, they are you. The good news is that you didn't know this. Through simple awareness, you can take charge of your life, maybe for the first time, and achieve the potential that is every man and woman's natural right by birth. After all, *success is something that you consciously experience*. If you want to be successful, you must first take control of your life!

POINTS TO PONDER

Success is not comfortable for those who have not yet achieved it.

If you respond, you can change your life.

If you have not achieved financial success, you need to change your life.

In order to achieve long-lasting success, you need a healthy, positive self-image.

Success is something that you consciously experience.

22

The Taming of the Shrew (Ego)

Character is like chiseling a statue; one has to knock
off huge hunks of selfishness, which requires self-discipline.
Only then does character begin to emerge.

— Fulton J. Sheen, clergyman (1895-1979)

Your ego has had years of being in control and will not give
up this control so easily. What follows is a set of exercises to help you tame
the savage beast so that you no longer have to be its slave.

For those of you who aren't sure that the ego exists by itself, that it
has its own mind and is not always in your control, I offer this example.
Have you ever had a song in your head that just kept playing and playing and
you couldn't seem to get rid of it? Very often when I wake up in the morning, I have a melody or song that keeps playing in my head. After a while,
it even becomes annoying. Sometimes it happens during the day, but most
often in the morning. Where did the song come from? If it came from me, if
I decided to play the song in my head, why can't I get rid of it? If it wasn't me
who decided to play and continually replay the song, then who was it? The
ego, that's who! Don't ask me why it chose a particular song, I couldn't tell
you why.

Personally, I love music. I can escape into music, but that also means
I can be distracted by music. I use the mornings for concentration, to prepare
myself for the day, and a song—it's a different one every morning playing in
my head—distracts me. One of the things I try to accomplish every morning
is to suppress my ego, through meditation, so that I can write.

That leads us to the first exercise—meditation. We've already discussed the technique, the how-to of meditating, but there are a few things
more to be said. Meditating quiets the ego. It sounds rather simple, but it
is more difficult than it sounds because the ego doesn't want to be quiet. It

enjoys the constant chattering and the resulting confusion. In meditation, you simply think of nothing, which is hard to do, but it gets easier with practice. The trick is to not try too hard. Just give way, release control, and let the experience take you where it will. Not being in control is scary for most people, the humor of which is what they think is their control is really the control of the ego. The past, the future, controlling what happens next, all are the realms of the ego. The higher self, the true self, has no need for these perspectives. There is only one true reality, and that is now. Meditating increases the awareness of now.

The second exercise is the suppression of the will. The first question you have to ask yourself is, "Is what I want really what 'I' want, or is it what my ego wants?" If it has to do with who you think you should be, who you want to be, or who you'd like to be, then it's the ego's will. If you're like most, you'll discover that much of what you want falls into the ego's category. The truth is that you already are everything you want to be. You're perfection in action. So what could you possibly want? *The only thing you really need is the awareness of what already is!* Try not to control your life for a day. Go where the path takes you. Encounter experiences, people, places, and things, and observe the lessons that each has to offer. Be aware of the lessons and be aware of the opportunities. There are many of each in a day, most of which escape the average person because *people are so busy trying to create reality that reality passes them by*. Get in the flow, and like the seed blown by the wind, it will take you to where you are supposed to be. It will take you where you need to be.

The next exercise is to do what you fear. There is magic in this action. Believe me when I tell you that I am a novice in many ways. The more I work on facing my fears, the more I realize that I continually need to learn. But the practice of encountering your fears creates great leaps in knowledge about yourself and everything else. *The conquering of fear is the beginning of wisdom.*

What is it that you fear? Heights, water, the dark, animals, the unknown? Whatever it is, plunge yourself into the middle of it. Sure, it's dangerous. That's why we're afraid. But overcoming that fear is about as rewarding as life gets. You'll feel a surge of energy and confidence. Your mind, your life and its horizons, will expand. Encountering fear is living! You'll know the world of Columbus, Einstein, Freud, Plato, the astronauts, and all the other adventurous souls who dared to encounter the unknown, the fear. Fear is the ego's way of keeping you in check. If you had no fear, the ego would have no power. I don't know if it's possible to be completely fearless; perhaps that is unreal, but I do know the freedom that the conquering of fear gives you. It's the freedom to be who you are—the freedom of no limitations. You see, fear puts you in a little box. It defines the parameters of your existence. As you erase each fear, you expand your world.

It's like the story of Plato's "Allegory of the Cave." Three men are chained from birth inside a cave facing a wall, with the cave entrance behind them. They are chained in such a way that they can only see straight ahead. When the sun rises, they see light on the wall. At night the wall is dark. Occasionally they see shadows pass across the wall, but they don't know why. One day one of them breaks loose of his chains and walks outside the cave. What he sees is amazing, and he hurriedly runs back to his friends and tries to persuade them to come with him. He explains how outside the cave, there is a whole world of wondrous things—plants and animals and sky and sea. But they refuse to believe. They reply that the shadowed cave wall is reality. They refuse to follow him. He enters the real and wondrous world alone while the others let their fear control their lives. Is this your story? Are you interested in the wonders of other worlds, or are you a cave dweller whose fear forces you to believe that life is the shadows on the wall? Break your chains and see the world as it really is. Live a life in the world of wonder instead of the safety of a life you control, in a cave!

The fourth exercise in taming the ego is to do what you don't want to do. It takes great self-discipline to go against your feelings, your thoughts, and your attitude about something. Initially, until you make a concerted effort to do otherwise, the ego will command control of these functions, and that's what makes it so difficult. For example, one night I received a phone call from my seventeen-year-old, who was at work, asking for her mother. I told her that her mother wasn't at home and asked why she wanted her. She said that she was hungry and wanted her mother to bring her some food, but since her mother wasn't home, I was to forget about it as she herself would be home in a few hours, and that's where we ended our conversation.

I was in the midst of relaxing, undressed, and preferring not to be interrupted by anyone or anything. The thought sprang into my head of bringing her dinner myself, but I didn't want to. I began to rationalize that she didn't deserve it because lately she had been very uncooperative and unloving, as teenagers sometimes are. I realized that she didn't ask me to bring her dinner because she was aware of her behavior too. I had every good reason in the world not to do anything but relax. But I wanted to be better than that, so I brought her a dinner, prepared with love.

I received no reward for my action other than the self-fulfilling feeling of going beyond the selfishness of my ego and being a better person for it. I walked a little taller, I held my head a little higher and, for a brief moment, I felt divine. I look forward to the day when I will always feel that way, when it becomes a way of life as opposed to a specific incident in my life. By doing something unselfish I took one more step up the ladder to becoming my higher self. What could you get away with not doing? Find that action that goes against every grain of your body, although deep down you know you should do it, and do it! Immediate growth will occur, and you will have taken one more step in mastering your ego.

The fifth exercise is very demanding and highly challenging. In fact, most people can't do it. It involves becoming passive to the things that annoy you. Passivity does not merely mean putting up with the annoyance. It is not a separation, like ignoring or denying that the annoyance is occurring. It's a kind of submissiveness. The dictionary states that being passive is being the object instead of the subject of an action. It entails being actively involved in the annoyance and changing your actions and awareness from having it bother you to allowing it to happen and then doing nothing about it. It is a completely different perspective than we are accustomed to. Ideally, it moves us to a state of awe and amazement about what we see.

To start, you have to first identify what annoys you. Since we all have our own annoyances, petty or otherwise, I'll use the examples in my own life. Three that come to mind immediately are waiting in line at the supermarket, being stuck in traffic, and flies. Yes, flies.

Which reminds me of another annoyance, yellow jacket wasps at a barbecue or a picnic. Are they a pain or what? These are the things that get me ticked off. These are the annoying examples of what calls me to action to do something. And that something is what I want to do to them. When I'm sitting in the midst of a traffic jam, or in a long line at a supermarket, I get angry. I start making judgments and become critical of the actions of others. I can remember while living in New York, using the horn of my car as a way to express and release my anger. So did everyone else. They still do it today.

The trick is to not get caught up in all that. Remove yourself from being the object of the traffic jam and the long line to being an observer.

Stewart Wilde has a great way of looking at it: "Right now, we're doing traffic." For a moment, sit there and observe, in awe and amazement, everybody and everything that is occurring around you. Don't make judgments, just observe. Then insert yourself back into the middle of all that is happening, and your experience will change. You may even begin to enjoy the annoyance and the chaos. The behavior and the scenery become amazing and even entertaining. Try it.

Once, while attending a preparation seminar for a "fire walk" sponsored by my company, the rest of the group and I were attacked by hundreds of flies. They were very distracting and annoying. Everybody was swatting, swinging and slapping. It was so bad that we couldn't pay attention to the seminar. After about forty-five minutes of participating in this peculiar dance, I decided to change my reality, which wasn't hard to do because the present reality wasn't working. Instead of continuing to be the subject of the action, swatting and swinging as a result of being the object of the annoying flies, I stepped out of the picture and observed what was happening. I noticed something peculiar. The flies weren't biting. I began to wonder why they were so insistent in swarming around us. I also noticed that, in general, they were landing on the parts of our bodies that weren't covered with clothing.

I decided to get inside the fly's head and try to see what it was thinking. Then it occurred to me—salt! They were after the salt from the perspiration on our bodies. I decided to be magnanimous and let them have it. After all, the salt wasn't of any use to me anymore. I let them land on my legs and ignored their tickling, itching presence. I mentally communicated with them that they could stay and have all the salt they wanted, but there was no biting allowed.

All of a sudden, the flies were attracted to me in droves. I was wearing shorts and my legs were outstretched while I was sitting there listening to the speaker. The flies kept coming and coming to a point where it became very noticeable. The people around me were looking in amazement. There were flies everywhere, covering both legs. Being seated in the front, the speaker also noticed what was happening, and at one point stopped the seminar to remark, "They really like you, don't they?" I was sort of "The Lord of the Flies."

This continued for about an hour, until the end of the seminar, and I can remember twice feeling a fly beginning to bite. As soon as I mentally said, "No," the biting would stop. I can assure you that I had a different experience than everyone else at the seminar, and it became a different experience for many others there. I turned a very annoying situation into one of the most amazing experiences a person could have. You may initially be repulsed by the image you conjure up in your mind when you begin to imagine what it looked like. But believe me when I tell you that my experience was far from repulsive. In fact, it was enjoyable. I took an annoying, repulsive situation and turned it into one of the most memorable, enjoyable experiences of my life.

This reality switch, this change in causation, is the mother of invention. By changing the input, you change the output. This yielding, this passivity, takes reality and recreates it. In the process you are first the object of the action. Then you become the subject as you begin to respond, then catch yourself and become the object again by submission to the event. This takes you out of the pattern of automatic response and creates a different experience than that experienced by most. It takes you out of the conditioned-response world of the ego and puts you into the reality-inverting world of the higher self. Try it yourself the next time you're in the midst of an annoying situation, and see how your experience of that situation changes.

This last exercise will be easier for some, and for others it will be more difficult. It will be easier for some people because it's a physical exercise. It involves changing the habitual pattern of your life. Most people get into a rhythm of existence and can experience an entire lifetime without changing a thing. This habitual rhythm has hypnotic, trance-like qualities that create comfort and order, yet deter advancement and creativity. For those of you who want to be successful, hear this: *Comfort is **not** the objective of existence, growth is!*

If you get up at a fixed time every morning, say 7:00 A.M., try waking up at 4:00 A.M. Take up walking or some other form of physical exercise. Change your eating patterns. Do something! These physical changes will not necessarily lead you onto the spiritual path of success by themselves, but not changing your physical patterns is almost a sure way of not getting there. The thing I find most amazing about people is their lack of understanding about the following universal truth—*if you want to change your life, you have to first change your life.* Its simplicity is inarguable, and yet its wisdom escapes many. I can't tell you how many people I've met who said they wanted their lives to be better, more prosperous, more fulfilling, but they were not willing to break out of their comfort zones. Considering this insight, I know of no better way to conclude this chapter than by restating this quote: "Keep doing what you're doing, and you'll keep getting what you're getting."

POINTS TO PONDER

The only thing you really need is the awareness of what already is.

The reality switch, the change in causation,
is the mother of invention.

People are so busy trying to create reality
that reality passes them by.

Comfort is **not** the objective of existence, growth is!

By changing the input, you change the output.

The conquering of fear is the beginning of wisdom.

23

The World of Illusions
(DON'T BUY THE HYPE!)

**Unhappy is he who mistakes the branch for the tree,
the shadow for the substance.**

— The Talmud

We've spent a good amount of time discussing how your individual conditioned values have been at the root of your lack of success. However, I would be remiss if I did not acknowledge that there is another set of conditioned values that you will encounter that can also undermine your efforts. These conditioned values are the illusion of life that is presented to us every day by society. In the Eastern philosophy, this illusion of life is described as a veil that obscures reality. It is called "Maya." On the street, they call it "the hype," and you will find it whenever and wherever an ego is present. You see, society has an ego, as do various groups and corporations. The smaller the group, the easier it is to see.

Let me give you an example. In many corporations, there are traditions and procedures that became part of the culture of the corporation. If you want to progress in that corporation, there will be a great amount of pressure exerted upon you to adopt that culture. So if someone at the top decides that playing golf is a good way to build camaraderie between managers, then golf becomes part of the culture. If you want to be "in," if you have aspirations for management, then you better learn how to play golf. Golf becomes important. It becomes a conditioned value of the company, and you are often looked upon as an outsider if you don't comply. This conditioned value becomes a reality as an unwritten requirement for management, but it is a false reality. You don't need to learn how to play golf to be a successful manager or for the company to be successful. However, you don't get to make the rules of the game, and that's the point. The corporate culture is just a game, an invention of man that obscures reality. There is, of course, nothing wrong with playing golf, until someone tries to sell it as necessary for success. There *is* something wrong with that. But if you want to climb the corporate ladder in that company, then you have to agree to play the game. And there is no sin in that either, short of committing something immoral, unethical or illegal, as long as you always keep in mind that it's a game and not reality.

Getting caught up in this false reality causes anxiety. Using the above example, you not only have to learn how to play golf, but you have to become proficient at the game. Generally, the greater your proficiency, the more favorable you become to upper management, especially to the one who made the unwritten rule. For those who buy-in to that reality, the anxiety to become favored causes them to do some strange things. It's not peculiar to see adults jumping up and down like children when they miss a putt, or to see clubs fly through the air, or to hear every curse imaginable uttered in record time. And this is not just true for those who buy-in to the corporate illusion, because society also maintains golf as a conditioned value that has its own culture, vocabulary, dress code, etc. The unwritten rule says that successful people play golf. So if you are successful, and especially if you want to be successful, you have to learn to play golf. And of course the value also dictates the false reality that your degree of proficiency will be directly related to your degree of success. Therefore, you need to become an expert at the game. After all, you do want to be highly successful and viewed as such, don't you?

The whole lesson here has nothing to do with the game of golf. It concerns the "game" that is presented to us as reality. We become duped into believing that the "game," in this case, golf, is necessary for us to experience a fulfilled life. This social construct is sold to us as necessary for us to experience happiness. If you don't think, your propensity for conditioning in order to be accepted causes you to adopt this false reality as truth, and you begin to live in fantasyland. Without intervention, you go through life and become one of those people who is one day heard to say, "Is that all there is?"

Let's take another example. Wall Street is an additional construct of society that is presented to us as reality, one "they" would have us believe is important to our financial welfare and future. There are people who live and die with the fluctuations of the market. Some have even committed suicide. They feed us "the hype" that Wall Street is important to our well-being. If you "buy the hype," then you buy-in to their fantasy world. So when the market's up, you feel good. When the market's down, you feel bad. When you respond this way, the fluctuations of the market really do determine your well-being. The feelings are real, but they have no basis in reality. The feelings people had as they thought about sailing off the edge of the Earth when it was believed to be flat had no basis in reality either. It's all a game that someone created and we bought-in to. But the game wasn't created for you or me to win. That's why most investors lose money. It's all "Maya," hype, fluff—it's a fairyland. Wall Street is Disney World with a ticker tape! But at least Disney World doesn't try to represent itself as being real. The feelings you get at Disney World are genuine also, but nobody would commit suicide because the roller coaster went downhill. In other words, the feelings don't produce thoughts and then actions as they do in the fairy constructs of society, which are presented to us as being important, as being reality. So you don't have to develop an appreciation of the arts, go to college, own the trappings of success, attend gala affairs, become politically influential, or live in a big house to become successful or to demonstrate your success. These, too, are the illusions of society. Once you step outside of these fairy constructs you see them all for what they really are: nothing. It's all hype!

So the question is, "Should I own stocks and bonds?" The answer is yes, if you want to, but know *it's all a game that wasn't designed for you to win*, and act accordingly. The game of Wall Street was designed by others for them to win, namely the market makers, the brokerage houses, the mutual funds, etc. And generally, their winning comes at the expense of someone losing. Robert Kiyosaki, in his book *Rich Dad, Poor Dad*, made the same discovery about owning a home. The system has fed us the fallacy for decades that owning a home is an asset. Robert exposed this illusion by simply stating that assets produce income, while liabilities are represented by an outflow of capital. So where most people are duped into "investing" in a home, Kiyosaki educates people about true investments, those that produce income.

The danger with buying into these fairyland constructs of society is that they distract you from the focus you need to become successful. The energy and time that you give to these false realities reduces the already limited time and energy that you can devote to your success. If you buy-in to enough of these false realities, you get duped into believing that you are focusing on success, when in reality you're just being "played." You engage in lots of activity, but you get nowhere. The Sicilians have an expression for that. It's called "digging a hole in water." The only solution is to concern yourself with what is real. *You can always test the reality of these conditioned values of society by examining the conclusions that they present, because the truth never contradicts itself.* So is learning to play and becoming proficient at golf necessary for success? The obvious answer is no. How about an appreciation of the opera, or having a college degree, or wearing a tie? Don't you wish it were that easy? Adam Smith probably stated it best in this quote: "No matter how thin you slice it, it's still baloney!"

Then how do you know what is reality? It may be a crude example, but ask a dying person that question and you'll find that it's an easy one for him to answer. If you had a definite time left on this Earth, would that item or activity in question be important? The answer to that question is the acid test of reality. All of the things or activities that still matter, even when you've been given a death sentence, are the realities of success that result in the truth.

The point of this whole chapter is "don't buy the hype!" A good rule of thumb is that *if it's natural, you can trust in its perfection. If it's man-made, be careful.* Don't buy into the false representations of success that they try to sell you as important. They will interfere with the attention that you need to give to your intention. They will prolong your lack of success.

POINTS TO PONDER

It's all a game that wasn't designed for you to win.

You can always test the validity of these "hyped" social constructs because the truth never contradicts itself.

If it's natural, you can trust in its perfection.
If it's man-made, be careful!

24

POTPOURRI

> Most jobs and many leisure activities—especially those
> involving passive consumption of mass media—are not
> designed to make us happy and strong.
> Their purpose is to make money for someone else.
> If we allow them to, they can suck out the marrow
> of our lives, leaving only feeble husks.
> — Mihaly Csikszentmihalyi in *Flow*

I entitled this chapter "Potpourri" because it doesn't contain one central theme or idea, but a multiplicity of themes and ideas. The first of which is the value of disagreement. We are programmed from birth to be agreeable. If not, there are consequences. No place is this more true than in the corporate world today. It's not true for every company, not the innovative ones, but unfortunately it is true of most companies.

Believe it or not, the "yes" man is still very much alive. The shame of it all is the wasted innovative ideas that never get to bear fruit. I heard a saying once that impacted me so much that, as a high-ranking executive, I try to keep it fresh in my mind. I don't know who said it, but it goes something like this: "When two partners (or two executives) agree too often, one of them is unnecessary." Disagreement is the seed of innovation because *you can't discover what you don't know based on what you know*. Progress is in the questions, not in the answers. How many questions never get expressed for the fear of appearing disagreeable, disloyal, or unsupportive? Everyone fears being "the square peg in the round hole," but innovation and progress belong to the square pegs. I once read that the number of great art works, inventions, poetry, songs, operas, musical compositions, and ideas that we enjoy today are miniscule in number in comparison to those that are buried in the cemetery, those that were never expressed. Henry Thoreau wrote that, "The tragedy of life was that most men lead lives of quiet desperation, and go to the grave with the song still in them." Are you one of those living tragedies? If you agree with the vast majority, who never experience financial success, then odds are that you will share their same fate. *Disagreement, seeing things differently, is an essential component of success.*

The second idea I would like to relate is the fact that there are no coincidences. Everything that happens to you, you cause to happen. *Everything happens for a reason—and you're it.*

Some people must be wondering, "How can I be the source of the unfortunate circumstances of my life?" It's simple (most great truths are), because "As ye sow, so shall ye reap." For ages this truth has been spoken in different ways by every wise person who ever lived, and even now people just don't get it. By your thoughts, by your beliefs, by your actions, you determine the world that you experience. "Oh, yeah? Well, what about the people who die in plane crashes?" My answer is—what about the people who don't? There are numerous stories about people who didn't get on the plane, or at the last minute changed their plans for reasons unknown to them. Maybe those who were in the crash received the same premonition but didn't pay attention to it.

I've saved myself many a problem by not doing something because "something told me not to." That something is your inner self. It's that mystical part of yourself that speaks to you through intuition. It's the wiser part of who you are, but how many of us listen to its wisdom? Instead, we try to be logical. We've been programmed to not trust ourselves, and because of that, we experience "apparent" misfortune. Listen to yourself! You already know the answers; you just need to find the questions. Life is not luck. What you sow is what you reap—only tenfold. That's the underlying truth behind positive thinking. No matter how people moan and complain, everyone is exactly where they decided to be, exactly where they planned to be. Life lives up to your expectations or not, but where you are in life is a direct result of the decisions you've made or have not made. Whether you plant negative seeds or positive seeds, they will return to you tenfold. The point to be made here is that if you want to be successful, you must take full responsibility for the results of your action, or lack of action. *Success is a science. It's not about luck. It's about cause and effect.*

Time management is another one of those areas that give people great difficulty. Distractions test commitment and resolve. As stated earlier, you just have to learn how to say no. Everyone wants to be a "good guy," and we often search for the opportunities to prove it. If we look closer though, we realize that the reason why we do things for other people, even if our acts don't become known to anyone else but ourselves, we do so that we can feel better about ourselves. Everything everybody does is connected to personal gain in some way, shape, or form, and there is nothing wrong with that unless we foolishly try to believe otherwise. The woman who unselfishly takes care of her children does so to feel like a good mother. The man who stops working to play with his son wants to feel like a good father. The man who doesn't stop working to play with his son wants to feel like a responsible businessman or breadwinner. Everything we do is for personal reasons, whether we realize it or not. When traveling the road to success, unconsciously exhibiting personal-gratification behavior can be costly.

Time doesn't come cheap, and in the beginning, you need every bit of time you can get your hands on to get your success plan off the ground. It's very much like sending a rocket to the moon. When NASA launches a moon shot, there is more energy expended in the first few minutes just getting the rocket off the launch pad than it takes to propel the rocket for the rest of the trip. The same thing is true when you decide to launch yourself toward success. It takes a great amount of time and effort when you start to get yourself rolling toward your objective. In fact, it takes *all* of your time and effort. And except for the basic survival necessities, and even some of those are questionable, all of your time and effort *must* be devoted to your success plan.

Somewhere along the line, we got the idea that "working hours" are 9:00 A.M. to 5:00 P.M., five days a week. Well, I guess they are if you want to wind up like the 93 percent that achieve mediocrity. This is one of the programs that most of us have been conditioned to believe that results in making the achievement of success so difficult. The Bible says that even God worked six days and rested on the seventh! (Do you think God is a good role model to follow?) In the beginning, every waking hour of every day should be devoted to your attainment of success. Only then will you have a chance of realizing it. The good news is that, like the rocket, once you really get the ball rolling, it won't take a lot of time or energy to keep it going. Then you can devote yourself to those other "good" things that you would like to experience in your life.

Another thief of our time is the television. Someone aptly named it the "boob tube" because that's what you turn out to be when you watch too much of it—a boob! I often wonder if people who watch a lot of TV, especially the soap operas, aren't living their lives through the TV programs. Are their lives so dull that a make-believe life on a screen is better than their own? Some of them know more about the families on those soap operas than they know about their own families.

And what about the guys who are sports nuts? What's the motivation? They know every player, statistic, standing, point spread, etc., that there is to know. For what? I could never figure it out. The only time I came close to knowing was in my horse betting days. I knew every jockey, trainer, horse, time trial, etc., that anyone could know. For what? For nothing! All I ever did was lose money, crowd my mind with nonsense, and feel emotions that had no basis in reality. Maybe that's the answer. *Maybe people need something to fill their minds, to fill the void, to feel alive.* Heaven forbid they have a quiet moment of introspection. They might discover the truth. There is someone who would prefer that didn't happen and that someone is your ego—you.

Behind every loss of time and energy lies our old nemesis, the ego. It is the ego who gets ingratiated when we do something that makes us feel like the good guy. It's the ego, through deception and confusion, that keeps us glued to the tube or buried in the sports pages day after day, week after week, year after year. The ego thrives on the social excitement of those mediums where we see ourselves as the guy who scores the goal or the woman who rises up after being scorned by her lover. I guess it's okay if you want to engage in those fantasies, as long as you know that's what you're doing! I once wanted to be James Bond, Agent 007. My life today, my real life, is more exciting than any of his movies, and I've seen them all.

This is the basis of the spirituality of success. It's not mysterious, or magical, or eerie. *True spirituality is simply being mindful of what you're doing and why you're doing it while you're doing it.* From that comes the growth. From that comes the conquering of the ego, so that you no longer have to live in the dizzying, insecure, unrewarding confusion that people today call life. Once you clear that hurdle, the road to success is easier. You'll be amazed at how quickly success will materialize in your life. The time has come to master your destiny!

POINTS TO PONDER

You can't discover what you don't know based on what you know.

Everything happens for a reason—and you're it.

Disagreement, seeing things differently,
is an essential component of success.

Success is a science.
It's not about luck. It's about cause and effect.

Maybe people need something to fill their minds,
to fill the void, to feel alive.

True spirituality is simply being mindful of what you're doing
and why you're doing it while you're doing it.

25

VOICES OF SUCCESS

Make Something of Yourself.
Try your best to get to the top, if thats where you want to go,
but know that the more people you try to take along with you,
the faster you'll get there and the longer you'll stay there.

— James A. Autry, writer

I interviewed a number of successful people because I know that the more input you receive from successful people, the greater is your possibility of becoming successful. I chose the "Entrepreneur of the Year" award winners because winning this title is a generally accepted standard in the business world as an indicator of success. The process they engage in to pick their award winners is very elaborate and takes place on many levels. Ernst & Young provides the financial expertise. I chose the awards given in New York because of the quantity and quality of the competition. The six award winners I interviewed were:

Wade Saadi, President, Pencom Systems, Inc.

Frank Sciame, President, F.J. Sciame Construction Co.

Irwin Sternberg, President, Stonehenge Unlimited

William Ungar, President and CEO, National Envelope Corp.

Aubrey Balkind, President and CEO, Frankfurt Balkind Partners

Kurt Adler, Chairman, Kurt S. Adler, Inc.

These six award winners weren't the only ones I requested to interview, but they are the ones who responded favorably to being interviewed for your benefit. In my estimation, that is the final test of true success—their willingness to help you unselfishly.

I asked them questions that I thought you would ask, such as:

Their background and education level?

How much money they personally had to start their business?

How they felt, competitively, in a fledgling business?

If they set goals and used any specific goal-setting techniques?

How they viewed risk?

What advice they would like to give you, the reader?

These winners have gained a wealth of knowledge from their experience, and I tried to capture the physical, emotional, and spiritual aspects of that experience in my interviews. If you really want to know what it takes to be successful, then read on. What you will find is the truth and not just the generally accepted beliefs and principles that are taught today. In fact, you might find some of the answers shocking!

For the sake of continuity, I have included the actual interviews at the end of the book, so that you may review them at your leisure. Personally, I had a great time conducting the interviews. There were many times during the process that I felt privileged to be conducting them. Believe me when I tell you that these winners are just like you. The only difference is that they see things differently and have a different belief structure by which they operate.

As an example, only half of them graduated from college, and of the ones who did graduate, I don't think any achieved high honors scholastically. I got the impression that they viewed their time in college as the warm-up for the big race. I found it quite humorous that more than one of the non-graduates were claimed as graduates by their former colleges. Perhaps this was done for publicity purposes. Everyone wants to get into the act! In addition, none of them had the money they needed to get started, nor did they believe they needed it. Money to them wasn't important by itself. To them, it's a tool, a resource, and maybe a way of keeping score. I concluded that money was not their focus.

What I also found interesting and universal were their beliefs about risk. To them, *risk was simply the flip side of the coin of opportunity,* just like every coin has a "heads" and a "tails." They weren't nonchalant about it; in fact, they respected risk and cautioned about using evaluation before taking action; but they were not afraid of risk, even in the beginning. Nor did they fear competition, not even from the "big guys" in their business. In fact, I think they relished the prospect of competing with companies where the odds were stacked so lopsidedly against them. In watching them answer this question, I noticed the appearance of a gleam in their eyes at the memories, as well as at the prospect, of quality competition. They were all great competitors.

I guess that leads to another commonality they shared. They were all "players." Most people watch life from the sidelines, while these people played the game. *They didn't react to life; instead life had to contend with them!* They were a force to be reckoned with from the very beginning. They may not have had the experience, the resources, or the connections when they first started, but that didn't stop them. They had the dreams, the desire, and the will, which, as they demonstrated, are all you really need. They all faced adversity, some of them great adversity, even just to begin. But it didn't stop them and they didn't quit. Instead, they used their adversities as the fire that turns iron into steel. In the game of life, these people were true players.

One of the pleasant surprises that came during the interview process was their almost universal verification of what I call "the goal myth." In fact, it was kind of funny that most of them thought they were disappointing me when they answered the question on goals. They knew what the "right" answer was, the generally accepted answer to this question, but their honesty could not allow them to lie about it. What they didn't know was that my experience yielded the same answer.

Setting goals and the goal-setting techniques endorsed today do not work. In fact, they achieve just the opposite result. The most important factor in goal setting is flexibility, and a checklist or a detailed map will create the risk of eliminating your alternate possibilities. The proof of the importance of this is that most successful people are not in the business they planned to be in or in the way they envisioned it. On their roads to success, the people interviewed took advantage of the opportunities that presented themselves along the way. In fact, it wasn't even the particular business they were in that was important to them. What was important was the process of being "in business."

Today's teachings and knowledge about goals and goal-setting techniques are too confining, too restrictive for the kind of flexibility that is needed to achieve success. Perhaps Wade Saadi put it best when he said, "Companies use goals and business plans, not entrepreneurs [people]." I also found great wisdom and validation in the words of Aubrey Balkind when he said, "I believe chaos [uncertainty] is the oxygen that drives creativity. If you define things too much, like with goals, there is no room to maneuver." Whichever of these voices you choose to listen to, you get the same message —goal setting and its popular techniques don't work!

Another point that caught my attention was how they cared about you, the reader. They don't even know you, but you're the reason why they agreed to the interview in the first place. That impressed me even though I expected it. Caring about others, helping others has been a universally shared attribute of every successful person I've met or trained. The generosity of these voices of success was visible in many ways. They physically gave to causes and to others spiritually and emotionally. The secret that *helping others is the best way to help yourself was no secret to them*. They demonstrated it in many areas and on many levels, but their helping others had no ulterior motive. It was who they were, and according to the laws of the universe, they were repaid tenfold. Instinctively, they knew this, although it was not the reason for their actions.

I have listed other shared traits that were apparent during the interview process. I really could write an entire book about this experience alone, but their attributes and the importance of each are highlighted throughout this book. These successful people only verified what we each have to "be" in order to become successful. They all exhibited confidence, pride, passion, humility, depth, and a sense of adventure. They don't believe in luck, but believe that what happens to them in business, good and bad, is of their own doing. They take responsibility for the results—a trait that is missing in people who have not achieved success. They are also very grateful in general, and especially grateful to this country for the opportunity it gives to them and everyone else. They are patriots in the best sense of the word. Their lives are about continual self-improvement, and they spend a lot of their time broadening their experiences and their knowledge. They don't engage in the time- and energy-wasting activities that most people engage in. They don't have a "hump" day, and they don't say, "Thank God it's Friday." I suspect that they can't wait for Monday so they can get back to "playing the game."

Most of all, there is a spiritual and mystical thread that connects each of these men, their experiences, and their lives. They all believe that there is a greater purpose to their lives than the mundane existence for which too many people settle. I thank God for the experience and share their hope that these words will help make a difference in your life. It is truly their wish, as well as mine, to see your dreams come true.

POINTS TO PONDER

Risk is simply the flip side of the coin of opportunity.

Helping others is the best way to help yourself.

Don't react to life. Let life contend with you!

26

Quantum Physics: The Science of Success?

> ... cultivation of the personal life depends
> on the rectification of the mind.
>
> — *The Great Learning*, circa 450 B.C.

Quantum physics. These two words usually invoke looks of fear, confusion, or indifference from the average person. What does quantum physics have to do with success?

Humor me for a moment. What if I could show, through science, that there is scientific truth to many of the things I have said are necessary to be successful? When the current day's teachings talk about success, they usually do so in terms that have an airy-fairy quality. There is hardly anything that is really concrete, and that which is concrete, such as goal-setting techniques, usually don't work. They rarely speak of things that you can put your arms around and grab. They speak in abstract terms, such as desire, positive thinking, enthusiasm, perception, etc. What if I could give you the concrete of science as the foundation for your financial empire?

Why is that important? It's important because the entire Western civilization's belief structure is built on the foundation of science. If science shows a particular point to be true, then we Westerners proceed with an unwavering security, knowing that our truth has its roots in science. In other words, a scientifically proven "fact" instantly becomes our belief. *Belief is elemental to success.* In order to give you an unwavering security in the belief that the entire universe will conspire for your success, that you were destined to succeed, I will refer to quantum physics, the most advanced science we presently have, to illustrate it for you. As strange as it may seem, what occurs in the subatomic world is a model for what occurs in our larger world.

What is intriguing to me, as I learn more and more, are the similarities in the basic concepts upon which Western science, Eastern mysticism, and the science of success are built. In books like *The Tao of Physics* by Fritjof Capra, *The Dancing Wu Li Masters* by Gary Zukav, and *A Brief History of Time* by Stephen Hawking, the physicist/authors compare the new discoveries in modern physics to the age-old beliefs of Eastern mysticism. The same is true of *The Holographic Universe* by Michael Talbot and *The Six Roads from Newton* by Edward Speyer. They revel in the fact that Western science is becoming grounded in Eastern mysticism. What I find amazing is that Eastern mysticism is becoming grounded in Western science. The tireless Eastern concepts of the void or empty space not being empty, that material things are not made of anything material, and the interrelatedness of everything in the universe, are now being proved by modern physics.

Likewise, the science of success, as first explained by Napoleon Hill in his book *Think and Grow Rich*, is also being validated by Western science and Eastern mysticism. The landmark work by Napoleon Hill describes success as physical, mental, and spiritual. Many motivational speakers' material and many works on success and achievement are based on Mr. Hill's work. Unfortunately, not much has been done in the science of success since *Think and Grow Rich* was written. If it is truly a science, then it should develop, expand, and grow like the other sciences do. There has been some advancement in the science of success, such as *The Seven Habits of Highly Effective People* by Stephen Covey, but too few to keep pace with the degree of development experienced by the other sciences. That is why I chose to write this book in the way that I wrote it. My intent is that this book should pick up where Napoleon Hill left off.

So many developments have taken place in our awareness and knowledge that can be incorporated to further the science of success that I feel compelled to continue this work. Deepak Chopra, the man who prompted me to write this book, has brought modern physics and Eastern mysticism to the world of medicine. His work in the area of wellness has made serious inroads in helping people with their physical ailments. My objective is to use the same principles to help people with their financial ailments. *There is no concrete, valid reason why everyone shouldn't be able to experience and materialize their dreams of success*, and my intent is to drive that point home to the multitude. When one is poor or barely making ends meet, their hollowed dreams of success make the experience of a fulfilled life questionable. Now let's look at how science validates that not only can our dreams come true, but they are completely within our power to experience.

POINTS TO PONDER

Belief is elemental to success.

There is no concrete, valid reason why everyone shouldn't be able to experience and materialize their dreams of success.

27

WHAT IS REALITY?

There are no unnatural or supernatural phenomena,
only very large gaps in our knowledge of what is natural. . . .
We should strive to fill those gaps of ignorance.

— Edgar Mitchell, astronaut

$\mathbf{B}$ack in the days of Einstein, a revolution took place in the field of physics that forever changed the way we looked at the universe. Up until that time, everyone subscribed to Newtonian physics, which was a theory of physics developed by Sir Isaac Newton. As folklore would have it, he sat under an apple tree and, when an apple fell and hit him on the head, got an idea that resulted in the theory of gravity. The basis of his theory was the relationship between cause and effect. In Newton's time, his postulates were revolutionary in themselves because of what people believed, such as the Earth being the center of the universe. There was only one problem: Newtonian physics could not explain everything. That's where Einstein came in.

Let it suffice to say that there is a fundamental difference between the old physics and the new physics. The old physics saw the world as apart from us, as being "out there." The new physics sees the universe as participatory, where everything is connected to everything else and, in a sense, as being "in here"!

The prime example of this discovery came into being as a result of man's search to find the elemental particle of life. While searching for the basic building block of life, physicists made some interesting discoveries. In trying to measure the properties of subatomic particles, they found that, depending on what they were measuring, these subatomic particles, or quanta, were sometimes particles and sometimes waves. "What's so astounding about that?" you might ask. What is astounding about that is this: A particle has no wavelike properties and a wave has no particlelike properties. They are opposites.

It's like discovering that a particular animal is sometimes an elephant and at other times a fish! What determined whether the quanta exhibited the properties of a particle or a wave depended on what kind of measuring equipment that the scientists installed. If they installed wave-measuring equipment, they found the quantum to be a wave. If they installed particle-measuring equipment, the quanta were particles. Whatever the scientists wanted it to be, it was. Basically, they determined reality. The scientists determined the properties, the realities, of the quanta by their participation in choosing the equipment of measurement.

They also found that the same thing happened in trying to measure the position and the momentum of the quanta. John Wheeler, a well-known physicist at Princeton, wrote:

> Nothing is more important about the quantum principle than this, that it destroys the concept of the world, "sitting out there," with the observer safely separated from it by a 20-centimeter slab of plate glass. Even to observe so minuscule an object as an electron, he must shatter the glass. He must reach in. He must install his chosen measuring equipment. It is up to him to decide whether he shall measure position or momentum. To install the equipment to measure the one prevents and excludes his installing the equipment to measure the other. Moreover, the measurement changes the state of the electron. The universe will never afterward be the same. To describe what has happened, one has to cross out that old word "observer" and put in its place the new word "participator." In some strange sense the universe is a participatory universe.

He also wrote:

> May the universe in some strange sense be "brought into being" by the participation of those who participate?... The vital act is the act of participation. "Participator" is the incontrovertible new concept given by quantum mechanics. It strikes down the term "observer" of classical theory, the man who stands safely behind the thick glass wall and watches what goes on without taking part. It can't be done, quantum mechanics says.

Remember that this is not an Eastern mystic in an orange robe speaking. This is a world-renowned scientist talking about the material world. This discovery, that the scientist's results of an experiment are self-determinable, has led physicists to the point of asking some very interesting questions. According to Gary Zukav in his book *The Dancing Wu Li Masters*:

> Quantum physicists ponder questions like "Did a particle with momentum exist before we conducted an experiment to measure its momentum?" "Did a particle with position exist before we conducted an experiment to measure its position?" "Did any particles exist at all before we thought about them and measured them?" "*Did we create the particles that we are experimenting with?*"

Incredible as it sounds, this creation of the particles is a possibility that many physicists recognize.

However, what I think is even more incredible is that science has determined that the physical presence and feel of material things are products of our minds and senses. When you examine a molecule of matter, science tells us that it is composed primarily of empty space. There's nothing there! Within the molecules are the atoms, but the material content of the atoms is negligible in comparison to the space between the atoms. And to further compound the astonishment, when you go into the atom and examine the sub-atomic particles, you find that there is nothing material about them at all. They are simply energy impulses, and the space between them, again, is pretty much all there is to the composition of the atom. In fact, they've estimated that a molecule is 99.9999…% empty space, and that if you took *all* the matter in the universe and put it in one place, it would barely fill a football stadium. So what is it that we see? What is it that we grab hold of?

The reality is that the form and substance of the universe is a result of our thoughts, therefore, we live in a mental world. Everything has a vibratory frequency, and we take those vibrations and give them form and substance through our thoughts and through our senses. Without our minds and our senses, all there is is energy and space. If this is how reality works, and science tells us it is, then can you imagine how we can use this knowledge in the achievement of success? Your mind is the key to reality! This is echoed in the age-old quote from Proverbs 23:7, "For as a man thinketh within himself, so is he." Also the ancient saying, "As within, so without," tells us that the reality of life starts within, in the mind, and then it takes form in the material world. This is how spirituality manifests into the natural laws of the universe.

This leads us to the success principle that states *if you can think it, you can do it!*

We've taken the long route back home to a very simple truth that is so often quoted that it has almost lost its meaning: "Life is what you make it!" Never before has that phrase had so much validity as it has today because of the science of quantum physics. Up until now, it was one of those airy-fairy concepts of Eastern mysticism that everyone kind of "knew" was true, but there was no concrete proof. Science today provides us with the proof. You determine what reality is. It's not "What will be, will be." It's what you want to be, will be. So which do you choose—success or failure, affluence or poverty, happiness or sadness, or even worse, mediocrity? They are all *your* possibilities, and you get to choose.

A side effect of these discoveries is the discovery of the paradox of reality. The paradox of reality is simply that everything contains its opposite. Quanta can be particles or waves. They are both. You can be a success or a failure. You are both. And just as the scientists can determine which the quanta will be at any specific moment, so you too have that same power over success and failure. Scientific proof gives us the concrete evidence of this reality.

Furthermore, we know some of the determining factors of the choosing. As an example, I will use my vegetable garden. I have found that the only way to get a tomato to grow in my garden is to make a concerted effort to achieve that result. I have to plant a tomato seed. I have to take action. Inasmuch as that action is revealing in and of itself, what is even more revealing are the results of my inaction. If I don't plant tomatoes, I get weeds. My vegetable garden contains the possibility of both tomatoes and weeds, and it doesn't care which one it produces. I have the power to determine which one I will harvest. My planting of the tomato seed is an action, but my inaction to not plant the seed is also an action. In other words, *doing nothing is still doing something*, although that fact escapes most people. This unconscious action of inaction is why success escapes you. *Success is a choice, and so is lack of success!* And the universe or nature doesn't care which one you experience; it will give you either one.

One of the other properties in the choosing is one that we have already briefly discussed. It's that anything worthwhile in life cannot be pursued. It must be attracted. In fact, *the more we pursue success, the more we drive it away.* A story that dramatically affected my understanding of this principle tells of life being like two women named Success and Knowledge. A young man asked the question, "How can I achieve success in life?" The old philosopher said that if you pay too much attention to Success, you will drive her away. But if you pay more attention to Knowledge, Success will become jealous and pursue you.

Oscar Wilde said, "There is only one class of people that thinks more about money than the rich, and that is the poor. In fact, the poor can think of nothing else." What escapes them is that their preoccupation with money and their pursuit of affluence are what creates their poverty! For many years I pursued success with a vengeance only to have it elude me every time. My actions were always determined by what was best for me to become wealthy and successful. Little did I know that I was the source of my own poverty and failure. This little-known "secret" has been published millions of times in different words and shouted from every mountain that man could climb, and yet it remains a secret. Jesus Christ said it: "Love thy neighbor as thyself." What he was saying was that if you love your neighbor, you love yourself. Zig Ziglar said it also: "I believe you can get everything in life you want if you will just help enough other people get what they want." Again I heard it often as a child: "It is better to give than to receive." In short, the only way to experience authentic, long-lasting affluence and success in your life is by making a concerted effort to make it appear in the lives of others.

The third property involved in the choosing is learning to become comfortable with the uncomfortable. The fact that reality is a paradox, that everything contains its opposite, that quanta can be waves or particles is not disconcerting to nature or to the universe. In fact, nature and the universe are very comfortable with things being that way, because that's the way it is. The universe and everything in it are constantly in a state of flux, changing in polarity, but people continually struggle for life to be unchanging and constant when it's impossible. When change occurs, some people get bent out of shape and lose all sense of direction. Instead of seeing change as the essence of life, as the stuff opportunity is made of, all they can see is their discomfort. "When God closes one door, He opens another" is a great description of what happens when change occurs. The problem is that most people keep their eye on the closed door and lament instead of using their energy to find the open door. We need to become comfortable with change. Change is good. Change is wonderful. *Change is reality!*

POINTS TO PONDER

If you can think it, you can do it!

Doing nothing is still doing something.

Success is a choice, and so is lack of success!

The more we pursue success, the more we drive it away.

Change is reality!

What Is Time?

Time is the image of eternity.
— Plato

Eastern mystics speak of the past, present, and future all taking place at the same time, and the objective they strive for is to be fully aware of the present moment. They see the power of life in the present moment, and they've had this belief for thousands of years. What is similar to their beliefs is Einstein's theory of relativity.

In the theory of relativity, time is relative. The past, present, and future exist simultaneously within a sea of consciousness. This is, of course, not readily apparent, but with the help of physics and astronomy, it becomes glaringly clear. The present I assume needs no explanation, although I may be too innocent in my assumption. But assuming that is true, through physics we know that when we look up at the evening sky, we are not seeing things as they are, but as they were, hundreds and thousands of years ago. In fact, the light from the closest star, other than the sun, takes almost *four* years to reach us. So what we are actually seeing in the present is how that star looked four years ago. We are viewing the past in the present. In fact, the actual star may no longer even exist, but the light it generated years ago makes it look like it is still there. Amazing stuff!

Seeing the future in the present is a little more complicated, but through the power of visualization (focused daydreaming), we can peer into the future. Maybe you've experienced this in some aspect of your life, if you've given yourself permission to, but it is not something everyone has done. I have experienced it, and I use visualization today in just about every aspect of my life. I do it because it works.

Visualization engages the creative ability that we all possess. It is the thought or intention that is likened to the scientist choosing his measuring equipment. *Visualization produces the creative spark that is the basis for all creation.*

What further fans that spark into the raging fire of reality is the emotional belief that one invests in it. What is truly amazing is that this awesome power is quite easy to initiate. There is nothing supernatural about it. It's almost exactly the same as daydreaming. It works through the principle that the brain thinks in pictures, and cannot tell the difference between a real event and an imagined one. Simply imagine or "see" your objective in your mind. Notice that I did not use the word goal. Remember the difference? With a goal the emotion comes first and then the thought. It has all the right steps of the creative process, but it has them backwards, and that's why it doesn't work. Be careful not to visualize an objective down to the minute details as in goal setting. Leave room for flexibility. As with setting an objective, the creativity of visualization works best when success is a residual effect of keeping the success of others foremost. There is great creative power in that combination! Once you have done that, let go and trust in the fact that the universe will correctly guide you from that point forward to the best possible result. You just need to watch for the signs. You already have the ability; you were born with it. Now you just need to practice!

I have found that what I visualize very often comes into being, like the first time my sales team achieved top honors in the country. The lead my opponents had was insurmountable by logical calculations, but I visualized my team passing them in sales one by one, and we secured the lead in the last week of the year. I even visualized the awards ceremony and how I would give the credit to those who really deserved it. If I hadn't used visualization so many times, I would have been amazed, but sometimes reality and truth *are* amazing.

As seeming proof of having experienced the future in the present is the phenomenon of "deja vu." Deja vu is the feeling that you've actually experienced before what you are presently experiencing, sometimes down to the smallest details. It is the seeing of an event in the present that was previously viewed through an involuntary visualization or higher state of consciousness. Most people, I believe, have had this experience, and although they weren't able to explain it, they "knew" they had "experienced" it before. This alone should be proof enough of having experienced the future before it occurred, but it doesn't really fulfill our need of sensory validation for us to believe it to be true.

However, if you ever stood in the path of an oncoming storm, you have watched the future coming, and although there are probably many other examples of the past, present, and future all being visible at the same time, we don't readily notice them. The reason for that is that they all converge in the here and now, in the present moment.

In Einstein's theory of relativity, he discusses time and space to be so closely associated that they are inseparable. It's like having a dog that is half collie and half St. Bernard, but you can't separate the collie half from the St. Bernard half. That's how closely space and time are associated. They call it a space-time continuum. In fact, no physicist today uses the word "space" or "time" independent of each other anymore. The space-time continuum adds the fourth dimension to what we know as a three-dimensional world. This is where it gets sticky, because our minds cannot comprehend a four-dimensional world. In fact, we cannot even explain it using the language of English, but it is easily explained with the language of mathematics.

Understanding it isn't as important, for our purposes, as knowing that this realization is a commonly accepted premise in quantum physics. To understand the space-time continuum, we can use the analogy of an endless wall made up of space-time. We can pick any point on the wall and say this is the present, and anything to the right of that present point is the past, and anything to the left of that present point is the future, but the wall is there in its entirety all the time. No matter what point we pick on the wall to be the present, the past, present, and future are always present on that wall of space-time. In the book *The Dancing Wu Li Masters*, Gary Zukav writes:

> This is the space-time continuum. In this static picture, the space-time continuum, events do not develop, they just are. If we could view our reality in a four-dimensional way, we would see that every thing that now seems to unfold before us with the passing of time, already exists <u>in toto</u>, painted, as it were, on the fabric of space-time. We would see all, the past, the present, and the future with one glance.

As you can see, modern physics is annihilating our conceptions about our physical world. The problem is that we have become too reliant on our five senses for the truth. Our lack of awareness leads us to believe the physical feedback that we receive from those five senses until we have come to believe that *only* that which our five senses can experience is true reality. Nothing could be further from the truth! We cannot see x-rays or infrared light, but we know they exist. Dogs can hear sounds that our ears don't hear.

Sharks can smell blood miles away, and we have no such ability. Rocks and trees appear to be standing still, while the truth is that the rocks, trees, and we are hurtling through space on this hunk of land we call Earth at unbelievable speeds, we just don't feel the movement. Science has brought us to a reality beyond our five senses, and it's time we become conscious of it.

But what does this all have to do with achieving success? Well, if the past, present, and future all exist at the same time as quantum physics tell us, then everything we do affects all three, and for our purposes, the effect on the present and future are most important. Every action, every thought, every emotion could be likened to the planting of a seed. And every seed bears fruit, good or bad. So thinking that *anything* that we do may be inconsequential is sheer lunacy according to modern physics. *Everything we do, everything we think, and everything we feel matters and has consequences.* The consequences, good or bad, may not be readily apparent, but every seed bears fruit eventually. This knowledge should prompt us to redefine our behavior, our thought patterns, and our beliefs, not only in regard to success, but also to life in general. *Remember—negativity kills!*

POINTS TO PONDER

Visualization produces the creative spark that is the basis for all creation.

Everything we do, everything we think, and everything we feel matters and has consequences.

Remember—negativity kills!

29

THE RELATIVITY OF TIME

Finally, the sense of the duration of time is altered;
hours pass by in minutes, and minutes
can stretch out to seem like hours.

— Mihal Csikszentmihalyi, in *Flow*

Einstein's theory of relativity, according to Gary Zukav, states that: "A moving clock runs more slowly than a clock at rest, and continues to slow its rhythm as its velocity increases until, at the speed of light [186,000 miles per second], it stops running altogether."

In other words, time slows as the speed increases, which is amazing enough. But what is more important is the relativity of time, which states that time is relative for everyone depending on the speed at which they are traveling. In *The Dancing Wu Li Masters*, Gary Zukav offers the following example:

> Suppose we are aboard a spacecraft outward bound on an exploration. We have made arrangements to press a button every fifteen minutes to send a signal back to Earth. As our speed steadily increases our earthbound colleagues notice that instead of every fifteen minutes, our signals begin to arrive seventeen minutes apart, and then twenty-five minutes apart. After several days, our colleagues, to their distress, find that our signals arrive every two days. As our velocity continues to increase our signals become years apart. Eventually, generations of earthlings come and go between our signals.

> Meanwhile, on the spacecraft, we are entirely unaware of the predicament back on Earth. As far as we are concerned, everything is proceeding according to plan, although we are becoming bored with the routine of pressing a button every fifteen minutes. When

we return to Earth, a few years older (our proper time) we may find that we have been gone, according to Earth time, for centuries (their relative time). Exactly how long depends upon how fast we have been going.

This scene is not science fiction. It is based upon a well-known [to physicists] phenomenon called the twin paradox of the special theory of relativity.

The twin paradox, very simply stated, says that if one twin blasts off into space at high speeds and the other one stays on Earth, the one who took the space trip will return to Earth younger in relative time than the one that stayed on Earth.

"Wild stuff," you might say, "but what does that have to do with success?" Humor me and I will bring it all together for you. Isaac Newton stated that time "flows equably" for everyone. This Newtonian principle of time was proven incorrect by Einstein's theory of relativity, which states that everyone's experience of time is relative—not equal. The problem is that everyone still believes Newton's invalid assumption that all people experience the passage of time in the same way. It's one of those insidious, invalid programs that are continually passed on from generation to generation. The understanding of the truth about time is infinitely important to your quest for success, because time is one of the essential factors that one must contend with in order to become successful. As an example of the relative quality of time, Deepak Chopra offers the experience of visiting the dentist and makes the statement that time passes slowly if you're sitting in the chair compared to the passage of time that the dentist experiences. If you've ever had a root canal or dental surgery, you know that it's true. It seems to take forever. But if you look up at the clock when it's over, you realize that it only took a few minutes! What Chopra and Zukav are both acknowledging is that time has a subjective quality and is different for everyone.

In addition, Gary Zukav offers the following supposition in *The Dancing Wu Li Masters*:

> If, at the quantum level, the flow of time has no meaning, and if consciousness is fundamentally a similar process (a quantum process), and if we can become aware of these processes within ourselves, then it also is conceivable that we can experience timelessness.

Well, I promised to bring it all together for you, so here goes. Did you ever wonder why successful people seem to be able to get more work done than the average person in the same period of time? Is it because they work harder? Well, maybe, but my personal experience is that, for many reasons, successful people do not engage in hard work. The primary reason is, of course, that "if you are doing something you love to do, you'll never do a hard day's work in your life." This bit of wisdom is often passed on from generation to generation, but I believe it's more than that. I believe that modern physics has the answer for us in Einstein's theory of relativity. The secret lies in the fact that time is not rigid, but instead has an elastic quality that can be manipulated. *Time can be controlled and you have the power to control it!*

We already know that thoughts, and I believe emotions, too, become molecules called neuropeptides, and that these molecules can be projected. In order to do that, it means that the molecules have to be able to move. Projection indicates movement. Well, if we bring in some age-old sayings like "your mind is running away with you" or "your mind is racing" or you are "heavy in thought" or "have the weight of the world on your shoulders" and look to Einstein's theory of relativity, you notice some interesting connections. And, if we add in the most important ingredient in success, focus, we also arrive at some interesting questions. What if the ability to focus allowed a person to increase the velocity of his neuropeptides of thought? What if focus allowed us to speed up these thought molecules dramatically in relation to the speed of light? What we would experience is a slowing of time! Isn't it focus that slows time down when you're sitting in the dentist's chair? Isn't it that high concentration of focus that makes any experience seem to be longer, and sometimes much longer, than it actually is? If focus allows us to consciously or unconsciously control time by speeding up these neuropeptide molecules, then can you see the value in doing it consciously in order to help you to attain success?

The other effect of increased velocity toward the speed of light is the effect it has on mass or matter. According to the special theory of relativity, Gary Zukav states:

> When particles travel at velocities that are fast relative to the speed of light, their kinetic energy makes them behave as though they have more mass than at lower velocities. In fact, the special theory of relativity shows that the effective mass of a moving object *does* increase with velocity.

So the speeding up of the neuropeptides of thought through focus not only affects the elasticity of time by stretching it out and giving you more time (relatively), but it also increases the mass or density of those thought molecules, those neuropeptides. In physics, the greater the mass or density of an object, which is simply a collection of molecules, then the greater its magnetic attraction. By increasing the mass of the neuropeptides, their attractive qualities increase. This attractiveness is what pulls success to you, since success must be attracted and not grasped. In reality, the field of attraction around you is not newly created. It was always there. It is simply enhanced and made stronger.

Earlier, I mentioned that man is composed of different energies, i.e., electrical, atomic, magnetic, etc. *Everything and everyone already has a field of attractiveness surrounding them.* We call it "magnetic," but perhaps our century-old definition and understanding of it is much too elementary to reflect its reality. Science tells us that every material thing has a field of attractiveness, which we call magnetic, but I believe that this also applies to the non-material world, the spiritual world. In metaphysics, they refer to this field as a person's, or a thing's "aura," and metaphysically, as the person progresses and experiences higher and higher states of consciousness (awareness), his aura becomes more and more pronounced. This progression into higher states of consciousness, metaphysically, is exactly what you must do to experience the success, physically, that you dream of. *Successful people operate on a higher plane of consciousness than most people do.* They are more aware. They "see" things differently. And because they do, they increase the field of attraction that surrounds them, drawing to themselves the experience of life that they focus upon. What they want finds them, even though it appears to be the other way around. To the uneducated, they seem to be very lucky. Everything they touch turns to gold. We know these people when we meet them because we can sense something special about them. We don't know what it is, but we are drawn to them. The catchphrases that have been invented to describe this phenomenon are that the person has a "magnetic personality," or "animal magnetism." What we sense is that their field of attraction has been enhanced to a point where it is greater than those surrounding them and the person "stands out in the crowd." Quantum physics gives us the knowledge and understanding to scientifically create this phenomenon at will, which will in turn propel us toward our objective, or more precisely, propel our objective toward us.

Now when we look at the catchphrases "heavy in thought" or "the weight of the world on your shoulders," we can be amazed at the innate wisdom contained in many of the age-old sayings. How could they have known long ago that the mass of a thought molecule may actually increase with the increased velocity of concentrated thought and actually get heavier? It's further proof of the fact that there is nothing that isn't known, just unrealized or unexperienced.

More important are the implications that these conclusions have for us in the achievement of success. Successful people can accomplish more than the average person in the same amount of time, because, through focus, they gain control over their relative time and slow it down by increasing the speed of their thought molecules so they have more "time" to get things done! In addition, the increased speed of the neuropeptide molecule creates an enhanced field of attraction that draws to itself that upon which you focus. Success becomes effortless!

Based on these observations, we should create a college course to teach people how to focus because of its importance in actually accomplishing anything. For me, the ability to focus is a natural extension of my obsessive personality. In fact, I have to be careful that I don't focus or obsess too much because it leads to negative results in other areas of my life. I overlook people and events. What I have noticed in the hundreds of successful people whom I have had the good fortune to associate with, is their ability to also have this laser-beam, pinpoint focus. My guess is that for most of them it comes naturally.

If my suppositions are correct, there's a very good chance that your lack of success is due to the fact that your ability to focus is not something that comes naturally. But it can be learned. In Eastern mysticism, people strive for the ability to focus. It is a learned skill, and mystics have been successful in teaching it to their followers for thousands of years. And if they can do it, you can do it.

This revelation alone should be worth all the time, energy, and money that you've put into this book. If I were you reading this, I'd be jumping up and down celebrating the realization that my lack of success wasn't due to my lack of ability. Let me state that again—*your lack of success is not due to your lack of ability!* This revelation supported by modern physics and Eastern mysticism should give you control over your destiny. It should change your life!

POINTS TO PONDER

Time can be controlled, and you have the power to control it!

Everyone and everything already has a field
of attractiveness surrounding them.

Your lack of success is not due to your lack of ability!

Successful people operate on a higher plane
of consciousness than most people do.

30

"The Field" of Dreams

All advancement and progress come through ideas,
not through physical force or mechanical force.
— Ralph Waldo Emerson

The space, the air, the "ether" between us is unseen and appears to be non-existent. And yet it is made up of the same atoms and molecular combinations of hydrogen, oxygen, nitrogen, etc., that our bodies and all other material things are made of. Because we can see our bodies, they are real, but because the molecules in the air do not register in our sight range, they do not "exist" and therefore the space between us appears "empty." This is about as far as we can get from the truth. Science calls this empty space, "the field."

The scientific study of biology has made discoveries to help us understand more about the "space" we live in. We have already discussed that scientists have found that thoughts are transformed into molecules called neuropeptides. Soon they will discover that the same is true for emotions. Emotions are the feelings we get as a result of what we believe, what we think. *Emotions are thoughts on a sensory level.* This discovery explains certain mystical and supernatural phenomena. Did you ever walk into a room and get the uneasy feeling that you've walked into the middle of a conflict? How did you sense that? Very simply, you came in contact with one of the neuropeptide molecules floating in "empty" space produced by one of the people in that room. In fact, you can "sense" what previously happened, even in an empty room. You can sense "trouble in the air." This is much closer to the truth than we have ever known before. The molecules of "trouble," anger, or whatever emotion are truly in the air and able to be intercepted and registered, even with our limited sensory capabilities. On the road to success, this information becomes valuable.

In order to better and more easily become successful, one must understand how the medium of "empty space" operates so that it can be used to one's best advantage. For instance, over 65 percent of the way people communicate is nonverbally accomplished through this medium, and your ability to communicate effectively is essential to becoming successful. But nonverbal communication is only one of the many processes affected by and through empty space. This "ether" is also the corresponding medium that engages in a sympathetic intercourse with other success principles such as visualization, intention and attention, and the power of positive thinking. So knowledge of the operation and properties of empty space gives one an advantage, while lack of knowledge about it relegates one to experience consequences.

That which we call empty space is a communicative medium in which are located the lines of attachment that connect all things. This living medium that we "see" as empty space connects all of us to each other and to everything. As an example, let's look at another life-sustaining medium that we can actually see, and search for clues and similarities to help us understand our medium better. The ocean is another living entity that sustains life and, I believe, is much like the atmospheric medium that we live in. The inhabitants of the ocean, such as fish and shellfish, can breathe in water the same way as you and I breathe in the medium we call empty space or air. However we cannot breathe in each other's medium. For that reason, water registers in our senses and I believe, our empty space, the air, registers in the senses of aquatic life.

The inhabitants of a watery realm are born into it, as we are into ours, and live their entire lives in this medium. Do you think a fish notices the water in which it exists? Do you think a fish can "see" the water that surrounds it? I believe that, like us, the inhabitants of the oceans have become so accustomed to being in the medium that they don't even know it's there. Sure, periodically they can feel it. The ocean has currents, but so does the wind. Fish can see things floating in the water and if you've ever seen the air lit up by a ray of sun, you realize that there are things floating in the air also. In the ocean and on land, there are creatures that live on the solid ground and those that live (fly or swim) above it. The turbulence in both mediums is greater at the top (waves and the jet stream) than it is at the bottom.

In fact, as you go deeper into each medium, the turbulence decreases. Both mediums also communicate to the sense of smell of its inhabitants as well as serving as a communicative medium for other sense data. In the ocean, a shark can smell blood from miles away, just as some animals on land can smell blood from far off. But since our sense of smell is not that acute, a better example for humans is the smell of burning wood or leaves, an odor we can detect from a great distance.

Sensory acknowledgment of vibrations is another similarity in both mediums. Our ears and our brain work together to convert vibrations into sound. Likewise, the ocean's inhabitants can sense vibration, although I don't know that they hear as we understand it.

The mediums also support extrasensory communication. Telepathic communications between humans and between animals is a generally accepted possibility, even though at this point we are not in full command of its techniques. Likewise, to watch a large school of fish change directions almost simultaneously makes a fair argument for extrasensory communication among aquatic creatures. But in our world, telepathy is often explained away as hunches or intuition. *Consciousness of space as a "living" medium is not a prerequisite for its existence*. Like the law of gravity, it works every time, even on those who know not of its existence!

This knowledge of space as a communicative medium is very valuable in your quest for success because, as previously stated 65 percent of communication between people is nonverbal and delivered through this space. In fact, even the vibrations that the ear and brain convert to sound must first travel through this medium. In sales, we teach people that when they are making a sales presentation the buyer is only faintly listening to the words that they are saying. The simple proof of that fact is that the buyer will be able to repeat very little of what the salesperson has just told him. What the buyer is doing, consciously or unconsciously, is "looking" for the truth. I tell them that the buyer is "listening with his eyes." What the buyer is trying to determine are the ethics and motivations of the salesperson. This is communicated through nonverbal means.

Many salespeople think that the purpose of a sales presentation is to convince the buyer that he needs that product. The reality is that if the buyer gave the salesperson an appointment, he already has determined, on some level, that he needs the product. This is especially true in the insurance business. The sale is already made. All the salesperson can do from that point on is lose the sale. If you understand that premise, then you understand why the buyer is only vaguely listening to the salesperson's words. The buyer knows that the salesperson has all the knowledge that the buyer needs to make an intelligent decision. So the buyer is "looking" and "listening" for the clues that will determine if he will buy the product from *that* salesperson and *that* company because, invariably, the buyer will ultimately purchase that product from someone. The buyer is looking for the intuitive sensory data communicated through nonverbal means. Body language, tone of voice, enthusiasm for the product, the initial handshake, and attitude are all more important to the buyer's decision than the words that the salesperson is saying. And what's more important than all of those is the "feeling" that the buyer "gets" about the salesperson. This "feeling" is communicated to the buyer by the salesperson's molecules of thought and emotion that travel through "empty space." Ultimately the buyer buys the salesperson because he has already determined that he needs the product, even if he has made that determination subconsciously. Nonverbal sensory feedback will help the buyer to determine how well the product performs, how price-competitive it is in the marketplace, and if the salesperson is there to help him or just there to make money. Once the buyer is satisfied that all three points are positive, he will then sign on the dotted line. Since *the ability to sell is part of every success*, in some way, shape, or form, our knowledge of buyer thoughts and feelings gives us the means to more quickly and definitively experience our dreams of financial independence.

The proof of space not being empty came to modern physics as a result of a phenomenon that could leave no other conclusion. The phenomenon was Feynman's vacuum diagram. In a vacuum, all of the air is removed. It's really empty. But even in a vacuum, they found that subatomic particles came into being from "nowhere" and then vanished again into "nowhere." Now, we know that this is not possible because, like the age-old saying tells us, "You can't get something from nothing" (or can you?). So where did these particles come from? And where did they go? Here are some interesting observations made by some world-renowned physicists and thinkers.

In *The Tao of Physics*, Fritjof Capra writes:

The distinction between matter and energy and empty space finally had to be abandoned when it became evident that virtual particles can come into being spontaneously out of the void, and vanish again into the void, without any nucleon, or other strongly interacting particle being present. Here is a vacuum diagram for such a process: three particles—a proton (p), and antiproton ($\bar{p}$), and a pion (π)— are formed out of nothing and disappear again into the vacuum.

According to field theory, events of that kind happen all the time. The vacuum is far from empty. On the contrary, it contains an unlimited number of particles which come into being and vanish without end.

Commenting about the same phenomenon of empty space not being empty, Gary Zukav writes in *The Dancing Wu Li Masters*:

> In this diagram no world line leads up to the interaction and no world line leads away from it. It just happens. It happens literally out of nowhere, for no apparent reason, and without any apparent cause. Where there was *no-thing*, suddenly, in a flash of spontaneous existence, there are three particles which vanish without a trace. This type of Feynman diagram is called a "vacuum diagram." That is because the interactions happen in a vacuum. A "vacuum" as we normally construe it, is a space that is entirely empty. Vacuum diagrams, however, graphically demonstrate that there is no such thing. From "empty space" comes something, and then that something disappears again into "empty space." In the subatomic realm, a vacuum is obviously not empty.

Michael Talbot relates an interesting extension of this discovery in physics in *The Holographic Universe*:

> Bohm's view that space is as real and rich with process as the matter that moves through it reaches full maturity in his ideas about the implicate sea of energy. Matter does not exist independently from the sea, from so-called empty space. It is part of that space.

To continue, Talbot says:

> According to our current understanding of physics, every region of space is awash with different kinds of fields composed of waves of varying lengths. Each wave always has at least some energy. When

physicists calculate the minimum amount of energy a wave can possess, they find that *every cubic centimeter of empty space contains more energy than the total energy of all the matter in the known universe!*

To understand this quote fully, you have to remember Einstein's theory of relativity. In it he says that $E=mc^2$, or energy equals matter times the speed of light squared. Energy and matter are the same thing in different form, like water vapor and water. In fact, in physics, it's called a matter-energy continuum, like the space-time continuum, because they are so closely related that they are inseparable. So what the quote is saying is that every cubic centimeter of empty space has more matter-energy than all the *visible* matter-energy of the universe combined. In fact, it contains so much matter-energy that this quote came under Michael Talbot's section titled, "The Energy of a Trillion Atomic Bombs in Every Cubic Centimeter of Space."

Not only is empty space not empty, but conversely, it is full of more material than all the material things we can see combined. As it turns out, this field of empty space plays a greater role in the events that occur in our world than we have ever imagined. Now that we know this, we can make use of its properties to produce our desired results. In the words of the astronomer Fred Hoyle, we now know that:

> The field exists always and everywhere; it can never be removed. It is the carrier of all material phenomena. It is the "void" out of which the proton creates the pi-mesons. Being and fading of particles are merely forms of motion in the field.

All of this information led me to the realization that the empty space or the "field" must be similar to the earth in my vegetable garden. If you'll remember, my garden has many possibilities and always produces results. If I take an active role by planting a seed, the results will be desirable. Conversely, my inaction produces weeds, which are undesirable. My garden, the field, really doesn't care what it produces. It makes no judgments. It just performs. That's where you and I come in. *We are the creative force that causes, by action or inaction, all things to happen.*

When we feel an emotion or think a thought, the neuropeptide molecule we launch is the seed that we, consciously or unconsciously, "plant" in the field. This is called having the *intention*. Of course, after you plant the seed, you must give it *attention*. It needs to be nourished, nurtured, and cared for to reach its full maturity, fruition, or realization. But the seed will grow even if you do nothing. It may not be as fully developed as if it was cared for, but every seed produces a result. That's why we need to be careful about the emotions we feel and the thoughts we think.

That's why positive thinking has such power. When Norman Vincent Peale wrote *The Power of Positive Thinking*, he didn't really know why it worked; he just knew it worked. Through modern physics, we now know why. Through modern physics, we find that we can control the experiences of our lives (the harvest), by controlling the thoughts and the emotions that we allow ourselves to demonstrate (the seeds).

Michael Talbot explains the reason for this to us in an excerpt from *The Holographic Universe*. In it, he speaks about the work of the great physicist David Bohm:

> Bohm uses his idea of the implicate order, the deeper and nonlocal level of existence from which our entire universe springs, to echo the sentiment: "Every action starts from an intention in the implicate order. The imagination is already the creation of the form; it already has the intention and the germs of all the movements needed to carry it out. And it affects the body and so on, so that as creation takes place in that way from the subtler levels of the implicate order, it goes through them until it manifests in the explicate." In other words, in the implicate order, as in the brain itself, imagination and reality are ultimately indistinguishable, and it should therefore come as no surprise to us that images in the mind can ultimately manifest as realities in the physical body.

This is why visualization, or the imagination of reality, works. The brain cannot tell the difference between a real experience and an imagined one. If you repeatedly visualize an imagined event, it will become reality. This is the fundamental tenet behind psychosomatic illnesses. People imagine repeatedly that they develop the symptoms or reality of the illness even though there is no medical cause. This also may explain the "phantom limb" mystery where an amputee still feels the presence of the amputated limb. Likewise, it explains the "placebo effect" whereby patients are given sugar pills to treat their disease while being told by the doctor that it is a powerful new medicine that will cure them. The positive results of the patients believing that it is a powerful new drug that will cure them has been documented countless times. That leads us to an important ingredient in the visualization process. Along with the intention, you must have the belief. If the intention is the seed in sculpting your reality, then belief can be likened to the sun and the rain that nourishes the seed's development. The more sun and rain that the seed receives, the more it develops toward its maximum potential. Likewise, *the more the intention is nourished by belief, the greater it will manifest itself in reality*. So what you have are varying degrees of success determined, ultimately, by you.

Belief varies to the degree that we are emotionally sold on the possibility of the proposal. When you combine enthusiasm with belief and intention, you get constructive results. And the more enthusiasm, or emotion, you put behind the belief, the more you experience the reality of your visualization. This has serious implications for us not only personally, but also professionally as sales managers, teachers, parents, and any other position of authority where our intentions and beliefs enter into the equation. The effect of enthusiasm was illustrated in *The Holographic Universe* by Michael Talbot:

> Another factor is the attitude the doctor conveys when he prescribes the placebo. Dr. David Sobel, a placebo specialist at Kaiser Hospital, California, relates the story of a doctor treating an asthma patient who was having an unusually difficult time keeping his bronchial tubes open. The doctor ordered a sample of a potent new medicine from a pharmaceutical company and gave it to the man. Within minutes the man showed spectacular improvement and breathed more easily.

> However, the next time he had an attack, the doctor decided to see what would happen if he gave the man a placebo. This time, the man complained that there must be something wrong with the prescription because it didn't completely eliminate his breathing difficulty. This convinced the doctor that the sample drug was indeed a potent new asthma medication—until he received a letter from the pharmaceutical company informing him that instead of the new drug, they had accidentally sent him a placebo! Apparently, it was the doctor's unwitting enthusiasm for the first placebo and not the second that accounted for the discrepancy.

This verifies for us the need to avoid negative people because their intentions and beliefs are destructive. *The negative intentions and beliefs of other people have the effect of canceling our positive intentions and beliefs.* Unfortunately, sometimes these negative people are our bosses, our spouses, or members of our families. That's why success teachers often tell us to keep our dreams and aspirations to ourselves. If no one knows the positive intentions we are trying to experience, then they won't unwittingly have the opportunity to plant the negative seeds that will result in a canceling out of our positive intentions. This knowledge is one of the reasons I am successful. Early in my sales career, my sales manager, Fred Hill, advised me to avoid negativity at all costs. He said that if I was present when other salespeople were talking negatively that I should run—not walk, but run—to the nearest exit!

Perhaps you will want to read this chapter again because there is so much knowledge available in this section that you will need in your quest for financial independence. The realization that empty space is a fertile field, that our thoughts and emotions plant seeds in it that bear fruit, the concepts of intention and attention, the power of visualization, and the effect negative people have on our dreams are crucial to our pursuit of success.

More interesting is the two-thousand-year-old echo of the teachings of the Eastern mystics in these realizations of modern physics. The Eastern philosophers concept of "the void" as the fertile field from which "all that is" develops, and the Buddhist teaching that says "Form is emptiness, and emptiness is form," as well as many others, bring the wisdom of the East and the science of the West together from different beginnings, to define for us the fundamental principles in the science of success.

POINTS TO PONDER

Emotions are thoughts on a sensory level.

The ability to sell is part of every success.

Consciousness of space as a "living" medium is
not a prerequisite for its existence.

We are the creative forces that cause,
by action or inaction, all things to happen!

The more the intention is nourished by belief,
the greater it will manifest itself in reality.

The negative intentions and beliefs of other people have the effect of
canceling our positive intentions and beliefs.

31

No Man Is an Island

**For everything there is a season,
and a time for every matter under Heaven.**

— Solomon, Ecclesiastes 3:1

All things are already complete in oneself.

— Mencius

One of the most interesting discoveries of modern physics is that nothing in the universe stands alone. Everything is interconnected. Scientists studying chaos, which is the relationship of seemingly unrelated, random events, have found that the flutter of a butterfly's wings in India can result in a twister in Kansas! In fact, they have found that *there is no chaos. There are no random, unrelated acts.* All that occurs affects all that is, which then becomes all that was. The scientific principle behind this states that if you gain enough distance and perspective from the seeming chaos, you will discover a perfectly functioning system (order). Since there are no random, unrelated acts, *there are no accidents.* **There is no luck!**

How many times have you heard people say that in order to become successful, you have to be a little lucky? The unsuccessful say it all the time as a seeming rationalization of why they have not achieved their dreams. Often when people are not successful, they will blame any number of people or things outside of themselves for their lack of success. They do this so they can argue the point and convince themselves that it's not their fault. By virtue of its nature, chance is unpredictable and uncontrollable. If luck or chance is a factor, then it's not their fault. They're not responsible for their lack of success!

Surprisingly, it's not only the unsuccessful that point to chance as an explanation, but also those who are successful often refer to chance as a necessary ingredient in the formula for success. I have found this to be true in the success interviews I've conducted and in those I've heard on radio and television, as well as in the personal collaborations I've had with successful people over the years. Knowing intuitively that this wasn't true but not being able to substantiate it created a very perplexing situation for me in my early years as a trainer. How could I train people to become successful if luck was a factor? That would mean, like the unsuccessful argue, that all the sage advice in the world would be meaningless unless you were also lucky. If chance was a factor, there could be no such thing as a success trainer. There also could be no such thing as a science of success!

When I began to study quantum physics in order to substantiate and solidify each step I used to become successful so that I could communicate that knowledge to those I trained, the answers to my questions became clear. The first answer I realized was that there aren't very many people who study success as a science, and many of those who do are not employed in the corporate world where the effectiveness of their training is subject to constant scrutiny. Therefore most trainers do not need to understand success completely.

Second, successful people do not need to substantiate why they are successful, unless teaching success is their life's work. They don't need to define and explain the steps they took to become successful. Some of the things they did correctly were intuitive or already part of their personality, as the ability to focus was easier for me because of my obsessive personality. Thus the unexplainable was explained by using the word "lucky."

Third, the humility that is evident almost unanimously in successful people is a factor. Successful people do not like to think of themselves as special, i.e., better or smarter than anyone else. These are unwanted labels that society forces upon them. If you have money, you're smart, even if you're dumb. And people expect you to prove it all the time! Successful people are also sensitive to the fact that those who aren't successful sometimes feel "less than" in their presence. This makes them very uncomfortable, and they alleviate that tension and empathize with people by saying one needs to be a little lucky, even though they know, consciously or unconsciously, that it isn't true. And besides that, they really do know that there is nothing special about them, physically, mentally or otherwise. They just "see" things differently. They operate from a different vantage point than most people. They understand that no one becomes successful by himself, and that everything everyone does has an effect on everything and everyone else to a greater or lesser degree, in some way or another.

Understanding the interconnectedness of all things is essential to lasting success. Again, the example of the child's crib mobile will serve to illustrate how this works. If we had a mobile with connecting threads so thin that we were unable to see them, then it would appear that the objects on the mobile were unconnected and suspended in midair. Just because we cannot see the lines that connect them does not negate the fact that if you touch one object, they all move and adjust their positions to keep a "balance." Physics, astronomy, etc., are discovering that the universe works in exactly the same way. In psychology they speak of the interrelatedness of people. It is becoming increasingly clear to all fields of science that everything is connected to everything else, even though, we often cannot "see" the lines of attachment. Unfortunately, as sense-focused beings, we are taught that "seeing is believing," when more often than not "believing is seeing."

We look to modern science to validate the uniformity and connection of all things in the universe. In *The Tao of Physics*, Fritjof Capra writes about the interconnection of all things:

> Thus modern physics shows us once again—and this time at the macroscopic level—that material objects are not distinct entities, but are inseparably linked to their environment; that their properties can only be understood in terms of their interaction with the rest of the world. According to Mach's principle, this interaction reaches out to the universe at large, to the distant stars and galaxies. The basic unity of the cosmos manifests itself, therefore, not only in the world of the very small but also in the world of the very large; a fact which is increasingly acknowledged in modern astrophysics and cosmology.

Likewise, Michael Talbot relates in *The Holographic Universe* about the work of the famous physicist David Bohm:

> ...he believes that dividing the universe up into living and nonliving things also has no meaning. Animate and inanimate matter are inseparably interwoven, and life, too, is enfolded throughout the totality of the universe. Even a rock is in some way alive, says Bohm, for life and intelligence are present not only in all of matter, but in "energy," "space," "time," "the fabric of the entire universe," and everything else we abstract out of the holomovement and mistakenly view as separate things.

The insight that everything is inseparably linked leads us, in turn, to examine randomness, chance, luck, or whatever you want to call it, by again looking to the world of physics for some clues. The interrelatedness of everything is the first clue that implies that there are no chance occurrences, and we've already seen how many fields of modern science corroborate this principle. But how can there be no random events? How can tossing a pair of dice, spinning a roulette wheel, or dropping a plate have order to them? (The presence of order eliminates the possibility of randomness, or disorder.) That would mean that every time you dropped a set of pick-up sticks, the pattern that was formed by the dropped sticks would be "predictable."

A newspaper article led me to the conclusion of complete order in the universe. The article said that a certain individual was banned from playing roulette in all of the casinos in Atlantic City and Las Vegas. The reason he was banned was because he developed a system for winning at roulette that obviously worked. Now I've been to enough casinos, and played enough roulette, and read enough gambling books in my lifetime to know that the only way to predict the outcome of a roulette wheel would be if there was faulty equipment, or if the same person kept spinning the wheel with the same force. However, I'm sure the casinos took these two possibilities into account and made the appropriate adjustments to protect themselves before they banned him from *all* the casinos. It was the ban from all of the casinos that got my attention. That meant they had concluded that he could predict the outcome of *any* roulette wheel, *anywhere*! So much for what I thought I "knew." So much for the randomness of a roulette wheel.

David Bohm worked with a fellow physicist named Yakir Aharonov at Bristol University in England to come up with an interesting example of complete order in the universe. In *The Holographic Universe*, Michael Talbot relates that:

> Bohm and Aharonov found that under the right circumstances an electron is able to "feel" the presence of a magnetic field that is in a region where there is zero probability of finding the electron.... As Bohm delved more deeply into the matter, he realized there were also different degrees of order. Some things were much more ordered than other things, and this implied that there was, perhaps, no end to the hierarchies of order that existed in the universe. From this it occurred to Bohm that maybe things that we perceive as

disordered aren't disordered at all. Perhaps their order is of such an "indefinitely high degree" that they only appear to us as random (interestingly, mathematicians are unable to prove randomness, and although some sequences of numbers are categorized as random, these are only educated guesses).

What further convinced Bohm that he was correct was a demonstration he saw on television. In this demonstration, a drop of ink was floating, motionlessly, on top of a jar of glycerin. When the glycerin was stirred in one direction, the droplet of ink slowly "disappeared" into the glycerin and was no longer visible. But when they stirred the glycerin in the opposite direction, they made an interesting discovery. As the number of times they stirred the glycerin counterclockwise began to approach the number of times they had, originally, stirred it clockwise, a faint line of ink began to appear, which eventually re-formed the original droplet of ink.

If you did this experiment with three drops of ink, you would get the same result. If you put a droplet of ink on top of the glycerin and turned it once, the ink would "disappear" into the glycerin. If you then put in a second drop of ink and turned it again in the same direction, the second drop would disappear and then, finally, if you did the same thing with a third drop of ink, it would disappear also.

If you now reversed the direction of the stirring, you would notice something pretty amazing. After turning the glycerin one revolution in the opposite direction, one droplet of ink would reappear, after the second turn, a second droplet, and after the third turn, the third drop of ink would reappear. In response to this phenomenon, the physicist David Bohm wrote:

> This immediately struck me as very relevant to the question of order, since, when the ink drop was spread out, it still had a "hidden" order that was revealed when it was reconstituted. On the other hand, in our usual language, we would say that the ink was in a state of "disorder" when it was diffused through the glycerin. This led me to see that new notions of order must be involved here.

These scientific experiments confirmed my belief that there is no chance; there is no luck. *There is order to every outcome in the universe, and it is predictable.* Just because we cannot uncover the pattern of order does not mean that it doesn't exist. Eastern mystics have been espousing this for thousands of years. Here again, Western science, Eastern mysticism, and the science of success come together from different points of origin to meet in a pyramidlike convergence that points to the truth. That truth is this: *When it comes to cause and effect in your life, consciously or unconsciously, you cause your effects!* You are in control of your destiny; you are the master of your fate. There is no chance. There is no luck!

POINTS TO PONDER

There is order to every outcome in the universe and it is predictable.

Understanding the interconnectedness of all things
is essential to lasting success.

The study of chaos reveals that there are no random, unrelated acts.
There are no accidents. There is no luck!

When it comes to cause and effect in your life,
consciously or unconsciously, you cause your effects!

32

"I'M OKAY, YOU'RE OKAY"

Therefore the sage places himself in the background,
but finds himself in the foreground.

— Lao Tzu

This chapter title was the slogan for the intellectual awareness movement of the '60s and '70s. Little did they know that they were
espousing two of the major concepts of modern physics—perfection and
unity. The "living" air, the ether, the empty space of which we have spoken
connects all things to create unity and perfection in the universe. This unity
and perfection is what the Eastern mystics call enlightenment. In *The Tao of
Physics*, Fritjof Capra writes:

> ...quantum theory has made it clear that a subatomic particle can
> only be understood as a manifestation of the interaction between
> various processes of measurement. It is not an isolated object but
> rather an occurrence, or event, which interconnects with other
> events in a particular way. In the words of Heisenberg, "...one
> has divided the world not into different groups of objects but into
> different groups of connections.... What can be distinguished is the
> kind of connections which is primarily important in a certain
> phenomenon.... The world thus appears as a complicated tissue of
> events, in which connections of different kinds alternate or overlap
> or combine and thereby determine the texture of the whole.

In *The Holographic Universe*, Michael Talbot relates:

Most mind-boggling of all are Bohm's fully developed ideas about
wholeness. Because everything in the cosmos is made out of the
seamless holographic fabric of the implicate order, he believes it is

as meaningless to view the universe as composed of parts as it is to view the different geysers in a fountain as separate from the water out of which they flow…. Dividing reality up into parts and then naming those parts is always arbitrary, a product of convention, because subatomic particles, and everything else in the universe, are no more separate from one another than different patterns in an ornate carpet.

This takes us beyond the interconnectedness of everything to the interdependence of everything. The unity of the universe means that everything is one, and we are part of that oneness. An example can be displayed by using our own body as a model. If our body represented the entire universe, upon examination we would find that parts of the body seem to have no connection at all to each other, for instance, your feet and your teeth. However, we know that at a deeper level, they are not only connected but interdependent on each other, part of the one body. No cell lives in isolation; no man is an island. We are all part of the one body, the universe. This is unity.

One of the interesting aspects of unity is that every part reflects the whole. In the movie *Jurassic Park*, the scientists recreate the dinosaurs by extracting their DNA from fossilized mosquitoes. I thoroughly believe this is possible. In our own bodies, every cell is stamped with our DNA. It is the great blueprint from which we are constructed. Every cell in our body reflects the whole. Every "piece" of the universe reflects the whole.

An interesting example of this occurs in the field of holography. A hologram is a three-dimensional image produced by using lasers in the photographic process. A three-dimensional holographic image looks real, but if you try to touch it, you find that it isn't there. It's a virtual image of the flat photographic film that seems to have height and width, but it is merely a man-made mirage. What is really interesting is that if the holographic film is cut up into a thousand pieces and you then take one of those thousand pieces and again pass a laser beam through it, the original hologram comes back *in its entirety!*

Amazing stuff, but it's no more amazing than cloning a man or a dinosaur from a DNA molecule. They've already done it with sheep! Physics tells us that the whole universe is this way. Everything is the universe, and within each thing, lies the whole thing. This truth is reflected not only in street slang when they say "Everything is everything," but also in the arts through a poem by William Blake:

To see a World in a Grain of Sand
And Heaven in a Wild Flower,
Hold Infinity in the Palm of your Hand
And Eternity in an Hour.

For those of us on the road to success, the realization that within each thing lies the whole reflects a previously stated truth. You first have to be a success on the inside before you can be a success on the outside. Success is not just financial independence, but rather financial independence is a reflection of the successful person. *Every area of your life is crucial in the pursuit of long-lasting success.* You can't be a child molester and expect to find lasting success. Even if you make a lot of money, you'll never keep it. Somehow you will find a way to self-destruct because you know, and the universe knows, that you don't deserve it.

I'm not saying that we have to be perfect, but that we have to be the best we can be in every area of our lives. "A chain is only as strong as its weakest link" applies to success also. There are varying degrees of success, but whichever degree we choose to achieve, its longevity will be determined by how unilaterally successful we are in our entire lives. This is the unity of success, which reflects the unity of the universe as confirmed by modern physics and by Eastern mysticism.

One of the other aspects of unity is perfection. It pervades the entire universe, and a prime example of that is that nature is already perfect. If we look at nature, we see patterns of perfection. How tall can a tree grow? As tall as it is able. Everything in nature develops to its fullest despite our judgments to the contrary, which is where all of this gets to be kind of humorous. *We humans constantly strive to make things better when they're already perfect to begin with.* Every technological advance carries negative consequences that make life better for some and worse for others. We've invented the power to completely destroy ourselves through nuclear technology. We have epidemics of disease from medically treated mutated viruses that kill thousands if not millions. Even our own hospital systems have become a major cause of illness. Where did it begin? Where does it end? *Unknown to man is the consequence of fooling around with perfection. That consequence is to cause imperfection!* For instance, in the sales profession, there comes a point in the perfecting of a sales presentation where it loses its effectiveness. It is simply fixed so well that it doesn't work anymore! In this process, once you pass the point of perfection, you cause imperfection.

But to return to the perfection aspect of unity, *The Dancing Wu Li Masters* by Gary Zukav tells us:

> A vital aspect of the enlightened state is the experience of an all-pervading unity. "This" and "that" no longer are separate entities. They are different forms of the same thing. Everything is a <u>manifestation</u>. It is not possible to answer the question "manifestation of <u>what</u>?" Because the "what" is that which is beyond words, beyond concept, beyond form, beyond even space and time. Everything is a manifestation of that which is. That which is, is. Beyond these words lies the experience; the experience of that which is.
>
> The forms through which that which is manifests itself are each and every one of them perfect. *We* are manifestations of that which is. *Everything* is a manifestation of that which is. Everything and everybody is exactly and perfectly what it is....
>
> We might say, "God's in his heaven and all's well with the world," except that according to the enlightened view, the world couldn't be any other way. It is neither well nor not well. It simply is what it is. What it is is perfectly what it is. It couldn't be anything else. It is perfect. I am perfect. I am exactly and perfectly who I am. You are perfect. You are exactly and perfectly who you are.
>
> If you are a happy person, then that is what you perfectly are—a happy person. If you are an unhappy person, then <u>that</u> is what you perfectly are—an unhappy person. If you are a person who is changing, then <u>that</u> is what you perfectly are—a person who is changing. That which is is that which is. That which is not is that which is. There is nothing other than that which is. Everything is that which is. We are a part of that which is. In fact, we are that which is.

Zukav goes on to say that if you substitute the words "subatomic particles" for "people" in this concept, then you have a pretty good approximation of the conceptual dynamics of particle physics. In other words, this is the way it is in the subatomic world! It's not so important that you get it as it is that it gets you. The mind expanded by a new idea can never again regain its original shape. If the ideas presented in this book cause you to think, you will be miles ahead of the average person, who, for the most part, thinks very little. Most people go through life as victims, reacting to the circumstances that are delivered to them on a daily basis.

If they would just think, they could exert whatever control they personally had and have their lives unfold in more of a planned manner. But the obvious and the simple are usually the most difficult to comprehend.

This pervading perfection that is present throughout the universe verifies a point made earlier in this book. We all constantly strive to become better when we came into this world perfect to begin with. You already are everything you need to be. What's holding you back are the shackles and chains of conditioning and programming that you picked up along the way. Since you were born perfect, *failure for you is a learned trait.* It's been passed on from generation to generation, but it is not part of your DNA, so you can do something about it. You can make the decision that, after generations of failure in your lineage, it ends with you. The buck stops here!

The other point this concept of modern physics validates for us is that you were destined to succeed. Like the tree that grows as tall as it is able, you were born into this world already predisposed to develop to your own personal potential. It comes with the rest of the package. It is part of the oneness and unity and perfection that permeates the entire universe. This predisposed and perfect ability to develop to one's own full potential is a great definition of success for each of us. This is your birthright. This is your destiny. No longer allow circumstances and people to cheat you out of what you are naturally born to realize—***you are success!***

POINTS TO PONDER

Every area of your life is crucial to long-lasting success.

We humans constantly strive to make things better
when they're already perfect to begin with.

The consequence of fooling around with perfection is imperfection.

Failure for you is a learned trait.

You are success!

33

Who Said the Dice Weren't Fixed?

**When the sun is at noon, it is setting;
when there is life, there is death.**

— The Logicians, circa 350 B.C.

Before we get too far away from the discovery of predestined perfection by modern physics, consider one more point. The predestined ability to realize one's full potential negates the necessity for goal setting, or certainly negates, at least, the necessity for the goal-setting techniques that are being taught today. *If we allow nature to take its course, then we will reach our maximum potential.* It's already a done deal. To do otherwise is like setting goals for our birth after we're born! If we are all each reflected in the other, if we are all part of the same oneness, this perfect unity that pervades the universe, then what other part of this oneness sets goals or needs to engage in goal-setting strategies?

Does a tree set a goal for how high it will grow? No, it naturally grows as high as it can. So it is with us. The only thing goal setting will accomplish for each of us, for the most part, is to let us focus on becoming less than we are destined to become. Because of our poor self-image, our ego, conditioning, environment, and programming, *we will choose goals that will be below our natural-born potential.* We will underestimate ourselves. The worst thing we can do under these circumstances is to succeed—to succeed in spending a lifetime achieving our goals and ultimately accomplishing mediocrity, less than we were predestined to accomplish!

The reason why we don't naturally reach our full potential is explained by modern physics in the second law of thermodynamics. Physicists call it the tendency of everything, without intervention, to "entropy" or become disordered. In *A Brief History of Time*, Stephen Hawking says:

A precise statement of this idea is known as the second law of thermodynamics. It states that the entropy of an isolated system always increases, and that when two systems are joined together, the entropy of the entire system is greater than the sum of the entropies of the individual systems.... It is a matter of common experience that disorder will tend to increase if things are left to themselves. (One has only to stop making repairs around the house to see that!) One can create order out of disorder (for example one can paint the house), but that requires expenditure of effort or energy and so decreases the amount of ordered energy available.

What this law of physics says is that without directed effort to cause the contrary, everything will have a tendency toward disorder, which we see as a negative result. For example, if we don't make an effort to nourish our body, we die. However, before we go any further, it's wise to realize, based on everything we've learned through physics about the universe, that in this perfect system there can be no such thing as disorder. If everything is already perfectly "that which is," then entropy is part of "that which is" and is likewise perfect. In other words, the disorder is order. The reason we run into trouble is because we humans have a need to separate everything into opposites.

This is part of the paradox of reality (it's a paradox for us, not for nature). Since every particle has its antiparticle that it *needs* to exist, and since every "this" has a "that" which it *needs* to exist; physics tells us that they are complementary, not opposite. This is true reality. It is reflected in the *Yin* and the *Yang* of Eastern philosophy. *Seeing things as opposites is merely a bad habit, the constant repetition of which has created a need to separate everything into positive and negative, good and bad.*

A good analogy of this can be obtained by looking at a coin. A coin has two sides—heads and tails. Neither one of them is better than the other. Neither one of them is good or bad. They are both needed to complete the coin. However, if we decide one day that heads is the preferable outcome, that heads is good, then we have decided that tails is bad. And now we have opposites, when the reality is that heads and tails are complementary sides of the same coin, and one cannot exist without the other. This concept alone has a wealth of knowledge for those of us on the road to success. If we could break the bad habit of seeing everything as opposites, then we would simply see "that which is." Our vision would clear, the clouds would lift from our eyes, the "Veil of Maya" the Eastern mystics speak of would be removed, and we would "see" the path to our ultimate potential simply and clearly before us.

But going back to the idea of the tendency of everything to entropy or become disordered without intervention, there are a few lessons, courtesy of modern physics, which validate many of the principles I have learned in my pursuit to further the science of success. One of the interesting points that can be deduced from the second law of thermodynamics is one already briefly discussed. It's that we see disorder as a negative result, an undesirable result. Stephen Hawking uses the example of how a house "entropies" when we stop making repairs. In my garden, it means that if I don't make a direct effort to plant a tomato seed, I get weeds. It also means that *if we don't make a direct effort to have positive thoughts, we will have negative thoughts*. If we don't make a direct effort to be successful, we will be failures. If we don't make a direct effort to live, we will die. This is also why cold (negative) displaces heat (positive). It is the law of physics that gives credence to the wise old saying, "You're either busy growing or you're busy dying."

This leads us to an interesting set of questions. In what ways are you growing? What direct efforts are you putting into growth? On your road to success, what kind of books have you read? And how many? What kind of tapes have you listened to? And how many? If you don't make an effort beyond that made by others, how can you ever hope to experience anything other than the disorder in life that they experience? If you don't make a direct effort to expand your mind so that you can think on a higher level, how can you ever expect to *think differently* than the average person and achieve above-average results? This law of physics and the resultant questions amplify the call to change for those of us who wish to experience success. If you don't change, then, "If you keep doing what you're doing, you'll keep getting what you're getting."

As if the knowledge that we have a tendency toward the negative if we don't make a direct effort to be positive wasn't enough, the law of entropy also demonstrates, through physics, the danger of associating with negative people. Remember, the law, according to Stephen Hawking, says, "The entropy of a system [you are a system] always increases, and that when two systems are joined together, the entropy of the entire system is greater than the sum of the entropies of the individual systems." In other words, for our purposes, the law of entropy says that when one negative person comes in contact with another negative person, the combined destructive power of their negativity is greater than the sum of the destructive power of each individual's negativity.

This is why, if we want to be successful, we have to avoid negative people at all costs, whoever they are. This may sound like a harsh truth, but it is crucially important for those of us who have yet to achieve financial success. The reason for this is until we have gained power over our negativity, of which success is the acid test, then we have a tendency toward the negative. That tendency is enough to destroy our efforts when it is amplified by the presence of other negative systems (people). I have to conclude by this law, that if a positive system comes in contact with a negative system, we get a "zero" effect, and we want to accomplish more than "zero." Even if we make our best effort to be positive, the contact with negative people will destroy our efforts.

Also in the equation, which gives further credence to the destructive power negative people will have on your dreams, is the fact that the sum of two negatives is more than two. Even if you are successful, and especially if you're not, the sum of their negativity and your tendency to be negative will completely overpower whatever positives you've been able to muster. And if you are in contact with two other negative systems (people), you're a dead man! (Affluently speaking, of course).

This second law of thermodynamics also validates what I have learned about personal energy, or the need for each of us to be conservation-minded when it comes to the ways we expend our energy. As Stephen Hawking said, "One can create order out of disorder...but that requires expenditure of effort or energy, and so decreases the amount of ordered energy available." Sound familiar? Well, now we have physics telling us the same thing. There is only so much "ordered energy" available that we can use to create order out of disorder, to create success out of mediocrity.

So how do you spend your energy? What are the energy drains of your life? Based on this law, might it be a good idea to rethink the amount of time and effort that you spend watching TV, being a sports fanatic, engaging in leisure-time activities, or even reexamining the activities you engage in for socially accepted or ego-satisfying reasons? *The achievement of success requires the commitment of all available energy other than that needed to satisfy the bare necessities!* If you want success, that's what it takes.

To sum up the points made in this chapter: first, setting goals will tend to result in achieving less success than we are capable of achieving.

Second, if we don't make a *direct* effort to experience success, the second law of thermodynamics demands that we experience failure. Third, *any* contact with negative people will result in dilution, if not complete destruction, of all our efforts to experience financial success. These are the principles of the science of success, courtesy of modern physics, that we "know" to be true. If you use these insights, you can change your life and experience your dreams.

POINTS TO PONDER

If we allow nature to take its course, then we will
reach our maximum potential.

Entropy states that if we don't make a direct effort
to have positive thoughts, we will have negative thoughts.

We choose goals that are far below our natural-born potential.

Seeing things as opposites is merely a bad habit,
the constant repetition of which has created the need
to separate everything into positive and negative, good and bad.

The achievement of success requires the commitment
of all available energy other than that needed
to satisfy the bare necessities!

34

SEEING IS BELIEVING?

**Experience is not what happens to a man.
It is what a man does with what happens to him.**

— Aldous Huxley

**Great is the Way of the sage!
He goes over the old so as to find out what is new.**

— The Doctrine of the Mean, circa 200 B.C.

Earlier, I related the idea that success lies in what you "see." *In the achievement of success, your point of view is everything. As you perceive, so shall you achieve.* In my many years of activity in the business world, I have seen some people crumble over an incident in their lives, and I've seen other people prosper when that same incident occurred in their lives. Much of the difference had to do with whether or not people saw themselves as victims, like a passenger in the car of life instead of the driver. Somewhere along the way, we each individually adopted the belief that we can make life and the universe bend to our will. And when it doesn't, we're the ones who get bent out of shape.

About fifteen years ago, I heard a truth that had a dramatic effect on my life. The truth was that "Life unfolds as it should, despite what we think." Life happens to everyone—the different interpretations of life's happenings, how we each individually "see" it, determines the difference, ultimately, in each of our experiences. In the words of Charles Swindoll, "I am convinced that life is 10 percent what happens to me, and 90 percent how I react to it." This same principle is echoed by John Homer Miller: "Your living is determined not so much by what life brings to you as by the attitude you bring to life; not so much by what happens as by the way your mind looks at what happens." So how do you see life? When you look at life with its twists and turns, what do you see?

Right now you might be saying, "What the heck is he talking about? I see what I see, how can I see anything else?" Which is exactly the point I wanted to arrive at. Do we really see what we see? Do we see what really is? We can look to physics to help us understand the reality of seeing. In *The Tao of Physics*, Fritjof Capra writes:

> ...when you identify an electron, you may do so by cutting through some of its connections to the rest of the world in different ways, by using different observational techniques. Accordingly, the electron may appear as a particle, or it may appear as a wave. What you see depends on how you look at it.

"What you see depends on how you look at it."

This is a physicist's description of our physical subatomic world. It goes back to the notion that a quantum can be either a wave or a particle, depending on what we measure for, and the choice of the measuring instrument is determined by us. In other words, we determine beforehand whether the quantum is a particle or a wave, and then we find that it is whatever we believed it would be.

I want to go one step further, Michael Talbot tells us in *The Holographic Universe*:

> Perhaps most astonishing of all is that there is compelling evidence that THE ONLY TIME QUANTA EVER MANIFEST AS PARTICLES IS WHEN WE ARE LOOKING AT THEM. For instance, when an electron isn't being looked at, experimental findings suggest that it is always a wave.

What creative power there is in how we see things! Unfortunately, to the same degree, there is destructive power included in our ability to "see." This is where conditioning, programming, and the second law of thermodynamics (entropy) come into play. If you are not conscious, if you are not awake, if you are not aware of the choices you make when you're making them, then you will "see" yourself as a victim, or someone that life happens to, and then that will be your experience. You will cause your own negative reality. The other thing that could happen, which would be even worse in my mind, is that you are completely unaware of what is happening and don't even choose. This is in itself a choice, because without direct effort all things will entropy and will tend to flow to the negative. Not choosing gives the same negative result.

The only solution is to wake up!

Wake up to the realization that sight is a recollection of past events and images. It is as much affected by conditioning and programming as our mind is. In fact, this is true of all our senses. There is a deep need within us to create the known from the unknown. Every time we hear, touch, taste, smell, or see something, there is a subconscious need in us to create familiarity. As an example, I will pick an experience that is probably common to everyone. If we taste something that we've never tasted before, we generally respond with "It tastes like…" and we do this at the slightest hint of familiarity. This generally subconscious need for us to file all of our experiences neatly into little boxes keeps us from experiencing true reality. By being conscious of this subconscious need, we "wake up" to reality. This is a key factor in enlightenment. This is an essential part of the truth sought after by generation after generation of wise men seeking "the Way."

Science tells us that no two snowflakes are alike, and yet when we see snow falling, it's hard to make that distinction. Upon closer inspection, however, the truth is revealed. Notice that I did not say that the truth reveals itself to us, because the truth was always there. Our need for familiarity causes us to see all snowflakes as the same. *Insert consciousness and we see differently.* The truth is that no two of anything are the same and consciousness of this fact will change your life. That is why every moment is precious. That is why the "now" is so important. The appreciation of the paradox of the separateness *and* the oneness of all things leads to a full appreciation and gratitude for and of our existence. *At the moment of conception of appreciation and gratitude, the world and everything in it becomes yours to command.* Success, or anything else you desire, is yours. You simply need to see!

POINTS TO PONDER

In the achievement of success, your point of view is everything.

What you see depends on how you look at it.

As you perceive, so shall you achieve.

The only solution is to wake up!

Insert consciousness and we see differently.

At the moment of conception of appreciation and gratitude, the world and everything in it becomes yours to command.

35

Success Is Infinity

The place whereon thou standest is Holy ground.
— Exodus 3:5

The most recent photos sent back by our deep space probe have caused science to reevaluate the numbers of galaxies that were thought to exist. Scientists had to revise their estimates upward by 60 percent and have ascertained that there are about 100 billion galaxies containing about 100 billion stars in each galaxy. What they forgot to say is "That's what we have discovered—so far!" The truth of the matter is that the universe is infinite. It has no edges. It doesn't begin or end anywhere. Try to imagine that and you will find it impossible because everything we "know" has a beginning in "our" world.

Deepak Chopra put it well when he said, "Science is not stranger than we think," rather "science is stranger than we *can* think!" He cites that the immediate problem we encounter when we entertain the possibility that the universe had a beginning is "What was there before the beginning?" If we entertain the idea that the universe has an end, the problem that arises is "What is there after the end?"

We live in a highly complicated, multidimensional universe that has at least four dimensions when we can only understand and comprehend three (time is the fourth dimension). Science today is entertaining the possibility of more than four dimensions. What is a human to do? I don't know about you, but it makes my everyday concerns seem small and inconsequential in the grand scheme of it all. The average person's worries about bills, social status, etc., seem to evaporate into the shadows of this brilliant revelation. Existence is a gargantuan concept!

Likewise, it does us no good to go from the macro world to the micro world. Originally, man thought that the smallest piece of matter was the molecule until he discovered the atom. Man then thought he had finally found the basic building block of everything. Then he discovered the sub-atomic world, and he's been discovering more and more particles ever since. Every time he thinks he has come to the end, he makes a new discovery. One day, man will conclude what I already know—no matter what direction we go in this universe, we will find infinity. *Infinity is the epitome of success!*

What is true for the physical world holds true for the spiritual world. When I meditate and go within, I once again find infinity. There is no end to the layers and layers of spiritual existence. Likewise, the self has no boundaries. We, each of us, are infinite. Spiritualists and psychologists have created graphs to demonstrate the various levels of mind and consciousness. To what they've already discovered, I would like to add one more level—the infinite self, the infinite mind. Try to fathom the possibilities!

What we are talking about here is you. *You are the boundless, infinite perfection that contains the ultimate potentiality.* Is success your destiny? Don't ask such a ridiculous question. It was a done deal from the beginning of this beginningless universe. Success is there, waiting to unfold before you. It only awaits your acknowledgement of its truth. No matter where you go in the universe, conscious or subconscious, atomic or subatomic, micro or macro, Yin or Yang, there you will find infinity. You will find perfection. Are you destined to succeed? *Perfection does not question its perfection.* It just achieves its full potential. Wake up to your spirituality of success! Wake up to *your* infinite self! Open the door to the success and perfection of you! *You already are, now you need to become.*

POINTS TO PONDER

Infinity is the epitome of success!

You are the boundless, infinite perfection that contains the ultimate potentiality.

Perfection does not question its perfection.

You already are, now you need to become.

ADDENDUM

Interviews With
the Voices of Success

What follows are the actual questions and answers from the interviews with the "Voices of Success." Although chapter 25, also titled the "Voices of Success," contains a summary of these interviews, there remains much to gain from hearing the responses of these successful people in their own words.

Most of the interviews are preceded by an introduction, courtesy of one of their co-workers. This was done because it is often difficult to get successful people to talk about their qualities or the personal traits that led to their success. This is perfectly logical because it is ingrained in their minds that no one becomes successful by themselves, and the way that you attain success and get what you want in life is by helping other people to become successful in getting what they want in life. These beliefs produce a humility that is difficult for an interviewer to penetrate; thus the reason for the introductions.

I can only wish that you will thoroughly enjoy reading these interviews as much as I enjoyed participating in them.

Vinny

INTERVIEW WITH WADE SAADI

President of Pencom Systems, Inc.

Introduction by Joy Venegas

According to his close associates, Wade Saadi is a fair and humble man. His humility, however, cannot overshadow the light he brings when he enters a room. He is a smart businessman, who is a friend to most of his employees because he has allowed them the freedom to grow beyond what they believed were their capabilities. He is described as reliable, visionary, nurturing, and a lover of life. He has many hobbies and appreciates family and relationships. Some other words used to describe him are "trustworthy, punctual, efficient, and orderly."

What follows is an interview with Wade Saadi, the 1996 New York "Entrepreneur of the Year" award winner in the field of technology.

Question: Can you give us an insight into your background?

Wade Saadi: I was born and raised in Brooklyn, New York, and I still live there. I was the oldest of four children in a close-knit Arabic family. We still feel very close to each other. I experienced a lot of love growing up, and regardless of how Dan Quayle is teased about it, family values played a tremendous part in my life. A lot of that has flowed over into Pencom, that family feeling, where everyone is on a first-name basis. We have a group of 1,000 close-knit employees, and I get close to as many as I can even though we have eight offices nationwide.

Education-wise, I attended Brooklyn Technical High School where I majored in chemistry, and I attended college at Brooklyn Polytech where I majored in chemical engineering, but I only stayed there for one and a half years. I got impatient, I guess, and I didn't see the value of education because I had seen a lot of people who had degrees but couldn't get jobs at that time. The fields of chemistry and science had crashed a few years before I went to college, and I found engineers making as much as cab drivers. It just didn't make any sense. I also saw many people who didn't have a college education making money in business. I thought college was going to be a great time. I thought I'd learn so much. When I got there, I was kind of disappointed. It wasn't what I expected. It wasn't what it was built up to be. Now, one of the regrets I have in life is that I never finished college. Maybe I would have been better off going away to a college with a campus where I might have been able to build up a network of friends, instead of attending a local college.

I read a lot. I always have. Not novels, but periodicals, nonfiction, and educational books. I also have many hobbies. I have a voracious appetite for reading. I don't watch much television. My reading and my hobbies distract me from the rigors of everyday business.

Question: What inspired you to take the risk involved in starting your own business?

Wade Saadi: My dad had his own business. He was a partner with another fellow in the ladies' garment business. My uncles were almost all self-employed in one form of business or another. And most of them were without a college education, as were their friends who also did very well. They were immigrants or children of immigrants. They had a certain spirit, which I inherited.

As a child, I would sell Kool-Aid. I had a paper route. I worked after school in the local Key Food supermarket. I sold candy for the Boy Scouts, and around Christmas I would stick candles in plaster of Paris and go door-to-door selling them in the apartment buildings. I liked to do that kind of work because it always challenged me.

When I opened Pencom, it wasn't a risk. It was just another chapter. You can't think of going into business as a risk, because you'll probably fail. Opening a business is an opportunity that has risks. Risks should be avoided, but opportunities that have risks should be examined. So, I opened Pencom because I liked business. I always had the desire to make money, to be in business. I loved to find ways to turn five dollars into ten dollars.

Before I opened Pencom, one of my very close friends and I opened a mail-order business, which was an abysmal failure. You learn to do things only after you have the experience. We studied for months before we did this, but that's not the same as having the experience. What we should have done was go to work for someone and learn the trade; that's how you get the experience. You don't reinvent the wheel.

Question: When you started Pencom, how much money did you have?

Wade Saadi: I didn't have a lot of money, only a few thousand dollars. I came from a middle-class background, and I didn't have a lot of money. I did have a lot of confidence, but financially I really didn't have anything to lose.

Question: What would you say are some of the characteristics that are necessary for people to be successful?

Wade Saadi: This goes back to what I was saying before. I don't think it's what you want to hear, but I think it has to be inherent in a person to want to be an entrepreneur. No matter what you teach, tell, or give to a person, if he or she doesn't have that desire, you can't teach them entrepreneurial desire. You have to want to [be successful]!

I've got a friend who has been a ski instructor for twenty-five years, and he's unhappy with it, but he likes his summers off and the other advantages. Water seeks its own level. That's the way he wants it, and it's okay. You either have it [the desire] or you don't. If people have the desire, you can teach them. Salespeople are entrepreneurs by nature. My definition of an entrepreneur is someone who goes out and re-earns his living every day. Salespeople have to prove themselves time and time again. It keeps them from becoming stale.

Question: In light of that statement, would you say that it's important to love what you do?

Wade Saadi: You have to love what you do. You need to have a passion, not necessarily for the products, but you have to love the business. I think all entrepreneurs have sales ability, and they love what they do. If computers became illegal, I still think I'd be in the forefront of some other business. I don't have a particular passion for computers or software. They don't mean anything special to me. What does mean something to me is this company and the people who work here. Together we're having a lot of fun, making money, doing something that's challenging, expanding, and growing. It's not the computers; it's the process.

Question: If you could reminisce back to when you first started the business, do you remember setting goals or using any specific goal-setting method?

Wade Saadi: No. I know I'm probably disappointing you again, but in the high-tech business, because it changes so rapidly, you have no idea where you're going to be in two years. Companies use goals and business plans, not entrepreneurs.

Question: In conclusion, Wade, what kind of advice would you like to give to people reading this book?

Wade Saadi: If they're going to build a company, never be deceptive to anyone, ever! Whether it's the client, the employee, or yourself. Know thyself! Be open and honest in all your dealings, because you can only lose your name once, and once you've lost it, your credibility goes with it and there's nothing left. Without credibility you're just an empty shell, no matter how much money you acquire.

Another thing is that you should autograph your work with excellence. Never let a product out of the door that isn't the very, very best that you can make. Otherwise, people see you at less than 100 percent, and there's no reason to do that. It's better to be late and on target than early and disorganized. Always make sure it's right before it goes out the door. It kills me to read a résumé or a letter or advertisement that has a typo. What people don't understand is that when you produce something, it is you. You're showing your inner soul, so why should there be an error in it?

The third thing is that you should never be afraid to surround yourself with people who are better than you. Your dream in life should be, that of all the people who surround you [that you employ], you should be the dumbest and least aggressive. When the chips are down, they can carry you. I surround myself with the finest people I can find. A lot of business owners are apprehensive about doing that for fear that someone might steal their secrets. So what's the alternative? Surround yourself with idiots? It's important to surround yourself with the very best people you can get. And last, the most important thing is to have fun. You have to enjoy what you're doing. It has to be exhilarating and a constant challenge, and it has to help people.

Post-Interview Reflection

The first words that come to mind when I recall the interview with Wade Saadi are the words "calm assurance." His aura of serenity and security are part of the reason why his coworkers value him so much. For them, he is an oasis in the desert, and at other times, he is a safe port in a storm. One cannot help but believe that there are much greater things that this man will accomplish.

Interview With Frank Sciame

President of F. J. Sciame Construction Company

Introduction

According to his close associates, Frank is known for his loyalty, his commitment, and his ability to be able to get projects through honestly and on time. This is rare in the construction industry. Frank started out from modest beginnings, worked his way through college as a carpenter, and started off with very small jobs. He went out on a limb, so to speak, and today has built some of New York City's most highly profiled projects. These include the Virgin Records Megastore in Times Square, the Warner Brothers Studio store on Fifth Avenue, the New Victory Theatre on Forty-second Street, the New Nike Town in the Trump Tower complex, and the renovation of "Windows on the World" in the World Trade Center.

What is interesting about Frank is that he is one of those guys you have heard about. Everything he touches turns to gold. Frank cares about people, and that comes back to him tenfold. He is known for doing a lot of good works, many uncelebrated, and the people who receive his generosity, his kind words and help, always keep him in mind and somehow pay him back one way or another. Frank's team has a commitment and a camaraderie that is not found in most teams. They actually care about each other, and that comes from the top because Frank cares about them. You can tell that everything filters down from the top, because he is one of those people who gives credibility to the expression, "The speed of the leader determines the speed of the pack." Frank's team members certainly try to measure up to their leader in his vigor, vitality, loyalty, and camaraderie.

What follows now is a question-and-answer period with Mr. Frank Sciame, the 1996 New York "Entrepreneur of the Year" award winner in the construction field.

Question: Can you give us some insight into your background?

Frank Sciame: I went to a Catholic grammar school, St. Michael's in East New York, Brooklyn. I went on to Thomas Edison Technical High School, then attended junior college at the State University of New York in Farmingdale for two years, studying civil technology. Following that, I attended City College studying pre-engineering for one year and then transferred to the City College School of Architecture for the second year. I received a BS degree from City College School of Architecture. While I'm glad my parents encouraged me to get my degree, I think there are a lot of people much more successful than I am without degrees. On the whole, obtaining a degree makes you more well-rounded and allows you to communicate with confidence on the same level as other people who have college degrees.

As far as my family background is concerned, my mother was a housewife and worked part-time as a saleswoman at a women's clothing store in Brooklyn. My father was a union painter, a lifetime member.

Question: Where did you get the confidence to start your own business? And with how much money did you start?

Frank Sciame: The confidence to start my own business was, basically, an unquestionable belief that I could do for myself what I was presently employed to do for a company. Not making a very high salary at the time, the safety net was that I could always put on a tool belt and support my new wife, Barbara, and our planned family if my business failed. So there never really was a doubt that I could make money in the building trades. The company that I worked for gave me exposure to the different parts of the construction process—estimating, project management, etc. I added the entrepreneurial spirit, and all of it together created the confidence to start my own business.

Financially, I started with $7,500. My wife, Barbara, and I saved $2,500 and I borrowed $5,000 from my parents. That was in June 1975. By November of that year, I was able to repay my parents and give my mother a mink coat as interest. It felt great. I had very little money initially, but as you can see, you don't need a lot of money to become successful.

Question: When you initially started out, Frank, or even today, do you use a stringent goal-setting method? A lot of the successful motivators today have people concentrate on their goals almost obsessively. I am not saying whether that is right or wrong. What I am trying to find out is what do successful people really do?

Frank Sciame: I don't set goals. Two years ago, for the first time after nineteen years of doing business, the company set some goals in terms of growth, but as a rule, we don't set goals. I never have set goals. My one objective is profitability. Just put your head down and work very hard. Goals can distract you from quality performance. In my opinion, setting goals could have you concentrating and expending lots of energy on the wrong things.

Question: What would you say are the characteristics that people need to be successful?

Frank Sciame: I think they need to have a lot of energy and enthusiasm. They have to be optimistic and willing to work very long hours. Couple all that with some basic ability and you have a winning formula for success.

Question: Would you say it's important to love what you do?

Frank Sciame: I think it's absolutely imperative that you love what you do. I don't remember who said it, but it has been said that if you love what you do, you'll never work a day in your life. I think there's a lot of truth to that. And, I think it's important that you love what you do so that you don't view your career as work. You can't look at the clock, and you won't look at the clock if you love what you do.

At a peak period in our business, I was accused of running a sweatshop because of the long hours our people were required to work in order to get the jobs done. I really took that to heart, and it troubled me because I wanted people to enjoy working for Sciame Construction. Then, it finally occurred to me that in this industry, and in any profession that you choose, if you want to be at the top of your field, you have to expect to work long hours. If you intend to be a top tennis player, you will have to play tennis ten to fourteen hours a day, seven days a week. If you want to be a top litigator, and perhaps litigate a trial as famous as the O. J. Simpson trial, long hours are a given. The hours don't count. The only way you can become capable of being the best in your field is by working the long hours early on in your career because you love what you are doing and you love learning more and more about your field. You do this over and over again and then suddenly one day you realize you have mastered your profession and people are now looking to you for the answers.

So, again, I believe a love for what you do is imperative for real success. A young individual who loves what he or she does is who I want working for me. That person does not see working for Sciame Construction as a job. He sees it as a tremendous opportunity to learn the profession from one of the best companies in the construction industry. Loving what you do is the key to success at any level, whether it's success as an employee or success as a business owner.

Question: What is it exactly that you love?

Frank Sciame: I love the building, putting things together and solving problems. But I also love making money. I would like to qualify the "making money" by saying that early on in my life, I saw that my parents weren't able to have many of the things that others had. They didn't have the vacations they deserved. They didn't have the nice furniture or the new car that they deserved. I was determined to provide these things for my family. So, making money for me, meant being able to make life more enjoyable for my family and for other people. To put it another way, I didn't love the money, but loved the experiences that money could buy and the inconveniences that money could avoid...and it's the way you keep score in business!

Question: Who is Frank Sciame, spiritually?

Frank Sciame: I always, inwardly and outwardly, try to put myself into the position of the other person. I think that's very helpful in many different aspects of business. In basic relationships with people, I believe you should treat people the way you want to be treated. Do unto others as you would have them do unto you.

I'd like to think that spiritually I have a high level of character and a good moral and ethical baseline to draw on when I make important decisions in life. I think good ethics is good business, and good morality is good business. I think that's so important. Spiritually, for me, that means being a good Christian.

Question: What advice would you give to people who are trying to create success in their lives?

Frank Sciame: I would like to tell them to pursue their dreams in the area of their life that most excites them. Then I would tell them to find a way to make that dream pay the bills, and at the same time take advantage of the opportunity to achieve the success that they deserve by aspiring to become the best in their chosen field. I think they should trust their gut feelings. They should take the risk required to become successful, and at the same time try to be realistic about the downside possibilities. It's always difficult to realistically assess the downside without putting a damper on your enthusiasm; you need to assess the general risks without dwelling on every potential problem. You need to be prepared to handle the downside risks if they occur. I think risk is what stops most people from achieving the success they're capable of achieving. Perhaps outside investors can be found to protect the downside risks, but in the final analysis, I would like to advise them to go for it. It will be an emotional rollercoaster, but it will be one hell of a ride—follow your dream!

Post-Interview Reflection

My interview with Frank Sciame was a lesson in humility. The only way to find out about his great accomplishments was by speaking to his associates, because he certainly doesn't publicize them. It was almost as if he protected his humility, by downplaying any inference to his greatness. I could hear the caring concern in his voice as he spoke of his associates, his family, and the readers of this book, whom he hasn't even met. His loving nature was apparent to me and is obviously one of the reasons for his amazing success.

INTERVIEW WITH IRWIN STERNBERG

President of Stonehenge Limited

Introduction by Dean Wilkerson
National Executive Director of MADD (Mothers Against Drunk Driving)

When you first meet Irwin, you are struck by his contagious enthusiasm and optimism, his amazing energy, and his excitement in talking about his industry.

Irwin genuinely cares about helping people and good causes. He delights in bringing joy and beauty to the world. These principles have guided the neckwear collections he has produced and have made him very successful.

The men's neckwear industry is fortunate to count Irwin Sternberg among its members. In the past five years he has revolutionized fashionable neckwear and, perhaps more importantly for the industry, has elevated its importance in the public's mind.

The following is an interview with Mr. Irwin Sternberg, the 1996 New York "Entrepreneur of the Year" award winner in the field of apparel and textile.

Question: Mr. Sternberg, could you give us some insight into your family life? Did you come from an entrepreneurial family? Were you an entrepreneur at a very early age?

Irwin Sternberg: I was not a young entrepreneur. I grew up in Baltimore, Maryland, in an average family that didn't have much, but we had enough to be content. My father worked for the government and my mother was associated with a private insurance company. Neither one of my parents was really successful according to the degree of education they had, but they were great providers for the family.

I was sick at a young age, and it cost me a year of schooling. That loss of a year also undermined my feelings of pride and accomplishment through grade school and high school. I did terrible in school, all the way through to the end of high school. In fact, I still remember my last year in high school when people started talking about going to college. I didn't realize that I could even think about going to college because of my grades. In fact, I thought no college would take me.

There was one college, the University of Baltimore, that accepted me after I interviewed with them. They gave me a chance. When I went to the university, I was, at best, a student struggling to get by because of the way I thought about education [after losing a year in school and giving up].

Psychologically, my insecurity made me feel so bad that I never really cared. But I graduated from the University of Baltimore and went to work for a clothing company in Baltimore called Jos. A. Bank Clothiers where I met two men, Dan Caplin and Howard Bank. Both of these men turned out to be great mentors of mine. Both of them have since died, and I miss them very much. But while they were alive, they taught me how to listen to what people were saying and not to listen to only what I wanted to hear. They taught me to give people the benefit of the doubt. It was a great education for me. I learned how to work with people and listen to new ideas.

After Jos. A. Bank was sold to Quaker Oats, I left to go to work in New York for a tie company named Bentley Cravats. A year and a half later I started a company, with my friend Natan Brach as a partner, called Stonehenge Limited. That was roughly fourteen years ago. It was the first time I had the opportunity to do something on my own.

I often have people ask me, "Did you ever think you would be as successful as you are today?" I don't know if anyone can answer that. I do recall having so much confidence when I left Jos. A. Bank that I really did believe that I could do anything that I wanted to do. I felt a sense of confidence that I could overcome a lot of things because I had a good background in my career.

Question: You talked about how you eventually started Stonehenge. Why did you start it, and did you have many financial resources? Many people believe that you need a lot of money to get a business started. Can you give us some insight?

Irwin Sternberg: As I said, we really didn't have much and I made only a modest income at Jos. A. Bank, but I loved working there. When my wife, my four-year-old twin sons, and I moved to New York, I can remember Natan telling me that we needed roughly $50,000 to start this business; and $50,000 back then was like someone saying you need a million dollars. I didn't have anything near that, but I begged and I borrowed and did everything I could to raise $50,000 to be his partner.

He had the finances and I didn't. I borrowed from members of my family and friends and everyone else I could find. I can remember to this day that I was short $3,000 and an aunt called me and said, "I understand that you need $3,000." She loaned me the money, and I always said that if I made it, I would return the money with 18% interest. That's how Stonehenge started, but I, personally, did not have the funds to start the business.

Question: It was interesting, when we were speaking before the interview, that you were talking about how the Stonehenge of today was born out of a declining business. When most people find themselves in that situation, all they can see is everything going down, but you found a way to bring everything up. Can you talk about that?

Irwin Sternberg: Sure. We started our company fourteen years ago. For the first four years, we created traditional handmade neckwear. Well, all markets change and all businesses go through peaks and valleys, and we certainly went through ours. As I mentioned to you earlier, the traditional business started to decline and the world of fashion started to become more and more important. People were no longer looking for that dumb-dumb red traditional tie or that Brooks Brothers-type stripe, and our business started to decline and decline rather quickly.

Fortunately, something happened that I will never forget, and as I look back, I can say that it was certainly one of the reasons why we are still in business. There was an art gallery in Soho, New York, called the Ambassador Gallery, and it was premiering the artwork of Jerry Garcia of the Grateful Dead. Tickets were sold out, and they had lines of people who wanted tickets. One of my employees came to me and said, "Do we have any contacts? Do you know how we can get tickets?" I always taught them that they should never give up. There are many ways to accomplish certain objectives. So, we called the art gallery, and I told the owner of the gallery that I was coming down to review the artwork of Jerry Garcia for a neckwear program.

He said, "No problem, how many tickets do you need?" Well, the employees were so excited that I decided to see it on my own, never even thinking about the reality of a partnership with Jerry Garcia. As I walked in, they had lines around the block and media from around the world. As I started to look at and review the art, I saw several very colorful paintings by Jerry which could easily be applied to a fashion concept.

Well, one thing led to another, and we went back the next day. We contacted the Jerry Garcia Estate, and they thought we were totally out of our minds. They said Jerry would never in his right mind wear a tie, nor had he worn a tie in twenty-five years, but they wanted to see what we were talking about. So we went to the mills with some of his art and we recreated some of the images on our ties. We tried four times to get them approved by the Jerry Garcia people.

After applying Stonehenge's creative color schemes to ties and mounting the ties on shirts, they called us back, very excited, and we signed a contract with Jerry Garcia. The first launch took place in Bloomingdale's in New York during the Democratic National Convention. The telephone system was knocked out of circulation because of the massive influx of calls from around the world, and over 3,000 ties were sold in a matter of a day or two.

The neckwear was reported in magazines as the biggest phenomenon ever in the fashion world of neckwear. It quickly became the number-one selling tie in America. Today, Jerry's name is a designer name, and we learned what marketing techniques were important and how to keep it exciting. It inspires people, because wearing a Jerry Garcia tie makes a statement.

Question: I find it interesting that the whole series of events that led up to the Jerry Garcia collection started with your wanting to do something for your employees. It started with you trying to help somebody. How important do you think it is for entrepreneurs to believe in the concept of helping other people in order to achieve success?

Irwin Sternberg: Oh, my God, it's incredibly important! We have built a very successful business helping other people achieve their objectives.

Question: Irwin, it's obvious that you love the business that you are in. How important do you think that is in becoming successful?

Irwin Sternberg: I think in order for you to be totally successful, you need to be totally committed to yourself and love what life is all about. I believe that to have success in a business, you need to truly love what you do. And if you don't, you haven't truly fulfilled your dreams and you need to continue to go and find different horizons. I absolutely have a love affair with my company, and I know it's helped me become a better person. I also believe it's helped give me the creativity to create growth. We help to raise funds, and at the same time we're helping people. Reaching that type of plateau in business is a dream come true.

Question: Do you set goals? It's obvious that the Jerry Garcia collection wasn't something you planned. It was a result of applying your creativity to an event you were exposed to. So, do you set goals? And, if so, how far in the future do you plan?

Irwin Sternberg: Those are great questions. I don't think, that as long as I've been in business, I've ever looked into the future. I've only concentrated on what I was doing today and never paid much attention to my competitors. I only believed in what we had the ability to accomplish. We were confident that we were setting the stage in fashion, and it was always a compliment knowing friends and competitors were trying to follow our guidelines.

Question: You mentioned earlier that a lot of the money you used to get started was borrowed. Obviously that represents a certain amount of risk. What was the extent of the risk you took personally to get this endeavor off the ground?

Irwin Sternberg: In the beginning stages, I had a real fear of failing. I didn't know if I would have enough capital. It was truly a fear having a young family and, for the first time, being on my own without support. It was a date with destiny that I had to survive. And I had to do it with a certain amount of class and respect. That's a rule I continue to live by even today.

Question: I am not as interested in Stonehenge, the company, as I am in Irwin Sternberg, the man. Is it fear that motivated you? I'm hearing that you used the fear of failure in a positive way. Is that true?

Irwin Sternberg: No question, but I also used the wisdom that people gave me, which brought me into a different reality of life. What's so amazing is that it comes down to confidence. If you really believe in yourself, then it doesn't matter where you went to school or what you studied. Also, part of my success is due to trying to give something back.

Question: As a result of all your success, you have been able to meet other entrepreneurs. What are some of the characteristics that they have in common that have led them to success?

Irwin Sternberg: I think they have a drive for life, a drive for love, a drive for giving of themselves for whatever the cause may be. I am generalizing, of course, but I have met many entrepreneurs who are worthy of that description. They are proud to be Americans. They are proud to be able to give back. The first thing that you see in them is humility. They always look at their company and say [about their employees], I couldn't have done it without them, and they start listing the names of people associated with them. A true entrepreneur is not a *me* kind of person. I think a business opportunity can help them become better people, but they are the ones who allow their companies to take them to those horizons.

Question: People are looking to better their lives, and one of the things I want to tell them is if they want to be successful, then they need to speak to the voices of success, a group to which you obviously belong. What would you like to say to the reader of this book? What kind of advice would you like to give them?

Irwin Sternberg: That's exciting; I could think of a gazillion things to say to them. Some things I could say are go for it; try it; don't give up; become what you want to be. I would say to beginning entrepreneurs, Do you think you could take a tie and present it to the Dalai Lama? They would probably think I was out of my mind. The point I am trying to make is that you can reach any plateau if you have common sense and an objective that is attainable. It really becomes a journey that's exciting and rewarding.

The best way I can tell you about a business being a journey is this. We created a neckwear program from the patterns of Tibetan carpets, each of which had a different spiritual meaning. I created a tie program from designers of Tibetan carpets and donated the proceeds back to the Tibet Fund, which is an organization that helps support Tibetan families that fled from China and lost their homeland. Well, the Dalai Lama heard about this and a representative of his called me and invited me to attend a conference with 3,000 people who came to hear the Dalai Lama speak in Louisville, Kentucky. I never, ever, thought that I would be called to the podium. But the Dalai

Lama presented me with a Tibetan prayer scarf for our fund raising efforts with the Tibetan Tie Collection. He wrapped it around my shoulders and blessed me for helping world peace. My company is only a tie company; I never thought it would take me to such exciting pleasures. So I would say to those budding entrepreneurs out there, you can reach, and grab, and obtain, any objective you want. You can obtain anything you want if you have a dream and let that dream take you where you've never traveled before.

Post Interview Reflection

Irwin Steinberg's work with various charitable organizations exemplifies the first rule of lasting success: those who give will receive. His enthusiasm for others makes one want to take up his banner and follow him wherever he goes. He is a lesson in leadership and success. He was so excited about his work with MADD (Mothers Against Drunk Driving) that I was inspired to help them achieve their objectives. MADD is a nonprofit, grassroots organization with more than 600 chapters and community action teams nationwide. MADD is not a crusade against alcohol consumption. Their focus is to look for effective solutions to drunk driving and underage drinking problems while supporting those who have already experienced the pain of these senseless crimes. Their mission is to stop people from driving under the influence of alcohol and support the victims of this violent crime. To support their efforts, call 1-800-GET MADD.

In working with Irwin, Dean Wilkerson, National Executive Director of MADD, reflected, "Discussing marketing and publicity with Irwin is like trying to drink water from a fire hydrant. The man is a fountain—a volcano—of creative ideas." Likewise, Doug Kingsriter, National Director of Marketing for MADD, commented, "Irwin is a gifted person and a brilliant marketer. He is a significant key to our success in cause-related marketing."

If I could manufacture a person who would have all of the characteristics of success, I would end up with Irwin Sternberg. Our interview lasted for three short hours, although it was originally scheduled for one hour. He was captivating, enthusiastic, intelligent, and powerful. Although I have known him only briefly, I know he would argue with the word "powerful," but that's because he is also humble. Humility, I find, is a common characteristic in successful people. It is very difficult to get them to talk about themselves. But it is part of the reason why the universe submits itself to their beck and call.

Irwin's power, as I observed it, came from within. It was not from his business, his contacts, his social position, or his money. Rather, they all flowed from the same source: the power within.

INTERVIEW WITH WILLIAM UNGAR
President & CEO of National Envelope Corporation

Introduction by Les Stern

According to his close associates, William Ungar is unique and greatly admired. He is a Horatio Alger story in living color. He was the only one of his family to survive the holocaust, and he believes he survived for a reason. It wasn't just coincidence. He has dedicated his life to show the world that "out of the ashes" the higher element of humanity always resonates. The higher level of decency always wins.

William Ungar came to America after the Second World War, on the first "displaced persons" boat out of Europe. He didn't speak a word of English and had only fifteen dollars in his pocket. He worked all day, went to school at night, and studied vocabulary into the wee hours of the morning. He knew learning the language would bring with it opportunity. He started his business in 1,600 square feet of space with five employees and three obsolete envelope machines, which he rebuilt himself. Today, the company has over two million square feet of space, approximately 3,000 employees, and manufactures 100 million envelopes a day.

They say he never sought to master other people but to master himself. He never substitutes words for actions. He always believes that people should be forgiving and honest in failure but modest in success. He lives his life believing that people should be strong enough to know where they are weak and brave enough to really look at themselves when they are most afraid. These are the principles he lives by.

The holocaust taught him that life was a risk and that gave him the confidence to risk starting a company. He doesn't get too high when things are good or too low when things are bad. When asked how he developed that difficult discipline, he replied, "When you've already lived the worst day of your life, everything else is relative."

His business is more than dollars and cents; it is a legacy. A legacy of triumph of good over evil—a statement that good people will win out. His business is also about families. He sees it as an opportunity to embrace the human aspect of business. The allegiance and loyalty flow to and from him and his employees. He is good to them and leads by example. He also gives to many charities.

To conclude, his associates say that meeting him makes one a better person, that he exemplifies modesty, simplicity of wisdom, and the meekness of true strength. In short, he is a very special person.

What follows is an interview with William Ungar, a New York "Master Entrepreneur of the Year" award winner.

Question: Mr. Ungar, you mentioned that when you first started, you didn't have much money. Do you think money is absolutely important in beginning an entrepreneurial venture?

William Ungar: To begin an entrepreneurial venture, one needs a nominal sum of "seed" money. Having a trustworthy reputation among friends and acquaintances, one will always find individuals who would be willing to make an investment with you. Ability and honesty are the two most important virtues to attract money for a business venture.

Question: How did you feel about competing with the large envelope manufacturers?

William Ungar: I began on a very small scale and was unnoticed by the large companies. At the onset, we concentrated on selling to the wholesalers, and when they learned that we were reliable, they favored us with orders and have remained loyal to our company. As a result, we continued to grow and expand.

Question: What role does risk play in being an entrepreneur?

William Ungar: Every new undertaking is, in itself, risk. The only difference is the degree of risk. If you have confidence in your undertaking and have objectives, the risk will diminish in time, and one will achieve positive results.

Question: Who were the people you consulted when you first started out? Who were your mentors?

William Ungar: The first person I consulted was the chief engineer at F. L. Smithe Machine Company, where I worked at my first job in this country. It was, and still is, a company that manufactured machinery to produce envelopes. He gave me the insight regarding the equipment and how to proceed in a business. He said that if I was willing to manufacture the envelopes at night and sell them during the daytime, that I would be successful. The other individual, a large paper merchant, was introduced to me by a sales manager from a paper mill. I told him what my intentions were in the envelope business. He told me that it was a crazy business. Nevertheless, I entered into the envelope field and have no regrets.

Question: So what you are saying is that one of the characteristics you need to be successful is that you have to be a little bit crazy?

William Ungar: The business may indeed be a crazy one, but one needs courage and conviction to be in it. I usually tell employees in the higher positions that they may note that we operate in a unique manner. In my opinion, we became successful for two reasons. The first was due to my technical ability and familiarity with the equipment. The second was because I employed people who possessed honesty, integrity, and diligence. They have contributed in large measure to our success. Today, I value people who work for us more than anything else; they are our greatest assets.

Question: What motivated you to succeed? What characteristics do you think are necessary for someone to become successful?

William Ungar: In my case, I like a challenge. I get great personal satisfaction in finding a solution and in getting results. One must have an inner initiative to do things and enjoy the results. It shouldn't feel like work. To enjoy what you are doing is the most important thing. My advice for others who want to become successful in their own businesses is to have their objectives in front of them and work hard. And with determination and dedication, one can achieve one's dreams in this blessed country like no other place in the world.

Post-Interview Reflection

William Ungar took a terrible experience, the holocaust, and made it work for him. Many others became victims of this human disaster, but William Ungar became the master of his experience. It was exciting to hear him reminisce about his start as an entrepreneur. I could see the gleam in his eye as he traveled back to his beginnings. It became obvious as I listened, that for him the challenge to succeed was everything. He would not be a victim. He refused to be a statistic. He overcame obstacles the likes of which are a lesson to us all. His life is a legacy of what a person can accomplish through self-discipline and desire. He is the personification of the American dream!

INTERVIEW WITH AUBREY BALKIND
President & CEO of Frankfurt Balkind Partners

What follows is an interview with Aubrey Balkind, a 1996 New York "Entrepreneur of the Year" award winner in the field of advertising and media.

Question: Aubrey, can you give us some insight into your childhood? Did you come from an entrepreneurial family? What was your economic background and education?

Aubrey Balkind: Yes, I came from an entrepreneurial family. I was born in South Africa and grew up there. My father had his own business, importing glassware and gifts from around the world and then wholesaling to retailers in the country. When I was a teenager, I would help my father as a traveling salesman. I wasn't very good at selling. I was very shy, and it was very difficult for me to introduce myself to strangers and ask them for an order, but I simply had to force myself to overcome my fears because, economically, my father's business needed the help.

Educationally, my undergraduate degree was in economics, after which I practiced as an auditor and accountant and then became the equivalent of a

CPA. I left South Africa to go to Columbia University in New York, where I received my MBA. I worked for Arthur Young (now Ernst and Young) for four years as a management consultant. While there, I studied at night for a Ph.D. in urban planning and design. Before I submitted my thesis, I decided to switch to communications and graphic design, where I educated myself. My education has helped me understand various businesses quickly, and my experience has helped me to become a communications expert.

Question: What motivated you to take the risk in opening your own business?

Aubrey Balkind: I felt unfulfilled by management consulting because there was no physical product at the end of the process. I always wanted to be an architect, which combines both right-brain and left-brain functions (creative design and logical engineering). What actually gave me the courage to start my own business was having a father who was an entrepreneur. I wasn't afraid to go out on my own and start a business. Although I had no money, because I had to pay back all my student loans, I felt secure that I always had a profession with decent pay that I could go back to if necessary. I was twenty-eight and naïve. I think you need some naïvete to follow your passion; your passion will drive you to reach your objectives. If you really knew all the obstacles you would confront [opening a business], you would never do it. But I had a dream, and the idea was to satisfy that dream. It has been a long journey, but the dream is still there. You never really attain it, it just grows and grows, and unless you have a passion for the process, you're never really going to get anywhere. You just constantly keep trying to meet and, possibly, surpass what you expect to accomplish.

Question: Do you think the passion that drove you to start a business is something that people can develop?

Aubrey Balkind: I think everybody has a passion for something, and they should try to get in touch with their passion. Some people want to lead and some people want to follow. For me, there is no doubt about that. Life is not an easy process. There are lots of hurdles and quite a few people, when they get beaten down, instead of getting up and learning from it, they start to blame what's going on around them for why they're not doing well. People will say,

"I've got to leave New York, change my job, or get divorced" as the reasons why they are not doing well. They need to take responsibility, themselves, to do better with their circumstances, instead of being controlled by outside forces. People can have much more control of their circumstances than they think. Some people are seen as lucky people, but they actually make themselves lucky by being in the right place at the right time. You have to make yourself available—not just looking, but looking and available when an opportunity comes along.

Question: As one of the voices of success, who was your mentor? With whom did you consult?

Aubrey Balkind: When I was practicing as an auditor and accountant, there was a man I worked with who showed me new ways of thinking. He taught me how to think through each problem from a very basic level. I now call it "zero-based thinking." You need to forget what you know, try to move away from all the preconceived ideas you have, and build your own logical structure around an issue. For me, it's being able to rethink things creatively from the ground up and build new logical structures around issues. Inventing new ideas actually requires an enormous amount of common sense or, phrased another way, strategic intuitiveness.

Question: How did you feel about competing with the "big guys" in your field when you first started?

Aubrey Balkind: You have to have a very strong sense of yourself. A sense of what's right and what's wrong and a good marketing plan. A lot of people have brilliant ideas, but you need to have a good understanding of what's good and what's bad about an idea. The first thing I realized is that the "big guys" are just people. Every organization, no matter how large it is, relies on a handful of key people. You just have to make sure that your key people are better than theirs. "Bigness" is an advantage, but it's also a great liability. Many of the large companies today are trying to function more like small companies, in many respects.

Question: They say you need to love what you do to be successful. Is it the field that you love, or is it being in business that you love?

Aubrey Balkind: I would like to phrase it a bit differently. Is it the field that you love or is it the process? I think you can love either and be successful. I think that it's easier to have a passion for the field. What I like about what I do now is that there's something physical at the end of the process—a product. I enjoy the elegance of the thinking, which I could get in management consulting, but I couldn't get the aesthetic beauty of what I do right now. Also, communication is very much based in popular culture, and that ties me to what's going on in life. It is important for me to help make life function better and be more enjoyable. That is where my passion comes from.

Question: What characteristics do you think a person needs to become successful?

Aubrey Balkind: I think you have to have an inner self-confidence. It can be based on your mind and your intelligence or on your social skills. You need to understand people—the ones you lead, the customers you serve, and in my case, the audience I am communicating with. You need to not be scared of failure. Realize that there are times when you are down, but you usually learn more when you're down than when you're up. It's a world of ups and downs. Success and failure don't mean that much in the short term—it's the long term that matters.

Question: When you first started the business, did you set any stringent goals for yourself or use any particular goal-setting method?

Aubrey Balkind: I think very long-term, and I think about very big issues, but I don't actually plan long-term. I don't plan more than a few weeks or a few months ahead because things change so rapidly. It's having an idea about where you're going and not so much about adhering to all the details along the way.

Question: What advice would you like to give the readers of this book?

Aubrey Balkind: Successful people never really think of themselves as successful. You never actually arrive at that place, and that's what keeps pushing them. I believe in continual learning, every day. I believe that when you do something, tomorrow you should be able to do it better. I've found that most destinations [success] are an illusion. The journey itself should be your destination. It's the passion, the wonderful experiences you have, that makes the journey so enjoyable. I believe chaos is the oxygen that drives creativity. If you define things too much, like with goals, there is no room to maneuver. A certain amount of chaos can be very productive. It helps fuel your passion.

Question: Who is Aubrey Balkind, spiritually?

Aubrey Balkind: I try to be clean; clean in thinking and knowing what's right and wrong, clean in how I live my life and how I balance what's important in life. That's what I strive for. I know people who have given their entire lives to their work. I think that it's important to strive for balance in life, which I am still working to achieve. You need to be honest with yourself.

Post-Interview Reflections

What struck me most about my experience with Aubrey Balkind was that his unassuming nature was hypnotic. His appearance was one of a typical successful businessman and yet, as the interview progressed, I got the sense that there was much more than met the eye. By the end of the interview, I was convinced I was not only in the presence of a successful person but I had also met a great man. I was most impressed with the depth of his insight of himself and the ease with which he was able to communicate it to me. His depth was obviously something he was familiar with, and, when he spoke, it was as if he was speaking of an old friend. His personal insights were among the many gifts I received from interviewing successful people.

INTERVIEW WITH KURT ADLER

Chairman, Kurt S. Adler, Inc.

Introduction by Karen Adler

According to his close associates, Kurt Adler is a very generous man who has a kind heart and is fair-minded. He invokes loyalty from people because of these qualities, and, as proof of this, many of his employees have been with him for fifteen to twenty years. He is an insightful man who has an eye for trends in a business that isn't very trendy. He also has the uncanny ability to know what the customer wants. He has a calm confidence about him that is very enjoyable, and the people who associate with him are proud to say so.

What follows is an interview with Mr. Kurt Adler, a 1996 New York "Master Entrepreneur of the Year" award winner.

Question: Mr. Adler, can you give us some idea of what kind of social and economic status your family had? What was the extent of your education? Give us a brief glimpse into your background.

Kurt Adler: It is really hard to compare 1996 in America to the situation in the 1920s in Germany. I came from an upper middle-class family. We lost everything under the Nazis, but my background was pretty solid.

Question: How about education? How far did you go?

Kurt Adler: I graduated high school and then went to night school here at a city college that keeps insisting that I graduated. But I never did graduate. I only completed half the credits. It seems my business success inflated my education success.

Question: What inspired you to get started in the business that you are in today?

Kurt Adler: Well, I can tell you that it didn't start with a desire to get into the Christmas decorations business. It doesn't work like that. After being in the United States Army for a while at the end of World War II, I made a decision that if I could help it, nobody was going to give me orders anymore.

I was stationed in the army in Honolulu, and I used the time to make contacts and become a buying agent for a wholesaler in Honolulu. He was in need of merchandise like everyone else, because the United States was the only country that had not lost its capacity to produce because it wasn't bombed. There was no Japan, no Germany, no England, so there was an immense need for finding sources of supply to get merchandise. The man was actually a Japanese-American businessman in Honolulu, and he made me the buying agent for everything he needed. Whatever he needed, I was to find it and he gave me five percent commission for my work, which paid a little better than having a job.

Actually, I have received most of my experience from one of the several jobs I had when I came to the United States. I worked at a pillow company, and the owner was a very successful man. I learned from him. He was a successful man and did it right, and I used him as a role model.

Question: When you talk about how you got into the business, what was it inside the man, Kurt Adler, that made you want to take that risk, made you want to be in business?

Kurt Adler: I came from a background where we had our own business. We came here with nothing; we had lost everything and that was the reason for me to make every possible effort to reestablish our family to our former position.

Question: How much money did you have to start with? You already said you had to leave everything in Germany. Did success in your own business come easy to you?

Kurt Adler: I started with three hundred dollars. Nothing comes easy; you have to work hard. I think there are several important things. You have to work hard, be willing to make sacrifices, be honest, and be reliable.

Question: Many entrepreneurs say, in order to be successful, you have to love what you do. Can you expand upon that?

Kurt Adler: I never did anything in my life that I didn't enjoy. Also I think that it is very important to have a spouse who supports you. I was fortunate to have a wife who was incredibly good and helpful.

Question: How did you feel about competing with the "big boys" in the business?

Kurt Adler: I liked that. It's easier to compete with the bigger ones than the smaller ones. It excited me to compete with them. I've enjoyed sports and love short-term success. I've been a fanatical tennis player all my life, and I've always been fair and ambitious in sports. I've used the same system in business. There's no Jekyll & Hyde. There are people who think you can cheat in business and be honest at home. It doesn't work that way. Either you are honest or dishonest!

Question: Did you set goals or use any specific goal-setting method when you started?

Kurt Adler: No. Setting goals doesn't work. How can you set goals when you need to go out and plug away and see what happens? The danger is that you can set a goal that is unrealistic or misdirected. My objective is to be profitable.

Question: For our readers, what characteristics would you say are needed to be successful?

Kurt Adler: There must be a need for what you do. When I first started out, I wasn't in the Christmas business. I was doing general exporting and importing. I liked the idea that I could take orders in the early part of the year and deliver them in the later part of the year. I didn't have to gamble with inventory. That was a deciding factor in the success of this business and why I chose the Christmas business.

Getting back to the readers, you need to make a good impression when you meet people. You need to always be dressed properly because you never know when you will meet someone who can help you. You also have to know your limits. That's most important. You need to work hard and invest in solid ideas that have a chance. You need to find someone to give you good advice, someone who is already successful, so he or she can help you to measure the gain versus the risk. That's very important. This will help you evaluate an idea in the real world because you don't conduct business in a vacuum. You have to be conservative in business.

Post-Interview Reflections

Kurt Adler has the confidence and the poise that typify the success that he is. After interviewing him, I walked away with the feeling that I had met someone special. I especially remember the pleasant look in his eyes as he reminisced about his childhood and the look of tragedy that came over him as he spoke of his family escaping Hitler's Germany. It reminded me that, even today, people are scrambling to reach America's shores, enduring unbelievable hardships in the process, just to taste the opportunity that you and I receive as part of our birthright as Americans. How often we take that for granted! Men like Kurt Adler remind us of that gift and exemplify what a man can do when given the freedom of opportunity.

Dear Reader,

Please feel free to contact me at the address below if you have any questions, suggestions, rebuttals, or comments. I would love to hear your feedback, so much so that I will offer you a free daily reminder of the **Points to Ponder** printed on Post-It® notes. Please include your name, address, telephone number and email address.

Also please use this same address or call 800-211-4261 (alternate 215-794-5196) for information about training seminars, audio cassettes, or additional copies of this book.

All the Best,

Vinny

Vincent M. Roazzi
P. O. Box 292
Lahaska, PA 18931

vinny@spiritualityofsuccess.com

Visit our web site at www.spiritualityofsuccess.com

ABOUT THE AUTHOR

Like many others on the streets of Brooklyn, Vincent Roazzi dreamt of becoming a millionaire by age 35. At age 36 he found himself in a drug rehabilitation center, on welfare, with over $100,000 of debts. Through his recovery, he discovered techniques and principles that he has used to first change his life and then change the lives of others.

This millionaire/author is the Executive Director of Marketing and Development for the Alliance for Affordable Services, a national association of 65,000 small businesses. Additionally, he is a success trainer for a large public corporation and has spent the last twelve years helping people to achieve their dreams of success.

His formula for success has been proven on the battleground, and in the trenches, of the business world. Vincent Roazzi was honored in 1999 by the National Association of Business Leaders with the "Small Business Leader of the Year" award for "his support and mentoring service to American small business."

The author is well versed in public speaking and is accustomed to speaking to audiences in every area of the country. He currently writes a regular column for the monthly corporate publication *Wealth Magazine* and has appeared on the PBS program *McCuistion* as a guest speaker for the episode entitled *The Drive to Over-Achieve*.

Vincent currently resides in New Hope, PA with his wife, Marlene, and their five children.